CONTEMPORARY HOLLYWOOD ANIMATION

Traditions in American Cinema
Series Editors Linda Badley and R. Barton Palmer

Titles in the series include:

www.edinburghuniversitypress.com/series/tiac

CONTEMPORARY HOLLYWOOD ANIMATION
Style, Storytelling, Culture and Ideology Since the 1990s

Noel Brown

EDINBURGH
University Press

Edinburgh University Press is one of the leading university presses in the UK. We publish academic books and journals in our selected subject areas across the humanities and social sciences, combining cutting-edge scholarship with high editorial and production values to produce academic works of lasting importance. For more information visit our website: edinburghuniversitypress.com

Edinburgh University Press Ltd
The Tun – Holyrood Road, 12(2f) Jackson's Entry, Edinburgh EH8 8PJ

First published in hardback by Edinburgh University Press 2021

Typeset in 10/12.5 Adobe Sabon by
IDSUK (DataConnection) Ltd, and
printed and bound by CPI Group (UK) Ltd,
Croydon, CR0 4YY

A CIP record for this book is available from the British Library

ISBN 978 1 4744 1056 4 (hardback)
ISBN 978 1 3995 0807 0 (paperback)
ISBN 978 1 4744 1057 1 (webready PDF)
ISBN 978 1 4744 1058 8 (epub)

CONTENTS

LIST OF FIGURES AND TABLES

Figures

TABLES

ACKNOWLEDGEMENTS

My first thanks go to the series editors, Linda Badley and Barton Palmer, for their enthusiasm for the book, and to Gillian Leslie, Richard Strachan, Anita Joseph, Fiona Conn and everyone at Edinburgh University Press for their professionalism, good humour and patience. (I first started work on this book in 2014, and there were times when the term 'suspended animation' wouldn't stop springing to mind . . .).

With typical intellectual generosity, Bruce Babington and Peter Krämer – two of the best scholars I know – read and offered invaluable suggestions on the book throughout the writing process. The book is richer for their ideas and constructive criticisms; quite a few of its flaws are no doubt due to failing to follow their advice more carefully.

I've had many conversations over the years with friends and colleagues that have informed the ideas in this book in one way or another. In no particular order, I'd like to thank Filipa Antunes, Robin Brown, Peter Clark, Joshua Gulam, Paul Johnston, Catherine Lester, Stephen McLoughlin, Lucy Pearson, Kimberley Reynolds, Jeffrey Richards, Michael Shaftoe, Susan Smith, Sam Summers, Yannis Tzioumakis, and my students on the BA Film & Visual Culture and MA Film, Media and Society programmes at Liverpool Hope University.

Finally, thanks and love to my parents, Alan and Kate, for all their help and support over the years; to my brother Robin and sister-in-law Helen, who put me up for a year and a half when I first moved to Liverpool; and to Mauricio, for keeping me relatively sane and for (mostly) putting up with my seemingly endless absences while writing this book.

1. CHANGE AND CONTINUITY: THE MAKING OF CONTEMPORARY HOLLYWOOD ANIMATION

Until the 1990s, animation occupied a fairly marginal presence in Hollywood. Today, it is at the heart of the industry. This transformation did not occur overnight; it reflects a number of seismic changes in industry and style. The most visible point of difference is the near-wholesale reinvention of a primarily cel-animated medium to one that is almost entirely computer-animated. However, we have also seen the emergence of several rivals to Disney's traditional pre-eminence in the animation marketplace, leading to a huge surge in production from the stop-start production rhythms of Disney's 'classical' era to the latter-day, year-round proliferation of major animated features; a broadening of the aesthetic and narrative horizons of Hollywood animation to encompass new genres and stylistic approaches; the continued rise of multimedia 'family entertainment' franchises built around tent-pole animated blockbusters; and, finally, an ongoing blurring of boundaries between animation and live-action. Put simply, animation is now at the centre not only of the film industry, but of contemporary popular culture.

This book charts the rise of the Hollywood animated feature since the 1990s. In the process, it investigates developments in industry and style, identifies narrative and thematic patterns, and explores how animation responds to and recapitulates the values, beliefs, hopes and fears of the nation. As Paul Wells observes, mainstream animation in the United States has the capacity to offer important insights into society, 'aligning with, and depicting the most human of needs, desires, thoughts and feelings'.[1] Equally, it reaches out towards an all-inclusive, global audience through the provision of narrative strategies and the recapitulation of humanistic values that resonate with international audiences of all ages and backgrounds. One of the aims of this book, then, is to illuminate the ways in which Hollywood animation is underpinned by North American values while, simultaneously, transcending national and cultural borders. Another aim is to convey the fact that animated films deserve to be taken seriously. While it continues to be denigrated in some quarters as part of an 'easily dismissed popular culture', mainstream animation in the United States engages with important philosophical beliefs and political issues under a cloak of innocence.[2]

Rather than trying (and inevitably failing) to be comprehensive in its coverage, this book adopts a selective approach to the field of contemporary Hollywood animation. Consequently, I am not concerned with practices of digital animation in putatively 'live-action' films (such as those that suffuse contemporary superhero films). Rather, I concentrate on the form and poetics of the mainstream animated feature – films that are produced, marketed and received as such. After considering the various changes and continuities that have underpinned the form since the 1990s, the book goes on to examine significant narrative, thematic and industrial trends with close analysis of key films, focusing particularly on the biggest critical and commercial hits.

In setting the scene, this opening chapter does four things. First, it surveys production trends in Hollywood feature animation from the 1930s to the present. Second, it presents an overview of the major changes in the Hollywood film industry since the 1970s, contextualising the resurgence of animation within developments in live-action cinema, family entertainment and multimedia conglomeration. Third, it examines the stylistic continuities and changes in post-1990s Hollywood animation, particularly with regards to the rise of computer animation. And fourth, it weighs the recurrent narrative structures and mythological influences on the form against more recent changes in storytelling conventions.

PRODUCTION TRENDS

It seems appropriate to begin a study of Hollywood animation with a (very concise) overview of the field of production. In very basic terms, we can divide the production history of feature animation in the United States into two broad eras: a 'classical' one (1937–89), in which relatively few films were made and Disney was almost entirely dominant; and a post-classical or 'contemporary' one (1990 to the present), characterised by much greater diversity in genre and style, a huge surge in production, and the ever-increasing centrality of animation within the film industry.[3] The most pertinent statistic, at this point, may

Table 1.1 Theatrically released animated fiction features
produced in the United States 1937–2019.

Period	Number	Percentage
1937–1969	31	8.2
1970–1979	23	6.1
1980–1984	7	1.9
1985–1989	25	6.6
1990–1994	24	6.3
1995–1999	29	7.7
2000–2004	42	11.1
2005–2009	67	17.7
2010–2014	60	15.9
2015–2019	70	18.5
Total	378	100

be this: since 1990, almost 300 Hollywood animated features have received
a wide theatrical release, as opposed to the 86 released in the 50-plus years
between the release of two iconic Disney films: Hollywood's first feature-length
animation, *Snow White and the Seven Dwarfs* (David Hand et al., 1937), and
The Little Mermaid (Ron Clements and John Musker, 1989), the film widely
perceived as reinvigorating Hollywood feature animation. Altogether, more
than 75 per cent of all major animated feature films released theatrically in the
United States emerged in the period 1990–2019. Table 1.1 shows a breakdown
of theatrical releases since the 1930s, and reveals the extent to which production has expanded since the 1990s.[4]

While some may nostalgically recall the first three decades after the release of
Snow White (1937–69) as a golden age for animation, it was a period in which
animated films were a relatively insignificant part of the Hollywood machine.
As we can see in Table 1.1, only 31 animated features received wide theatrical release, the majority of which were produced by Disney. In large part,
this is due to the fact that Disney had no real competitors: most of the major
Hollywood studios of the time produced animated shorts, but features were
viewed as prohibitively costly and resource-heavy (with an average incubation
period of between two and four years). The relative box office failure of the
two Fleischer Brothers features, *Gulliver's Travels* (Dave Fleischer, 1939) and
Mr. Bug Goes to Town (Dave Fleischer, 1942), both distributed by Paramount,
also served as a salutary warning to the other major studios to concentrate
on live-action films. Production increased somewhat in the 1970s with animation studios that operated principally in television, such as Hanna-Barbera and
Bill Melendez Films, making a handful of theatrically released features, while

independent animator Ralph Bakshi was at his most prolific in this period; his notorious, 'X'-rated comedy, *Fritz the Cat* (1972), became the biggest animated box office hit of the decade. Nevertheless, the majority of non-Disney animated features were low-budget releases that made little mark either in box office tables or the popular consciousness. Several of them were distributed by American International Pictures (AIP), known for its teen exploitation films of the late 1950s and 1960s. Most major studios had no presence in theatrical animation, and no interest in developing one.

However, in many respects, the period 1980–4 was the absolute nadir of Hollywood animation. Disney almost abandoned making animated features during the early 1980s, and most of its independent rivals dropped out of the theatrical market. Morale at the Disney studio was also hit by the departure of several high-profile animators who had become disillusioned with the pervasive artistic conservatism that had overtaken the company. One of them was Tim Burton, a future legend of leftfield Hollywood; another was Don Bluth, who formed his own studio in 1979 and became a considerable thorn in Disney's side during the 1980s, producing and directing box office hits such as *The Secret of NIMH* (1982) and, particularly, *An American Tail* (1986), a box office smash co-produced by Steven Spielberg's Amblin Entertainment which, at the time, was the most profitable non-Disney animated film ever made.

In comparison to the fallow first half of the decade, the second half of the 1980s saw a notable rise in the production of feature-length, theatrically released animation in the US. This fact is attributable to three sources: the slow recovery of the Disney animation division; Don Bluth's continued success as Disney's main rival in the business; and – most notably – a cycle of relatively cheap animated features designed to operate synergistically with children's consumer brands. The most notable examples include the Hasbro releases, *Transformers: The Movie* (Nelson Shin, 1986), *My Little Pony: The Movie* (Michael Joens, 1986), *G.I. Joe: The Movie* (Don Jurwich, 1987), and *The Care Bears Movie* (Arna Selznick, 1985), a co-production between Canadian animation studio Nelvana and the American Greetings Corporation, the owner of the line of stuffed toy animals on which the film was based. There were also numerous TV spin-offs, including Filmation's *The Secret of the Sword* (Ed Friedman et al., 1985), a compilation of episodes from its *He-Man and the Masters of the Universe* (1983–5) and *She-Ra: Princess of Power* (1985) series – themselves spin-offs from Mattel's 'Masters of the Universe' toy line – and *The Chipmunk Adventure* (Janice Karman, 1987), spun off from NBC's children's cartoon *Alvin and the Chipmunks* (1983–90). The majority of these films were sheer exploitation releases aimed squarely at children who already owned (or who might be encouraged to buy) the toys; few reached the wider movie-going public. Nevertheless, they offered up important lessons for Disney. Firstly, the fact that its flagship animated films, *The Black Cauldron* (Ted Berman and

Richard Rich, 1985) and *The Great Mouse Detective* (Ron Clements et al., 1986), were comfortably outperformed at the box office by *The Care Bears Movie* and *An American Tail* testifies to the extent of the studio's artistic and commercial decline since its heyday, and provided stimulus to Disney's attempts to re-establish its former dominance. Secondly, the continued under-performance of Disney's animated features exposed the lack of brand-name recognition that underpinned its corporate strategy in the 1980s.

Although the raw number of theatrically released animated features did not change substantially in the 1990s, significant industrial changes took place. As we shall see in the following section, Disney reasserted its dominance in the market, while new production companies emerged to challenge it. Equally, by the second half of the 1990s, there was a huge surge in the production of ani-mated features, although the vast majority were released direct-to-video (and, thus, are unrepresented in Table 1.1). The first half of the 2000s saw a further increase in theatrical releases, partly due to the emergence of studios such as DreamWorks and Blue Sky, as well as Disney's policy at that time of churning out sequels to its animated 'classics', such as *The Tigger Movie* (Jun Falken-stein, 2000), *Lady and the Tramp II: Scamp's Adventure* (Darrell Rooney and Jeannine Roussel, 2001) and *The Jungle Book 2* (Steve Trenbirth, 2003). A high proportion of animated films in the 2000s were still being released direct-to-video, so the figures do not relay the full extent of animation's centrality in Hollywood. Nonetheless, in this period, most films were still produced using traditional animation techniques (particularly cel animation). This changed after DreamWorks and Disney announced their abandoning of 2-D anima-tion to concentrate exclusively on computer-animated films in 2003 and 2004, respectively; Disney has since released only two cel-animated films, *The Prin-cess and the Frog* (Ron Clements and John Musker, 2009) and *Winnie the Pooh* (Stephen J. Anderson and Don Hall, 2011). The spike in computer-animated productions did not take place until after 2005, reaching a peak in 2006, and led to a much more significant upsurge in production as numerous studios jumped on the bandwagon, taking advantage of the significantly lower barriers to entry for computer-animated film.

Since 2005, the quantity of US-produced animated features receiving a wide theatrical release has levelled off at between 60 and 70 per five-year period, or between 12 and 14 per year. Nevertheless, there are some significant devel-opmental trends over this period. In Table 1.2, we can see the extent to which computer animation has superseded all other forms of animation, particularly cel animation, which was the industry standard until the early 2000s. We can also see that the terrain is dominated by an oligopoly of leading animation studios. As Christopher Holliday argues, these studios are roughly analo-gous to the 'majors' of classical Hollywood cinema; they include the 'big five' of Disney, Pixar Animation Studios, DreamWorks Animation, Illumination

Table 1.2   Theatrically released films by major US animation studios 1990–2019.

Studio	Cel animated	CG animated	Stop-motion	Total
Disney	29	27	2	58
DreamWorks	4	31	2	37
Pixar	–	21	–	21
Paramount (excl. DreamWorks)	10	10	1	21
Sony	–	19	–	19
Warner Bros.	6	7	–	13
Blue Sky	–	12	–	12
Illumination	–	10	–	10
Fox (excl. Blue Sky)	3	1	3	7
Laika	–	–	5	5
Total	52	138	13	203
Percentage	25.6	67.9	6.4	

Entertainment and Blue Sky Studios,[5] beneath which lies a second tier comprising Sony, Warner Bros., Twentieth Century Fox and Paramount. There are also several smaller animation studios (such as the Oregon-based Laika, the Texas-based Reel FX, the British-based Aardman Animations, and the more diversified, Australian-based digital effects company, Animal Logic) that depend on larger multimedia conglomerates to distribute their films internationally. However, within this list of companies there is a high concentration of ownership: Disney acquired Pixar in 2006 and 21st Century Fox/Blue Sky Studios in 2019, while NBC Universal owns both Illumination Entertainment (since 2008) and DreamWorks Animation (since 2016). Another important trend is that while direct-to-video remained a viable and profitable avenue of distribution until the early 2010s (particularly for companies such as Warner Bros.), more films are now released through digital streaming services such as Netflix, and receive only a limited theatrical release, or none at all. Indeed, it is conceivable that video on demand (VOD) will eventually become the most important means of distributing animated features.

ANIMATION AND HOLLYWOOD CINEMA SINCE THE 1970S

John Lasseter has claimed that there are only two turning points in the history of (US) animation. The first, naturally enough, is Disney's emergence in the 1930s, culminating in the release of *Snow White and the Seven Dwarfs*; the second, far less predictably, is George Lucas's sci-fi blockbuster, *Star Wars* (1977).[6] To understand how a live-action film – even one as influential as *Star Wars* – could possibly be placed at this level of importance in the field of animation history, we must broaden our scope to consider wider cinematic developments during the 1970s and beyond. It is well documented that the 1970s was a decade of mixed fortunes for Disney. On the one hand, it was a period of immense growth for the Walt Disney Company, with profits rising from $21.8 million in 1970 to $61.7 million in 1975 and $135.1 million in 1980.[7] However, this success was mostly accountable to Disney's consumer products and the popularity of its theme parks, Disneyland (est. 1955) and Walt Disney World (est. 1971). In contrast, the company's motion picture division endured a prolonged and increasingly serious malaise which extended well into the 1980s, with only two of its films – *The Aristocats* (Wolfgang Reitherman, 1970) and *Herbie Rides Again* (Robert Stevenson, 1974) – reaching the annual top-ten box office tables. By the early 1980s, Disney was no longer a significant player in Hollywood, with its share of the box office a meagre 4 per cent.[8] Equally, motion pictures were a relatively minor revenue stream for the company: films constituted less than 10 per cent of the operating income of $200 million in 1982.[9] By this point, Disney had ceased to be a major film studio in any real sense.

Disney's overriding problem during the 1970s was its failure to adapt to the changing requirements and composition of the movie-going public. The conditions were very much in place for the success of blockbuster tent-pole films aimed at an all-inclusive mass audience. The post-1960s trend towards horizontal integration more easily enabled the multimedia exploitation of film franchises, and the multiplex cinema (which developed in tandem with the 1970s US shopping mall) created the economies of scale required to exploit blockbusters fully. In an era when movie-going as a recreational activity was becoming far less popular, family-oriented blockbusters owed their success, as Krämer observes, not just to youth audiences, children and parents, but also to their ability to attract 'those people who rarely, if ever, went to the cinema'.[10] And while studios such as Universal were beginning to craft youth-oriented megahits such as *Jaws* (Steven Spielberg, 1975), Disney continued to ignore teenagers and cater to the classical-era conception of the 'family audience': young children accompanied by their parents. In 1977, Walt's nephew, Roy E. Disney, resigned from the company, claiming, 'I do not believe it is a place where I, and perhaps others, can realise our creative capacities. [. . .] Present management continues to make and remake the same kind of motion pictures, with less and less critical and box office success.'[11]

That same year, Twentieth Century-Fox released *Star Wars*, which became not only the biggest event movie of the decade, but almost single-handedly inaugurated the current era of franchise cinema. *Star Wars* was envisaged by Lucas as 'a modern myth', and an update of the children's serials of the 1940s and 1950s he had watched as a boy. Although promotional material strongly emphasised its universalistic, all-age appeal, Lucas privately viewed *Star Wars* as a children's film: 'That's what we're going for, eight- and nine-year-olds.'[12] However, fearing that its brash, pulp fiction, B-movie overtones, comic-book villains, space battles and colourful aliens would appeal *only* to children, Lucas subsequently lamented: 'I've made a Walt Disney movie [. . .] It's gonna do maybe eight, ten million.'[13] It is a measure of how far Disney had slipped that Lucas could associate the company with box office failure. His concerns appeared justified when he showed a rough cut of *Star Wars* to a group of friends and fellow filmmakers. Only film critic Jay Cocks and Steven Spielberg liked the film, and Fox studio executives were similarly unimpressed.[14] Upon release, however, it quickly became a pop-culture phenomenon. *Time* called it 'the year's best movie' and observed: 'it's got no message, no sex and only the merest dollop of bloodshed here and there. It's aimed at kids – the kid in everybody.'[15] Even more important was its influence on Hollywood. Described as 'the Holy Grail of licensing', *Star Wars* inaugurated a fundamental shift in the relationship between film and so-called 'ancillary' products. As David A. Cook observes, 'merchandising became an industry unto itself, and tie-in product marketing began to drive the conception and selling of motion picture products rather than vice versa'.[16]

Peter Krämer argues that there are four 'big players' who, collectively, have shaped the trajectory of animation and contemporary Hollywood: Disney, Pixar, George Lucas and Steven Spielberg.[17] The presence of Lucas and Spielberg on this select list reflects their unparalleled influence on post-1970s Hollywood cinema. Alongside Spielberg's *Close Encounters of the Third Kind* (1977) and *E.T. The Extra Terrestrial* (1982) and Warner Bros.' *Superman* (Richard Donner, 1978), *Star Wars* represented a new type of family film, which Krämer has termed the 'family-adventure movie'.[18] Repackaging the unpretentious action-adventure of the cheap 'poverty row' serials of the 1930s and 1940s within a blockbuster aesthetic that drew on new technological potentialities, the family-adventure movie nonetheless retained the emotive qualities of classical Hollywood family entertainment. However, while implicit didactic elements are still present, the overt moralism of films such as *The Wizard of Oz* (Victor Fleming, 1939) and the classical-era Disney features is routinely downplayed. As Krämer argues, since the late 1970s most of Hollywood's biggest hits are 'children's films for the whole family and for teenagers, too'.[19]

These releases, as I have argued elsewhere, are distinguished from earlier family films by their largely undifferentiated modes of address.[20] That is to say, they do not address notional child and adult spectators as separate entities, but rather assume – as Walt Disney did – that audiences of *all ages* may be attracted by specific patterns of fantasy. The post-1970s family film, as Robert C. Allen has argued, represents the 'earliest and clearest expression' of 'the rise of post-Hollywood cinema'.[21] Notable examples include the *Star Wars, Superman* (1978–) *Star Trek* (1978–), *Indiana Jones* (1981–2008), *Ghostbusters* (1984–), *Back to the Future* (1985–90), *Batman* (1989–2012), *Jurassic Park* (1993–), *Harry Potter* (2001–11), *Lord of the Rings* (2001–3), *Spider-Man* (2002–), *Chronicles of Narnia* (2005–10) and *Avatar* (2009–) series, as well as the films released under the umbrellas of the Marvel Cinematic Universe (2008–) and the DC Extended Universe (2013–). In each of these cases, films are always components in larger multimedia franchises. Although the initial film may be expected to produce several sequels and/or spin-offs, equally important is their scope for 'ancillary' revenues: licensing, merchandising (toys, clothes, books, games, etc.), pay-TV sales and home video. During the 1980s, Hollywood studios began to recognise that blockbuster family films, besides their considerable box office potential, also represent the best opportunities for exploiting entertainment across multiple platforms.

During the late 1970s and early 1980s, Disney made several faltering attempts to emulate the Spielberg–Lucas formula for family-adventure movies. In 1978, Walt Disney's son-in-law, former football pro Ron W. Miller, succeeded Card Walker as studio president. For Miller, luring an older (i.e. teenage) audience back to Disney movies was high on the agenda, and he regarded *The Black Hole* (Gary Nelson, 1979) – viewed as a space-opera version of Disney's 1950s live-action hit, *20,000 Leagues Under the Sea* (Richard Fleischer, 1954) – as a film capable of re-engaging 'that slightly older crowd [. . .] Ideally, this is the film that will take Disney to the all-important 15-to-30 year old group. The people who have seen *Star Wars* or *Close Encounters* two or three times.'[22] *The Black Hole* was the first Disney film to be released with a 'PG' rating, signalling its more 'adult' aspirations. However, it was a critical and commercial failure, no doubt partly because – as Disney's own audience testing had revealed – 'the Disney name was actually off-putting to young adults since they associated it with a world of childhood from which they were trying to graduate'.[23] The same problem afflicted *Tron* (Steven Lisberger, 1982), a visually impressive showcase for the technological potential of CGI which contained approximately 40 minutes of computer animation. Although *Tron*'s influence on the field of computer animation has been acknowledged by filmmakers such as John Lasseter, it was a substantial box office failure upon release – a fact that James B. Stewart partially attributes to the indifference of then-Disney CEO Card Walker, who allocated only meagre funds to its marketing and promotional campaign.[24]

In 1984, a new corporate team assumed office, headed by Michael Eisner (former president of Paramount Pictures) and backed by Roy E. Disney. Alongside executives Frank Wells and Jeffrey Katzenberg, Eisner oversaw Disney's gradual re-emergence from its prolonged malaise (which left it, as Stewart notes, 'ripe for a hostile takeover') to a fully diversified, multimedia conglomerate and the most successful studio in contemporary Hollywood.[25] The path was not always smooth. Initially, Eisner and Wells favoured shutting down Disney's animation division altogether until Katzenberg, convinced that animation represented 'a unique Disney asset', prevailed upon them to retain it; Roy E. Disney was made chairman of what became Walt Disney Feature Animation.[26] However, *The Black Cauldron*, Disney's first animated feature for four years, offered up further evidence that the studio was in need of a fresh creative impetus. As with *The Black Hole* and *Tron*, it was aimed at a slightly older demographic, and was rated 'PG' on account of its darker tone and occasional moments of violence. It was another commercial and critical failure, and reportedly left Roy E. Disney and Jeffrey Katzenberg fearful that its more 'adult' tone would damage Disney's reputation for family-friendly wholesomeness.[27]

Between 1983 and 1987, Disney's operating income increased from $300 million to $800 million, but this had little to do with its studio operations.[28] There were three primary factors in Disney's financial resurgence during this period. Firstly, the company raised admission prices at the theme parks and built more hotels. Secondly, at Eisner's behest, it expanded its roster of inexpensive live-action films that could be counted on to make modest but reliable profits at the box office ('singles and doubles' as he called them). Thirdly, and perhaps most importantly, Disney began releasing its old 'animated classics' on video. Home video represented an enormous but largely untapped resource for the major Hollywood studios. Between 1984 and 1986, VCR ownership in US households rose from approximately 15 per cent to 50 per cent.[29] Disney's first release priced for the 'sell-through' market, *Pinocchio* (Ben Sharpsteen and Hamilton Luske et al., 1940), was heavily promoted and sold 1.7 million copies; *Sleeping Beauty* (Clyde Geronimi et al., 1959) followed and sold 3 million copies, then *Cinderella* (Clyde Geronimi et al., 1950) sold 7 million.[30] By 1986, home video accounted for 40 per cent of overall revenue for Hollywood studios, compared to 28 per cent for box office receipts.[31]

For Hollywood, the dominance of the family market in the home video sector prompted a broader industry embrace of family film production. As Kristin Thompson observes, 'kids could watch [family films] time after time on the electronic babysitter'.[32] And for Disney, home video soon became the second most important revenue stream behind theme parks. Indeed, as Frederick Wasser points out, one of the main motivations behind Disney's expanded roster of animated features in the late 1980s and early 1990s was Katzenberg's desire to 'make new Disney classics to replenish the old ones', using the new money from home video to 'rebound' in the theatrical market.[33]

Two hugely successful animated films cemented Disney's recovery, and underlined the box office potential of animated films. The first was *Who Framed Roger Rabbit* (Robert Zemeckis, 1988), a live-action/animated hybrid co-produced by Steven Spielberg's Amblin and released under Disney's 'adult' banner, Touchstone; the second was Disney's animated fairy tale adaptation, *The Little Mermaid*. Whereas *The Little Mermaid* has been the subject of considerable literature as the first film of the so-called 'Disney Renaissance' period (1989–99), the importance of *Who Framed Roger Rabbit* has not always been acknowledged. With a reported budget of $60 million, it was the most expensive film ever made at the time of release. It was also the film that restored a good deal of artistic credibility to animation, a medium widely perceived in the United States as embodying juvenile vacuity. Importantly, the terms of the contract afforded Spielberg and Zemeckis full creative control, while Disney retained the merchandising rights.[34] Marked by self-referential, occasionally risqué humour, *Who Framed Roger Rabbit* consciously eschews the largely non-comedic wholesomeness of classical Disney animation, and anticipates the studio's pronounced reorientation towards comedy in the early 1990s.

In many ways, it is entirely appropriate that Spielberg and Zemeckis, two of the leading lights of the post-1970s family-adventure movie, helped restore Disney's moribund film division. In *Who Framed Roger Rabbit*, they implemented the same strategy that had worked on their own hit films, combining many of the traditional pleasures of Disney films with a hip, contemporary sensibility characterised by allusiveness and comic irony, and targeting older children, teenagers and their parents. This very same approach would underpin the 'Disney Renaissance' features, and the later films of studios such as Pixar and DreamWorks. Releasing the film under the Touchstone banner with a 'PG' certificate was also a prudent move, as it negated the possible impact of Disney's unwanted reputation as a purveyor of inferior kids' entertainment. Apparently, it was Roy E. Disney that advised Eisner that the film was too risqué for the Disney label, pointing specifically to one line – 'Is that a gun in your pocket, or are you just glad to see me?' – as anathema to Disney's patented brand of child-friendly wholesomeness.[35] In the event, *Who Framed Roger Rabbit* was audience tested mainly with teenagers, not children, and was a huge crossover hit, becoming the second highest-grossing film of the year and winning three Academy Awards.[36]

After the release of *The Little Mermaid*, Disney increased its rate of production for animated features. Hitherto, Disney had released a new animated feature every four years or so, a schedule that reflected the technical requirements of production and the fact that market demand appeared to be limited. Now, Disney would produce a new feature every 12 to 18 months, and animators were forced to abide by Katzenberg's mantra of 'bigger, better, faster, cheaper', an ethos that did little for his popularity amongst the rank and file but which ensured a consistent roster of box office hits.[37] Of the 'Disney Renaissance' films, *The Little Mermaid*, *Beauty and the Beast* (Gary Trousdale and Kirk Wise, 1991), *Aladdin* (Ron Clements and John Musker, 1992), *The Lion King* (Roger Allers and Rob Minkoff, 1994), *Pocahontas* (Mike Gabriel and Eric Goldberg, 1995), *The Hunchback of Notre Dame* (Gary Trousdale and Kirk Wise, 1996), *Mulan* (Barry Cook and Tony Bancroft, 1998) and *Tarzan* (Kevin Lima and Chris Buck, 1999) all made the list of top ten highest-grossing films worldwide in their year of release.

Elsewhere in Hollywood, there was a pronounced reorientation towards family entertainment. Time Warner was the first of the major Hollywood studios to announce plans to create a 'family film' production division. This announcement (in December 1991) aroused very little surprise in the trade press: *Variety* observed that it reflected 'industry-wide awareness that survival in the 1990s may be a matter of creating wholesome, family-oriented entertainment', and that similar discussions regarding 'increasing production of family films, if not creating family film divisions' were ongoing at Universal, Paramount, TriStar and Columbia.[38] An April 1993 article in *Entertainment Weekly* cited a recent report by entertainment research firm Paul Kagan Associates that advocated greater production of family films, having noted that almost half of the 46 movies that grossed in excess of $100 million between 1984 and 1991 were rated 'PG'.[39] In May 1993, Warner Bros. confirmed the formation of its 'Family Entertainment' banner. Over the course of the decade, Twentieth Century-Fox (Fox Family Films), Miramax (Miramax Family Films), MGM (MGM/UA Family Entertainment), Universal (Universal Family & Home Entertainment), Viacom (Nickelodeon Movies) and Sony (Sony Pictures Family Entertainment Group) all followed suit, creating specialised 'family' divisions oriented to the production and multimedia exploitation of live-action and animated films.

Disney still held a substantial competitive advantage in the theatrical family animation market. Many of the new family/animation divisions specialised in direct-to-video releases, a business that reached its zenith in the 1990s and early 2000s. 'Kidvids', as they became known, were cheap to make and distribute, and often highly profitable. *The Return of Jafar* (Tad Stones, 1994), Disney's direct-to-video sequel to *Aladdin*, cost an estimated $6 million to produce but sold 7 million copies, making it one of the top ten best-selling videos ever. Producer-director Tad Stones admitted that 'we didn't have Disney's best animators working on *Jafar*', but pointed out that 'you don't compare a TV movie-of-the-week to *Schindler's List*'.[40] In 2000, *Variety* noted that 'even a modest-selling video premiere can generate $25 million–$50 million in revenue for a studio'.[41] This dominance actually accelerated as DVD replaced VHS as the leading home video technology: by 2004, the annual revenue from 'kidvids' had increased to $3 billion.[42] Encouraged by animation's renewed box office appeal, a number of rivals jumped on the theatrical bandwagon. Matt Mazer, whose company, Nest Family Entertainment, made the $40 million production, *The Swan Princess* (Richard Rich, 1994), argued that new entrants to Hollywood's animation market needed to adopt the same 'mythic storylines' as Disney.[43] However, whereas *The Lion King* grossed over $200 million on initial theatrical release, *The Swan Princess* (distributed by New Line, owned by Turner Broadcasting) and Fox's *The Pagemaster* (Joe Johnston and Maurice Hunt, 1994) each recouped only about $10 million.[44] Terry Thoren concluded that 'fairy tale is a dirty word in animation now', and 'a cutting-edge niche' was required for non-Disney animated features to succeed.[45]

That 'cutting edge niche' was the rise of computer animation, signalled by the release of Pixar's *Toy Story* (John Lasseter, 1995). While 'Disney Renaissance' films such as *The Little Mermaid*, *Aladdin* and *The Lion King* established the basic idiom and narrative patterns of contemporary Hollywood animation, the extraordinary industrial resurgence of animation owes more to *Toy Story* and developments in CGI. The film's popularity upon theatrical release in 1995 proved that audiences were receptive to computer animation. Furthermore, the barriers to entry were much lower than for hand-drawn animation, since films could be made at a much faster rate. As a result, during the late 1990s and 2000s Hollywood's production of theatrically released animated features expanded greatly. The majority of them were computer-animated films, a medium described by *Variety* in 2008 as Hollywood's most reliable and lucrative 'genre'.[46]

The truth of this claim can be gauged by examining the number of Hollywood animated features in the top ten highest-grossing films per year worldwide between 1989 and 2019 (Table 1.3). Until the late 1990s, the only films to make this list were those produced by Disney. Furthermore, because all of Disney's 1990s films were primarily hand-drawn – a laborious, time-consuming process – the studio never released more than one major film per year; this is reflected in the fact that, throughout the decade, no more than two animated films ever made the top ten in any single year. Disney's monopoly was disrupted by the emergence of Pixar and the formation of DreamWorks SKG in 1994. The monopoly was later broken altogether by the appearance of other studios, like Blue Sky, Illumination and Laika, and the new animation divisions of established major studios, such as Sony and Warner Bros. It is notable that, since 1998, there has only been one year (2014) in which at least one animated film has not made the top ten. Furthermore, each of the 'big five' Hollywood animation studios (Disney, Pixar, DreamWorks, Blue Sky and Illumination) has produced multiple mega-hit films.

This point can be explored more closely by examining the box office performance of each studio's ten most successful films (Table 1.4). The numbers reveal the extent to which a film's box office success depends on its production company. Perhaps inevitably, Pixar, Disney and DreamWorks, the three most celebrated animation studies in the United States, occupy the top three spots. Nor is it especially surprising that the average gross of Pixar's top ten films ($900 million) is almost the equal of Disney's ($918 million). Although Pixar has released far fewer features than Disney, a particularly potent mythology of studio authorship – the idea that the films collectively espouse a coherent artistic vision – has formed around the studio, in conjunction with a reputation for unparalleled standards of quality control. By the early 2000s, Disney's own market research revealed that the Pixar brand was more trusted by the mothers of young children than Disney, the supposed champion of American 'family values'.[47]

Table 1.3   Number of animated films in list of top ten highest-grossing films worldwide per year 1989–2019.

Year	Quantity	Film and Production Company
1989	1	*The Little Mermaid* (Disney)
1990	–	–
1991	1	*Beauty and the Beast* (Disney)
1992	1	*Aladdin* (Disney)
1993	–	–
1994	1	*The Lion King* (Disney)
1995	2	*Toy Story* (Pixar); *Pocahontas* (Disney)
1996	1	*The Hunchback of Notre Dame* (Disney)
1997	–	–
1998	2	*A Bug's Life* (Pixar); *Mulan* (Disney)
1999	2	*Toy Story 2* (Pixar); *Tarzan* (Disney)
2000	1	*Dinosaur* (Disney)
2001	2	*Monsters, Inc.* (Pixar); *Shrek* (DreamWorks)
2002	1	*Ice Age* (Blue Sky)
2003	1	*Finding Nemo* (Pixar)
2004	3	*Shrek 2* (DreamWorks); *The Incredibles* (Pixar); *Shark Tale* (DreamWorks)
2005	1	*Madagascar* (DreamWorks)
2006	3	*Ice Age: The Meltdown* (Blue Sky); *Cars* (Pixar); *Happy Feet* (Animal Logic/Warner Bros.)
2007	3	*Shrek the Third* (DreamWorks); *Ratatouille* (Pixar); *The Simpsons Movie* (Fox)
2008	3	*Kung Fu Panda* (DreamWorks); *Madagascar: Escape 2 Africa* (DreamWorks); *WALL-E* (Pixar)
2009	2	*Ice Age: Dawn of the Dinosaurs* (Blue Sky); *Up* (Pixar)
2010	5	*Toy Story 3* (Pixar); *Shrek Forever After* (DreamWorks); *Tangled* (Disney); *Despicable Me* (Illumination); *How to Train Your Dragon* (DreamWorks)
2011	3	*Kung Fu Panda 2* (DreamWorks); *The Smurfs* (Sony); *Cars 2* (Pixar)
2012	2	*Ice Age: Continental Drift* (Blue Sky); *Madagascar 3: Europe's Most Wanted* (DreamWorks)
2013	3	*Frozen* (Disney); *Despicable Me 2* (Illumination); *Monsters University* (Pixar)
2014	–	–
2015	2	*Minions* (Illumination); *Inside Out* (Pixar)
2016	3	*Finding Dory* (Pixar); *Zootopia* (Disney); *The Secret Life of Pets* (Illumination)
2017	1	*Despicable Me 3* (Illumination)
2018	1	*Incredibles 2* (Pixar)
2019	3	*The Lion King* (Disney); *Frozen II* (Disney); *Toy Story 4* (Pixar)

Table 1.4   Top ten highest-grossing films of each major Hollywood animation studio.

Studio	Top Ten Highest-Grossing Films	Mean Gross
Disney	1. *The Lion King* (2019): $1.6 billion 2. *Frozen II* (2019): $1.4 billion 3. *Frozen* (2013): $1.3 billion 4. *Zootopia* (2016): $1 billion 5. *The Lion King* (1994): $970 million 6. *Big Hero 6* (2014): $650 million 7. *Moana* (2016): $640 million 8. *Tangled* (2010): $590 million 9. *Ralph Breaks the Internet* (2018): $530 million 10. *Aladdin* (1992): $500 million	$918 million
Pixar	1. *Incredibles 2* (2018): $1.2 billion 2. *Toy Story 4* (2019): $1.1 billion 3. *Toy Story 3* (2010): $1 billion 4. *Finding Dory* (2016): $1 billion 5. *Finding Nemo* (2003): $940 million 6. *Inside Out* (2015): $850 million 7. *Coco* (2017): $800 million 8. *Monsters University* (2013): $750 million 9. *Up* (2009): $735 million 10. *The Incredibles* (2004): $630 million	$900 million
DreamWorks	1. *Shrek 2* (2004): $920 million 2. *Shrek the Third* (2007): $800 million 3. *Shrek Forever After* (2010): $750 million 4. *Madagascar 3: Europe's Most Wanted* (2012): $750 million 5. *Kung Fu Panda 2* (2011): $665 million 6. *Kung Fu Panda* (2008): $630 million 7. *How to Train Your Dragon 2* (2014): $620 million 8. *Madagascar: Escape 2 Africa* (2008): $600 million 9. *The Croods* (2013): $590 million 10. *Puss in Boots* (2011): $550 million	$688 million
Illumination	1. *Minions* (2015): $1.1 billion 2. *Despicable Me 3* (2017): $1 billion 3. *Despicable Me 2* (2013): $975 million 4. *The Secret Life of Pets* (2016): $890 million 5. *Sing* (2016): $630 million 6. *Despicable Me* (2010): $540 million 7. *Dr. Seuss' The Grinch* (2018): $510 million 8. *The Secret Life of Pets 2* (2019): $435 million 9. *Dr. Seuss' The Lorax* (2012): $350 million 10. *Hop* (2011): $180 million	$661 million

continued

Studio	Top Ten Highest-Grossing Films	Mean Gross
Blue Sky	1. *Ice Age: Dawn of the Dinosaurs* (2009): $890 million 2. *Ice Age: Continental Drift* (2012): $880 million 3. *Ice Age: The Meltdown* (2006): $660 million 4. *Rio 2* (2014): $500 million 5. *Ice Age: Collision Course* (2016): $410 million 6. *Ice Age* (2002): $380 million 7. *Dr. Seuss' Horton Hears a Who!* (2008): $300 million 8. *Ferdinand* (2017): $300 million 9. *Epic* (2013): $270 million 10. *Robots* (2005): $260 million	$485 million
Sony	1. *The Smurfs* (2011): $560 million 2. *Hotel Transylvania 3: Summer Vacation* (2018): $530 million 3. *Hotel Transylvania 2* (2015): $475 million 4. *Spider-Man: Into the Spider-Verse* (2018): $375 million 5. *Hotel Transylvania* (2012): $360 million 6. *Peter Rabbit* (2018): $350 million 7. *The Smurfs 2* (2013): $350 million 8. *Cloudy with a Chance of Meatballs 2* (2013): $275 million 9. *Cloudy with a Chance of Meatballs* (2009): $240 million 10. *The Emoji Movie* (2017): $220 million	$374 million
Paramount	1. *The Adventures of Tintin* (2011): $370 million 2. *The SpongeBob Movie: Sponge Out of Water* (2016): $325 million 3. *Rango* (2011): $245 million 4. *Beowulf* (2007): $195 million 5. *The Rugrats Movie* (1998): $140 million 6. *The SpongeBob SquarePants Movie* (2004): $140 million 7. *Wonder Park* (2019): $120 million 8. *Barnyard* (2006): $115 million 9. *Rugrats in Paris: The Movie* (2000): $100 million 10. *Jimmy Neutron: Boy Genius* (2001): $100 million	$185 million
Laika	1. *Coraline* (2009): $125 million 2. *ParaNorman* (2012): $110 million 3. *The Boxtrolls* (2014): $110 million 4. *Kubo and the Two Strings* (2016): $80 million 5. *Missing Link* (2019): $25 million	$90 million

We can also gauge the level of Hollywood's dependence on hit sequels to hit films. With the exception of Disney and Pixar – which still produce a fairly diverse roster of films, partly to satisfy a business model that demands a regular supply of new, diversified content to feed the theme parks and ancillary revenue streams – almost all of the major players in the feature animation market are heavily reliant on one or two tent-pole franchises whose initial films generate several sequels (though often with gradually diminishing returns both critically and commercially): DreamWorks with *Shrek* (2001–10) and *Madagascar* (2005–), Illumination with *Despicable Me* (2010–), Blue Sky with *Ice Age* (2002–), and Sony with *Hotel Transylvania* (2012–). For studios that lack the established brand cachet of Pixar and Disney, the cultivation of long-running film series is a commercial necessity; Paramount and Laika, the studios with the lowest average grosses, do not possess any such franchises. Finally, although Sony's biggest hit films still scarcely rival those of the biggest players, it has achieved sufficient success to suggest that Holliday's notion of a 'big five' Hollywood animation studios (comprising Disney, Pixar, DreamWorks, Illumination and Blue Sky) might be widened to six.

These box office figures certainly bear out the centrality of family-oriented animation in contemporary Hollywood. However, it is important to emphasise that films are never self-contained entities, but rather form part of larger multimedia and transmedia franchises, and fit squarely within Hollywood's broader embrace of family entertainment since the 1970s. Family entertainment franchises – both live-action and animated – are central to the operations of the horizontally integrated, international multimedia conglomerates that produce Hollywood films.[48] These companies are driven by the need to realise their products across multiple platforms (e.g. films, television, publishing, games, comic books, toys, clothing and other merchandise), and such franchises present the best opportunities to access a broad, all-age international market. Consequently, not only must these films be accessible and appealing to mass audiences, but the brand images at their core must be exploitable across a number of media outlets. *Star Wars*, as we have seen, is the quintessential diversified, post-1970s family entertainment franchise, and it offered up a model to Hollywood-based multimedia conglomerates, especially Disney.

One of the most abiding lessons from the *Star Wars* multimedia franchise is the importance of 'synergy'. Roughly speaking, synergy refers to the ability to exploit a given product across numerous platforms within the same horizontally integrated multimedia conglomerate. Addressing Disney's perceived lack of synergy was high on Michael Eisner's agenda in the 1990s. He set in place a 'synergy boot camp' for divisional heads to reinforce that notion that Disney had to expand and diversify in order to survive.[49] He also instituted a permanent 'Synergy Group' to report to him directly, insisting that 'if you don't have synergy, you have nothing but new products. [. . .] If you have synergy, it goes on and on.'[50] Disney's need to generate additional synergistic outlets and licensable properties informed its subsequent acquisitions of Pixar Animation Studios for $7.4 billion in 2006, Marvel for $4 billion in 2009, Lucasfilm for $4 billion in 2012, and 21st Century Fox for $71.3 billion in 2019. In the aftermath of the Pixar deal, Disney executive Dick Cook enthused: 'You can't come close to calculating what [this acquisition] means in the long term for the company in terms of new characters, stories, and lands for films and parks and publishing and more.'[51] CEO Bob Iger made similar remarks after the Lucasfilm acquisition, predicting that the ownership of *Star Wars*, 'one of the greatest family entertainment franchises of all time', would 'give us a great footprint in consumer products globally'.[52]

The points apply equally to animation. Pixar's *Cars* series (2006–) epitomises the shift from a film-centred to a brand-oriented corporate model. While *Cars* is Pixar's most commercially successful franchise, the collective box office grosses of the films – which amount to approximately $1.5 billion – is small fry compared to the more than $10 billion earned by associated licensed merchandise. Although only a percentage of this revenue is returned to Disney, licences and merchandise are almost the very definition of 'easy money' for film companies, and serve as free marketing for franchises. *Cars* has been sufficiently lucrative for Disney that, by 2008, Iger could proclaim it 'the second most successful film-merchandising franchise in history after *Star Wars*'.[53] The reception of the *Cars* franchise reveals a curious disjuncture: although the films themselves are among Pixar's least popular releases, both in terms of their box office earnings and their critical reputation, the profitability of so-called 'ancillary' products comfortably outstrips that of more feted and iconic Pixar properties, such as the *Toy Story* and *Incredibles* series.

In turn, this points to a broader commercial reality in contemporary Hollywood family entertainment: films are merely constituent elements in larger multimedia franchises. This fact is often obscured by the hype that surrounds theatrically released content. *Toy Story*, for instance, is generally regarded as a landmark in contemporary culture. As such, it seems natural to think of its fast food tie-ins as little more than savvy marketing and a quick buck on the side (in the manner of Disney's pioneering licensing deal with merchandising executive Kay Kamen in the 1930s and 1940s). However, the relative box office underperformance of the *Cars* films illuminates the way that mainstream Hollywood animated films function as content vehicles for the brands at their core. Another notable example of this tendency is Illumination/Universal's *Despicable Me* series, and particularly the multimedia exploitation of its Minions characters, which appeared in the initial film and were then afforded their own bespoke feature, *Minions* (Pierre Coffin and Kyle Balda, 2015). The Minions themselves – small, benign, gibberish-speaking yellow creatures – exemplify contemporary Hollywood's tendency to build filmic narratives around multimedia brand properties. In *Despicable Me* (Pierre Coffin and Chris Renaud, 2010), their basic narrative function is to provide comic interludes (e.g. dressing up as female pop stars; singing with comic incoherence). An obvious concession to younger child spectators, their high-pitched nonsense-speak brings to mind children's television characters such as the Teletubbies (another instantly recognisable licensable property).

The Minions are ideal vehicles for global multimedia exploitation. Bright, happy, optimistic and instantly recognisable, they are perfect simulacra of Hollywood's ethos towards family entertainment. The inarticulate yellow blobs possess no language or cultural identity that might narrow the film's prospective international market beyond vague (and presumably deliberate) behavioural associations of human infancy and animality. In 2015, the year *Minions* was released, the brand appeared to attain near-ubiquity. As well as being adopted by distributor Universal as a sort of unofficial mascot, Minions appeared in restaurant tie-ins, a series of graphic novels and hundreds of licensed pieces of associated merchandising, all on top of a $600 million promotional campaign that Universal described as the 'largest and most comprehensive' in its entire history.[54] Nor are these promotional campaigns aimed exclusively at children; Minions licensees have included American Express and Kodak, firms which tailor their products mostly to adult consumers.[55] According to Universal executive David O'Connor, 'The Minions have permeated pop culture so [the film] has such a broad appeal from ages 3 to 84. [. . .] We started hearing from brands (around the world), so it was a very coordinated global effort; we worked with all the local offices around the globe.'[56] More than any other film, *Minions* underlines former Universal chairman Marc Shmuger's claim that 'brands are the new stars'.[57]

Critical appreciation of the film was comparatively muted, perhaps perceiving it as a blatant exercise in multimedia brand exploitation rather than an original and compelling story. Universal's Nick Carpou claimed that the Minions 'exist in the culture without even having a film attached to them', so it is hardly surprising that numerous critics viewed the narrative as perfunctory, or even expedient.[58] The *Chicago Daily Herald* identified 'a constant supply of slapstick violence and pop-tune references', *USA Today* noted the preponderance of 'juvenile humour' and 'Looney Tunes-style violence', and the *New York Post* claimed that 'The whole movie feels like filler, the equivalent of taking the Scrat slapstick that begins the "Ice Age" movies and stretching it to 90 minutes'.[59]

For companies that operate theme parks, the relationship between brands and creative content is even more important. One of the most famous examples of multimedia synergy is Disney's *Pirates of the Caribbean* series (2003–11), which is 'adapted' from nothing more substantive than a theme-park ride. As Siobhan O'Flynn observes:

> Where we might think of [Disney's] theme parks as ancillary to the films, the truth is in fact the reverse. Based on segment revenue reports in the 2017 fiscal year, the revenue from the parks and resorts segment earned more than double the revenue from all studio entertainment at $18.42 billion versus $8.38 billion, respectively, which includes the production and acquisition of 'live-action and animated motion pictures, direct-to-video content, musical recordings (including a substantial roster of artists and live shows), and live stage plays'.[60]

Artistry is still an important concern in the production of animated franchise films, of course, but primarily insofar that positive or negative reception directly affects the profitability and sustainability of the wider brand. Indeed, if we judge the *Cars* films in isolation, the two theatrical sequels to the initial film – which moved *Variety*'s Brian Lowry to comment that Pixar's 'enviable streak of creative triumphs' had come 'to a skidding stop' – hardly appear justified, either commercially or artistically.[61]

All of this underlines the fact that, in corporate and industrial terms, there is much less differentiation between live-action and animated product in Hollywood than there was in the classical era. The seemingly terminal decline of the mid-budget, adult-oriented film has encouraged the major studios to pursue a conservative creative strategy of making big-budget tent-pole films built around accessible brands that can be exploited across multiple media platforms. This policy reflects declining revenues across the board in the film industry in recent years, not helped by the bottom falling out of the DVD market in 2009. As Ben Fritz observes, 'in the franchise age of filmmaking, perhaps only one thing about movies remains unique: they are home to the biggest, most globally popular brands'.[62] The decreasing importance of the North American film market (which now comprises only about 30 per cent of the global box office) has also accelerated Hollywood's reliance on family entertainment. There are several reasons for this, including the more conservative censorship regulations in many territories, which therefore prioritise 'G', 'PG' and 'PG-13' films over adult-oriented ones; a tendency for non-US cinema-goers to attend fewer films, leading to a privileging of 'event' movies; and the fact, as Disney executive Mark Zoradi notes, that 'the fantasy genre' – which is closely aligned with family films – 'travels exceptionally well, partly because there's nothing that makes it geographically unique [. . .] and its themes are pretty universal – good vs. evil, loyalty, the family sticking together'.[63] In particular, as Ben Fritz observes, the growth of the Chinese box office from $248 million in 2005 to $6.6 billion in 2016 (making it the second-biggest film market in the world, behind North America) has fostered an increasing awareness of Hollywood's need to universalise its products.[64]

There are various other indications that live-action and animation production has moved further into alignment. For instance, whereas animated films used to be ghettoised to symbolic periods of family unity, such as Christmas (as with the Yuletide pantomime), since the release of *The Lion King* many of the biggest animated tent-poles have been given a summer release, bringing them in line with most live-action blockbusters.[65] At the time of writing, Disney's production strategy is divided into four major divisions roughly akin to the 'producer-unit' system of classical Hollywood cinema, comprising animation, live-action remakes of animated 'classics', Marvel's superhero films, and Lucasfilm's *Star Wars* series; each is headed by individuals whose role combines elements of film producer and brand manager.[66] This structure is designed to cultivate 'seriality'. As Bettina Kümmerling-Meibauer argues:

> A film series does not need to offer closure to the extent a single film does, and in fact, as important as closure for the current film is leaving room to carry the plot into a sequel. A singular film thus becomes an episode, which should be regarded within the greater context of the whole series, and the existence of the series creates the aporia of ending: the impossibility of determining whether a story is effectively complete or merely ends.[67]

Individual films thus represent 'episodes' or 'chapters' within larger, overarching stories. Just as the first film in the *IT* franchise (2017–) ends with an audacious title card announcing the end of 'Chapter 1', so Sony's *Spider-Man: Into the Spider-Verse* (Bob Persichetti, Peter Ramsey and Rodney Rothman, 2018) persistently asserts its seriality through its embedded strategies of universe-building. While audiences may eventually tire of reboots of iconic texts if they merely recapitulate familiar, and increasingly worn, mythologies, *Spider-Man: Into the Spider-Verse* takes 'world-building' a step further, conceptualising an infinite number of universes, all with their own, unique version of Spider-Man (or, in this case, Spider-Woman, Spider-Man Noir, Spider-Ham, and so on). This style of narrative is essentially polyphonic: not only does it present a 'central' story so complex that it must be told over the course of multiple narratives, but it also develops additional fictional universes that are simultaneously teased and delineated over the course of each film. Again, the pre-eminence in contemporary animation of universe-building and seriality (described by Henry Jenkins as 'the core aesthetic impulses behind good transmedia works') must be seen in the context of wider trends in Hollywood cinema and in digital popular culture more broadly.[68]

Finally, as we can see in Table 1.5, the budgets of animated films have risen in parallel with those of live-action blockbusters. Whereas in 1989–94 the

Table 1.5   Estimated budgets of top five highest-grossing Hollywood animated films per five-year intervals vs those of top-grossing live-action films of the same period.

Period	Top-Grossing Animated Films	Top-Grossing Live-Action Films
1989–1994	$31 million	$46 million
1995–1999	$85 million	$122 million
2000–2004	$109 million	$113 million
2005–2009	$107 million	$219 million
2010–2014	$152 million	$216 million
2015–2019	$151 million	$290 million

average budget of the top five animated films was $31 million as against $46 million for live-action films, by 2015–19 the figures rise to $151 million and $290 million, respectively. This to say, although animated films remain generally less expensive than live-action films – mostly a result of cheaper production and labour costs – the budgets of the top animated films place them squarely in the blockbuster category, and very far from cheap kids' fare.

While the evidence offered up in this section is merely the tip of a very large iceberg, the bottom line is this: if we wish to understand contemporary Hollywood animation, we cannot view it as a self-contained entity, but must instead consider how it relates to wider developments in Hollywood and the mass media.

STYLE AND AESTHETICS

It is now widely accepted that Hollywood animation (and Disney in particular) is characterised by a 'hyper-realist' aesthetic, what David A. Price describes as 'a stylised realism that ha[s] a lifelike feel without actually being photorealistic'.[69] The template, as Paul Wells observes, was laid down by Disney with *Snow White*, a film that mimicked not only 'real-world' physical laws, but also certain cinematographic tendencies of live-action cinema. In so doing, rather than advancing 'the language of animation' in ways that availed 'alternative aesthetic and socio-cultural perspectives' (in the manner of avant-garde animators such as Lotte Reiniger or Norman McLaren), Disney pioneered 'an art comparable to live action'.[70] Furthermore, as Chris Pallant notes, the guiding philosophy behind this style (as well as the development of key principles such as overlapping action and squash-and-stretch) was 'believability'.[71] Disney's approach largely eschewed formal experimentation in favour of a more conservative, transparent mode that, in the United States, became virtually synonymous with mainstream animation. Recognising the enduring supremacy of this hyper-realist aesthetic is vital to understanding the evolution of the form. Of course, this is not to deny that visual styles are constantly changing, even in a company such as Disney, whose popularity rests partly on the repetition of familiar tropes and conventions. Scholars such as Wells and Pallant point out that a number of distinct artistic phases can be identified in the history of Disney's feature films.[72] Even post-1990s Hollywood animation is marked by several important changes in visual style (responding to historical developments in fashion, industry and technology). However, these need to be understood in relation to the form's broader aesthetic commitment to hyper-realism.

The most significant technical innovations since the 1990s all pertain to the increasing sophistication of computer animation. In many ways, the story of computer animation in mainstream Hollywood begins, once again, with George Lucas, who formed a computer division at Lucasfilm in 1979 and hired Ed Catmull from the New York Institute of Technology to head a sub-division called the Graphics Group. The Graphics Group eventually produced a groundbreaking computer-animated short directed by the former Disney animator, John Lasseter: *The Adventures of André & Wally B* (1984). After Lucasfilm spun off the Graphics Group under the name of Pixar and sold the company to Steve Jobs in 1986, Lasseter produced four more acclaimed shorts: *Luxo Jr.* (1986), *Red's Dream* (1987), the Oscar-winning *Tin Toy* (1988), and *Knick Knack* (1989). Whereas the first Hollywood feature to make extensive use of computer animation, Disney's *Tron*, was concerned with CG effects primarily as locus of futuristic spectacle, Lasseter's shorts – rudimentary though they are in comparison with later films – demonstrated the potential for computer animation as a medium for narrative storytelling, and utilised many of the principles of traditional animation developed in the 1920s and 1930s.

At the same time, Disney's hand-drawn features began to employ new technologies. The most important was the Computer Animation Production System (CAPS). Through the use of Pixar Image Computers, CAPS allowed Disney animators, as Michael Eisner describes it, to 'digitise hand-drawn images into the computer, which gave them power to manipulate and three-dimensionalise [sic] characters and scenes in entirely new ways. It also dramatically enriched their colour palette.'[73] Although the 'Disney Renaissance' period is sometimes considered the last hurrah of 'traditional' animation, the computer animation era actually began, tentatively, with *The Little Mermaid*, the first film on which CAPS was employed. Disney adopted CAPS wholesale for *The Rescuers Down Under* (Hendel Butoy and Mike Gabriel, 1990), which became the first animated feature to be created entirely digitally and without the use of physical cameras. Computer technology was later used in various other ways: the backgrounds in the famous ballroom sequence in *Beauty and the Beast* was composed, animated and coloured digitally; behavioural modelling was used to create sequences such as the wildebeest stampede in *The Lion King*; and the 'Deep Canvas' programme allowed animators to simulate brush strokes digitally.[74] Perhaps understandably, Disney initially kept knowledge of its use of these technologies under embargo, fearful of accusations that it had lost its authenticity and artistry. In part, this reflects the fact that, unlike Pixar's early computer-animated films, Disney animation appeared to embody traditional craft. As J. P. Telotte notes, Disney's animated product of the 1990s 'still looked quite conventional – deliberately so – and it continued to be marketed as consistent with the long and popular tradition of Disney cartooning'.[75]

In contrast, much of the appeal of the early computer-animated films surely derived from their newness, their implicit challenge to shop-worn, traditional methods of manufacture and their celebration of technical ingenuity and advancement. Nonetheless, Pixar executives were mindful of the dangers of this entirely digital world being perceived as coldly alienating. Although photorealistic computer animation has usefully been employed in nominally live-action films since the 1990s, photorealism is rarely the aim in the computer-animated film. Instead, John Lasseter claims that *Toy Story* 'went beyond reality, caricaturing to make it more believable', a strategy underpinned by Pixar president Ed Catmull's belief that 'computer animation had to meet the expectations set by people's perceptions of everyday life'.[76]

Because of this, Andrew Darley argues that computer-animated films represent a 'further extension or development of the preoccupation with heightened realism first displayed by Disney'.[77] Nevertheless, films such as *Toy Story* represent a 'second-order realism' that 'produce old ways of seeing or representing by other means'.[78] Maureen Furniss observes that all animation exists in a continuum between the poles of 'mimesis' ('a desire to reproduce natural reality') and 'abstraction' ('the use of pure form').[79] Hollywood computer animation – with its deliberate 'realist' strategies – cleaves closer to the former, even though the expressive potentialities of the medium avail theoretical possibilities for excursions into pure abstraction. Indeed, abstraction in mainstream Hollywood animation has typically been confined to occasional punctuating interludes, such as the famous 'Pink Elephants on Parade' number in *Dumbo* (Ben Sharpsteen et al., 1941), or the shadow-puppet-inspired animated sequence in *Harry Potter and the Deathly Hallows – Part 2* (David Yates, 2011). Scholars such as Telotte, Holliday and William Schaffer all argue that computer-animated films voluntarily adopt a 'compromise position'.[80] The art of mainstream Hollywood animation, then, is partly predicated on self-abnegation. However, Holliday is right to point out that relatively few computer-animated films are intended to be mistaken for live-action films.[81] Rather than being driven by an inexorable, technological determinist push towards photorealism, computer animation has gradually adopted more expressive, 'painterly' aesthetic modes, partly as a means of differentiating the form from the kinds of photorealistic animation used in 'live-action' cinema.[82]

This is because Hollywood computer animation generally works on principles of familiarisation. This is evident in the delight that films such as *Monsters, Inc.* (Pete Docter, 2001) and *WALL-E* (Andrew Stanton, 2008) invite audiences to take in meticulously crafted everyday details and textures: hair, fur, plants, flowers, and so on. These tactile surfaces disavow the associations of plasticity and mechanisation that computer animation tends to evoke in viewers unfamiliar with the form. Strategies of familiarisation are also evident in the cinematic techniques used to bring these animated worlds to life. The digital animation used in *Toy Story*, Darley argues, 'does not just involve the traditional cartoon form as the model for emulation'; rather, this form has also 'been made to combine or become coextensive with the conditions obtaining on and within the live action set'.[83] According to David A. Price, 'to make the new medium feel as familiar as possible', *Toy Story*'s art department 'sought to stay within the limits of what might be done in a live-action film with real cameras, tripods, dollies, and cranes'.[84] They even went as far as to mimic the style of live-action directors, with a so-called 'Branagh-cam' and a 'Michael Mann-cam' to describe cinematographic techniques borrowed from Kenneth Branagh's adaptation of *Frankenstein* (1994) and Mann's iconic cop show, *Miami Vice* (1984–90).

Computer-animated films are replete with such instances of virtual camera systems 'performing' in a fashion that is similar to live-action equipment. They utilise cinematographic techniques such as manipulating focus (e.g. through the use of focus racks), appropriate stylistic tropes such as motion blur and slow-motion, and even simulate live-action 'errors', such as lens flares. Appropriations of this kind are not confined to the visual channel, but also encompass sound and music. Holliday notes that the 'isomorphism' of computer-animated film 'is rooted in a hyperrealist approach that eschews the comic possibilities of incongruous and inappropriate sounds' – of the kind that suffuse the classical-era Hollywood cartoon short – 'and aims instead for an emotive, rousing musical score that is closer to the effect of live-action cinema'.[85] This convergence in style is not by chance; several computer-animated blockbusters have employed live-action cinematographers, such as Roger Deakins and Pablo Plaisted, to educate animators on how to emulate principles of live-action cinema for aesthetic purposes.

DreamWorks' *How to Train Your Dragon* (Chris Sanders and Dean DeBlois, 2010), on which Deakins worked, is one of the more extreme examples of this practice. The film makes use of extreme close-ups, tracking shots, rapid cutting, and under-exposed 'night scenes'. The fluid, high-speed camera movements, high-octane battle sequences and the motion capture-like animation (which is sometimes photorealistic rather than hyper-real) are all reminiscent of live-action blockbusters that use computer animation for purposes of spectacularisation, such as the Marvel Cinematic Universe series. In this way, the film represents something of a mid-point between Disney/Pixar 'hyper-realism' and productions that use performance capture technology to recreate a live-action aesthetic, such as *The Polar Express* (Robert Zemeckis, 2004), *Beowulf* (Zemeckis, 2007), *A Christmas Carol* (Zemeckis, 2009) and *The Adventures of Tintin* (Steven Spielberg, 2011). Plaisted, who advised on the cinematography for *The Lego Movie* (Phil Lord and Christopher Miller, 2014), has spoken of his desire for audiences 'to believe they were seeing something that was real', but also to 'avoid the obvious computer controlled and floating camera seen in some animated movies' and instead evoke the 'subconscious language of cinema that people are used to'.[86] This suggests that, while computer animation is continuing to develop its own unique 'grammar', many filmmakers still wish to anchor the form to the familiarising conventions of live-action cinema. Indeed, Disney explicitly marketed its photorealistic computer-animated remake of *The Lion King* (Jon Favreau, 2019) as a live-action film, actively de-emphasising its status as 'animation'. In this way, the near-ubiquity of animation in digital Hollywood is working to destabilise traditional boundaries between animated and non-animated films. Perhaps the most important lesson to take from these examples of live-action/animation convergence is that animation has come to be regarded as a 'style' as much as a 'medium'.

One way of analysing stylistic changes in Hollywood animation over a larger time-frame is by comparing the average shot length (ASL) of a range of classical and contemporary films. Before proceeding further, it should be noted that what we are really talking about in animation is the *simulation* of 'shots', since animators are not actually cutting from one piece of film to another, but only appearing to do so for aesthetic or storytelling purposes (e.g. to signal changes in location and perspective). Since they are untethered by the physical constraints of cameras and other cinematographic equipment, we should not be surprised to see that animated films typically evidence a shorter ASL than live-action films. In theory, animated feature films could abandon standard editing principles altogether, but to do so would be to risk compromising their mainstream accessibility. The majority of film-goers are accustomed to classical cinematic storytelling conventions. Consequently, mainstream animated films usually retain a high degree of fidelity to live-action continuity principles: the shot/reverse shot pattern, the 180-degree rule, establishing and re-establishing shots, matches on action, and so forth. Largely in place by the 1920s, the continuity editing system remains, to this day, the most pervasive and effective means of organising on-screen space to convey a smooth, unobtrusive narrative flow.

As we can see in Table 1.6, there is a general, long-term tendency towards increasingly brisk editing rhythms. The same is true of live-action Hollywood films. According to David Bordwell, the typical ASL in the period 1930–60 was in the region of 8–11 seconds; it reduced to 6–8 seconds in the 1960s, to 5–7 seconds in the 1970s, and to 3–6 seconds by the end of the twentieth century.[87]

Table 1.6   Average shot length (ASL) of select Hollywood animated features 1941–2018.

Film	ASL (seconds)
Dumbo (1941, Disney)	5.8
The Little Mermaid (1989, Disney)	4.3
The Lion King (1994, Disney)	4.3
Toy Story (1995, Pixar)	2.9
Monsters, Inc. (2001, Pixar)	3.0
Finding Nemo (2003, Pixar)	3.3
How to Train Your Dragon (2010, DreamWorks)	3.3
Frozen (2013, Disney)	4.7
Minions (2015, Illumination)	4.7
Spider-Man: Into the Spider-Verse (Sony, 2018)	2.5

With an ASL of 5.8 seconds, Disney's 1941 feature, *Dumbo*, has a faster editing rhythm than was standard for the period, but it now feels relatively sedate.
The cel-animated 'Disney Renaissance' features, *The Little Mermaid* and *The
Lion King*, are closer to the period's live-action norm with ASLs of 4.3 seconds apiece. What is most striking about *Toy Story* (ASL 2.9 seconds) is the
way that digital storytelling avails a much faster editing pattern – particularly
during action sequences – in a way that reflects the rhythms of high-octane
live-action cinema. Many subsequent computer-animated features, including
Monsters, Inc. (ASL 3.0 seconds), *Finding Nemo* (ASL 3.3 seconds) and *How
to Train Your Dragon* (ASL 3.3 seconds) also average in the region of 3 seconds
per shot; again, this is roughly in line with those of live-action films since the
turn of the millennium.
    There are interesting and contrasting counter-examples in *Frozen* (Chris Buck
and Jennifer Lee, 2013) and *Minions* (both ASL 4.7 seconds) and *Spider-Man:
Into the Spider-Verse* (ASL 2.5 seconds) that require some discussion. Given their
seemingly sedate 'editing' rhythms, it might be assumed that *Frozen* and *Minions* are slow-paced, talky productions that revert to the more languid tempo of
cel animation. In reality, the slower editing rhythm in some recent computer-animated films is largely attributable to their utilising the technological potentiality
of digital cinema to convey the relentless, often dizzying kineticism of the moving
image in a more advanced way than 'first-wave' computer-animated films like
Toy Story, creating what David Bordwell calls 'a percussive burst of images'.[88]
Whereas live-action films (particularly those produced in the pre-digital age)
are heavily reliant on rapid cutting from shot to shot to engender kineticism,
computer-animated films can orchestrate complex camera movement through

tracking shots, aerial shots, pans, tilts and other 'reframing' techniques. Conversely, in *Spider-Man: Into the Spider-Verse* – a film which consciously evokes the aesthetic of a comic strip – an unusually brisk editing rhythm is employed; in conjunction with judicious use of the extreme close-up, this serves to engender suspense during the many action sequences while mimicking the thrillingly disorienting 'cuts' from one pane to another experienced by comic-book readers. However, as with *How to Train Your Dragon* and *Frozen*, the camera movement is still extremely fluidic; what emerges is a hybrid style that – in the manner of nominally live-action films that utilise CG effects, such as those of the Marvel Cinematic Universe – maintains an almost relentless kineticism.

Just as live-action film is becoming increasingly 'animated', then, so computer animation fuses principles of traditional animation and live-action filmmaking with its own unique aesthetic specificity. Holliday views computer animation as 'a specific genre of animation' that 'involves particular kinds of image-making techniques'.[89] Although the 'look' of many Hollywood computer-animated films evidences a certain uniformity (partly due to the fact that most commercial studios use Pixar's RenderMan for Maya programme), they also deal in visual currencies that were unattainable in the age of two-dimensional animation. As Holliday observes, the computer-animated film 'trades in flourishes of depth and dimension', creating digital worlds with 'a strong spatial imperative, with an impressive volume and heightened agency'.[90] In particular, he argues, the fluidic camera in these films transform the spectator from 'static contemplator' to 'mobilised anthropomorphic state', evoking what French philosopher Gilles Deleuze – in a description of the purity of vision of the non-human eye – called 'gaseous perception'.[91] Nonetheless, many computer-animated films self-consciously continue to ascribe to the conventions of live-action films, both in terms of editing techniques (e.g. average shot length) and, particularly, in the way that they seek to reproduce technical constraints (e.g. camera moves), while retaining much of the style, the tone, and the narrative ideology of traditional animation. Although Holliday speaks of 'live-action' and 'animated' genres, it seems increasingly difficult to uncouple them.[92] As we shall see, many of the key formal principles of post-1990s Hollywood animation can be viewed through the larger prism of engendering 'relatability': the spectator's capacity to engage fully with the films' diegesis is believed to rest on the creation of 'believable worlds', populated with 'believable inhabitants'.

STORYTELLING AND NARRATIVE

Although the formal developments in post-1990s animation may be profound, the storytelling conventions that underpin the form have remained fairly stable since the classical era. Most of Disney's early films were adapted from fairy tales and folk tales (e.g. *Snow White*, *Cinderella*, *Sleeping Beauty*) or children's literature (e.g. *Peter Pan*, *The Jungle Book*, *Alice in Wonderland*), but a high proportion of contemporary animated films are based on original screenplays. Nevertheless, they still adhere to classical storytelling principles, are intended for the consumption of an all-inclusive, mixed audience of adults and children, and are inherently intertextual, in the broadest sense of the term. To this extent, the films are locatable within larger traditions of children's fiction, narrative cinema (including children's film and family film) and deeper mythological structures that have their roots in numerous Western traditions of narrative drama and comedy.

The narrative ideology of contemporary Hollywood animation still derives, in large part, from classical (and principally live-action) Hollywood storytelling patterns, as outlined by David Bordwell:

> The classical Hollywood film presents psychologically defined individuals who struggle to solve a clear-cut problem or to attain specific goals. In the course of this struggle, the characters enter into conflict with others or with external circumstances. The story ends with a decisive victory or defeat, a resolution of the problem and a clear achievement or non-achievement of the goals. The principal causal agency is thus the character, a discriminated individual endowed with a consistent batch of evident traits, qualities, and behaviours.[93]

These 'canonic story' elements, Bordwell suggests, are inherited from specific historical modes of fiction: the well-made play, the popular romance and the late-nineteenth-century short story.[94] In turn, Jack Zipes contends that the canonical Hollywood story structure derives from the conventions of the literary fairy tale of the seventeenth, eighteenth and nineteenth centuries, as outlined by Vladimir Propp in his classic text, *The Morphology of the Folktale* (1928).[95] More abstractly, the majority of family-oriented features adhere to what Joseph Campbell calls the 'hero's journey', a syuzhet structure of home–away–home that recurs, with an almost infinite number of permutations, throughout the histories of Western oral and written storytelling. According to Christopher Vogler, the 'hero's journey' deals with 'childlike universal questions: Who am I? Where did I come from? Where will I go when I die? What is good and what is evil? What must I do about it? What will tomorrow be like? Where did yesterday go? Is there anybody else out there?'[96]

While employed as a story consultant at Disney in the mid 1980s, Vogler wrote a well-circulated memo that summarised the 'hero's journey' and advocated it as a foundation for all the studio's films. Vogler went on to advise in the writing of *The Little Mermaid* and *Beauty and the Beast* and received a story credit on *The Lion King*, and has worked as a story consultant for several other film studios. He claims that the 'hero's journey' is the essential foundation of

Hollywood storytelling. However, as we might infer from his 'childlike universal questions', the 'hero's journey' recurs most emphatically in child-oriented cultural forms. Indeed, most of the films that Vogler and fellow mythologist Susan Mackey-Kallis identify as expressing the 'hero's journey' in its 'purest form' – including *Star Wars*, *E.T.* and *The Lion King* – are quintessential Hollywood family movies.[97]

It is worth noting that the 'hero's journey' and the children's literary concept of the 'circular journey' – seen widely as underpinning almost all children's fiction – are essentially the same thing. Both concepts describe structurally simple, often Manichean narratives that express commonly held (if perhaps not quite universal) desires and fantasies, depict the processes of learning and eventual fulfilment undergone by their protagonists, represent the victory over internal and external difficulties, and typically end, unambiguously, with catharsis and a new equilibrium. Furthermore, both types of story meet social and ritual needs: bringing people together through the expression of shared values and desires. While there may be a good deal of semantic variation (plot, tone, mood, style) in how these stories are communicated – and it will be noted that Campbell and Vogler pare down the mythologies, slightly reductively, to their basic essence (what Campbell calls the 'monomyth') – the commonalities between the 'hero's journey' and many versions of the 'circular journey' in children's fiction reveals that the latter, far from being simplistic or meaningless, embodies many of the fundamental mythologies of human civilisation.

With relatively few exceptions, Hollywood animated features are intended for the consumption of children. As such, they tend to ascribe to what I have elsewhere identified as the broad, overarching generic conventions of children's films and family films: (1) the reaffirmation of family, friendship, kinship and community; (2) the foregrounding of child, adolescent and teenage figures (or childlike characters, including animals and other surrogate children) and their experiences; (3) the exclusion and/or defeat of socially disruptive elements; (4) the minimisation of 'adult' themes, including representations of sexuality, violence, crime, profanity, drug abuse, poverty and gore; and (5) a story that, while acknowledging the possibility of an unpleasant or undesirable outcome, is finally upbeat, morally and emotionally straightforward and supportive of the social status quo.[98] Films that target children (in whole or in part) are designed to meet their presumed aesthetic requirements, which often include some combination of magic, fantasy and adventure, song and dance, colour and visual humour. However, these conventions do not respond (at least, not solely) to children's preferred patterns of fantasy, or even to what producers believe children wish to see in their screen entertainment. They are prescribed by what (adult) society believes children *ought to see*. Determinations of this kind are based on social, psychological, ethical and behavioural considerations that are tied to the historical conditions of production and thus are liable to change, by degrees, in accordance with prevailing cultural attitudes towards childhood and adulthood.

While Hollywood animation may not be a 'genre', as some scholars (and many journalistic critics) have claimed, it is assuredly 'generic'. Just as narrative modes such as 'comedy' or 'tragedy' may be channelled into a wide array of forms, family-oriented animation is generically diverse and inherently hybridic, encompassing a broad, formally diverse array of sub-genres and media, including live-action forms as well as cel, puppet, stop-motion and computer animation. The generic horizons of Hollywood animation widened considerably in the mid 1990s to encompass traditions such as the suburban buddy movie (e.g. Pixar's *Toy Story*), sci-fi (e.g. Warner Bros.' *The Iron Giant* [Brad Bird, 1999]), fantasy (e.g. Disney's *Dinosaur* [Ralph Zondag and Eric Leighton, 2000]), biblical epic (e.g. DreamWorks' *The Prince of Egypt* [Brenda Chapman et al., 1998], self-reflexive genre parody (e.g. DreamWorks' *Shrek* [Andrew Adamson and Vicky Jenson, 2001]), and even horror (e.g. Disney/Touchstone's *The Nightmare Before Christmas* [Henry Selick, 1993]).

An important caveat to any discussion of the hybridity of contemporary Hollywood animation is that almost all this proliferation has taken place within the larger generic parameters of the Hollywood family film. Only a tiny minority of films, including low-budget 'indie' releases such as *Sita Sings the Blues* (Nina Paley, 2008) and *An Oversimplification of Her Beauty* (Terence Nance, 2012), and the occasional mainstream 'adult' animation, such as *Team America: World Police* (Trey Parker, 2004) and *Sausage Party* (Conrad Vernon and Greg Tiernan, 2016), are released with censorship ratings that restrict the attendance of children under the age of 12. Consequently, even in cases where Hollywood animated films appropriate, reference or subvert other genre tropes, they usually still adhere to the broad conventions of the children's film outlined above.

In structural and ideological terms, Hollywood animation – and Disney films, especially – adheres to fairly well-defined narrative formulae. As Janet Wasko has argued, prior to 1932 Disney's shorts were 'imaginative, magical, and open-ended', but what she calls the 'Classic Disney' style then began to emerge, characterised by 'closed fantasies with distinct beginnings and usually happy endings'.[99] Similarly, Nicholas Sammond contends that Disney's features 'repeat a formulaic narrative of generational succession in which the parent is left behind and the child discovers its inner resources as it overcomes seemingly insurmountable obstacles'.[100] In part, this embrace of pleasingly repetitive formulaic structures was accelerated by Disney's entry into the feature film market. Imaginative, open-ended narratives are considerably harder to sustain in a medium that relies so heavily on familiar moral fables as pre-texts, and in which (family) audiences routinely demand narrative closure, moral certitude and emotional uplift.

If we assume that genre operates (at least in part) as an unspoken contract between producer and consumer, we should not be surprised to see a large degree of consensus in how Disney portrays itself – a benign arbiter of universalistic family values – and the meanings that critics and audiences attach to the company. Michael Real's 1970s survey of 200 college students' responses to Disney, published in the book *Mass-Mediated Culture* (1977), found that Disney represented values of 'happiness', 'friendliness', 'honesty', 'innocence', 'industriousness' and 'cleanliness', while disapproving of 'sex', 'violence', 'greed', 'laziness', 'un-American activities', or 'leftist politics'.[101] The Global Disney Audiences Project (GDAP), which sampled over 1,200 responses to Disney films around the turn of the millennium, found that the overwhelming majority of respondents associated Disney with 'fun and fantasy', 'magic', 'good over evil', 'family', 'imagination', and 'love/romance'.[102]

Many of the narrative, thematic and ideological conventions of Hollywood animated films developed over a long period of time. As we have seen, the Disney model was influenced by broader mythological structures, while later studios such as Pixar and DreamWorks, in turn, inherited, refined and occasionally subverted prototypical story elements from Disney. Yet it is important to note that narrative development is an ongoing process that reflects changes in culture and society. Even Disney's early-classical period of feature animation is characterised by substantial narrative and ideological development. Whereas its first five features – particularly *Snow White*, *Pinocchio* and *Fantasia* (Ben Sharpsteen and Hamilton Luske et al., 1940) – exhibit an extraordinary graphic richness and impulse towards aesthetic innovation, Steven Watts has argued that the studio's creative output fundamentally changed after 1941, evidencing

> a new instinct to identify and uphold American values rather than playfully to probe or lampoon them. Individual achievement, consumer prosperity, family togetherness, celebratory nationalism, and technological promise became the beacons of the new Disney corpus.[103]

For Jack Zipes, however, Disney films are 'always the same':

> the disenfranchised or oppressed heroine must be rescued by a daring prince. Heterosexual happiness and marriage are always the ultimate goals of the story. There is no character development since all figures must be recognisable as character types that remain unchanged throughout the film. Good cannot become evil, nor can evil become good. This world is viewed in Manichean terms as a dichotomy. Only the good will inherit the earth.[104]

While this is a gross oversimplification, it is true that one of the fundamental difficulties for companies such as Disney is disentangling classical and much-loved story structures (which frequently have conservative inclinations) from the more pernicious attitudes towards gender, sexuality, race and class that often undergird them, and which are now considered offensive to large sections of the audience. By the late 1960s, in the midst of the counter-culture, leftist critics were able to lambast Disney for its 'unquestioning patriotism, bourgeois moral nostrums, gauche middle-class taste, racist exclusion, corporate profitmongering, [and] bland standards of social conformity', while a 'silent majority', as Watts puts it, viewed Disney as 'a defence of traditional American opportunity, entrepreneurialism, patriotism, middle-class decency, and moral uplift'.[105]

The commercial philosophy of Hollywood animation (and of family entertainment more broadly) rests on its ability to hold these apparently conflicting positions in delicate balance, pleasing as many and offending as few people as possible. While *The Little Mermaid* is often remembered as the beginning of the 'Disney Renaissance' – a bold new era for Disney that brought the studio into the attention of a new generation of American youth – it was its adherence to 'Walt's prescription for the animated classics: good versus evil, overcoming odds to realise a dream, and a happy ending' that most excited Jeffrey Katzenberg when he read the final screenplay.[106] Many subsequent films have attempted to retain the narrative attractions of the classic formula while updating it with new aesthetic elements and more contemporary attitudes to culture and society. On the one hand, most of the 'Disney Renaissance' films, as Paul Wells observes, continue to be predicated on the 'maturation plot', the 'coming of age' narrative that Sammond identifies as central to the 'classic Disney' formula.[107] On the other hand, these films adopt a 'spectacle as narrative' approach (particularly emphasising Broadway-style song and dance) drawn from the utopian tendencies of the 1950s MGM musical, one that is quite unlike the symphonic romanticism that characterises the sonic textures of the early Disney musicals.[108] Furthermore, as we shall see in later chapters, films such as DreamWorks' *Shrek* and Disney's *Frozen* consciously rewrite basic foundational elements of the classical-era Disney fairy tale that are no longer sustainable in the modern era because of changes in aesthetic conventions or majority-held political beliefs.

Indeed, in recent years, a number of critics have made the claim that certain post-millennial animated films advance radically progressive political agendas. The foremost advocate of this position, Judith (later Jack) Halberstam, argues in favour of a genre of contemporary animation known as 'Pixarvolt', which often centres on disorderly children who seek to escape from the stultifying confines of the conventional family. Pixarvolt films feature themes of 'revolution and transformation'; they 'revel in failure', 'make subtle as well as overt connections between communitarian revolt and queer embodiment', collapse social hierarchies and thereby articulate 'counterintuitive links between queerness and socialist struggle'.[109] The narrative form of the Pixarvolt film is a familiar one in which an individual is pitted against 'the conformist sensibilities of the masses', but unlike many critics, Halberstam sees films such as *Toy Story*, *Antz* (Eric Darnell and Tim Johnson, 1998), *Chicken Run* (Peter Lord and Nick Park, 2000), *Robots* (Chris Wedge, 2005), *Over the Hedge* (Tim Johnson and Karey Kirkpatrick, 2006) and *Bee Movie* (Simon J. Smith and Steve Hickner, 2007) as challenging selfish individualism and instead reaffirming 'collective action, anticapitalist critique, group bonding, and alternative imaginings of community, space, embodiment, and responsibility'.[110] Indeed, the protagonists of these films are rarely heroes, but rather selfish individuals who 'must be taught to think collectively' as part of a broader disavowal of conventional family structures.[111]

The 'Pixarvolt' thesis is rhetorically attractive in all sorts of ways; it ascribes progressive subjectivities to films often dismissed as merely perpetrating a vacuous, reflexive conservatism (indeed, Halberstam pre-empts this claim by labelling critics who tend towards such a view as 'cynical'). Nevertheless, in referring to the 'smuggling of radical narratives into otherwise clichéd interactions about friendship, loyalty, and family values', Halberstam implicitly concedes that it is an against-the-grain interpretation of these films.[112] Furthermore, Halberstam argues that the primary points of distinction between Pixarvolt and non-Pixarvolt animated films are that the latter 'prefer family to collectivity, human individuality to social bonding, extraordinary individuals to diverse communities'.[113] However, this seems to posit a false dichotomy. In the majority of contemporary Hollywood animated films, I will argue, collective thought is usually manifested in reaffirmations of family and friendship structures. Indeed, these functioning, surrogate families operate as microcosms of societies that, through the actions of the films' protagonists, are purged of destabilising agents. Equally, unsatisfactory forms of stability characterised by mechanistic or autocratic tyranny are often substituted for more appealing ones based on the kinds of peaceful utopianism that undergird most Hollywood animated features; this is certainly true of the films Halberstam singles out (*Antz*, *Chicken Run*, *Over the Hedge* and *Bee Movie*), and of several later ones, such as *Zootopia* (Byron Howard and Rich Moore, 2016) and *Isle of Dogs* (Wes Anderson, 2018).

It is undeniable that a much higher proportion of post-1990s animated family films present barbed criticisms of selfishness, bigotry, intolerance, conformism, mechanisation, and even the machinery of advanced capitalism. Where I am less optimistic than Halberstam (though not, I hope, cynical) is in my estimation of how radical this 'progressiveness' actually is. As I will argue at various points in this book, contemporary Hollywood animation rarely commits unequivocally to contentious political positions, and instead relies, as Ellen

Scott suggests, on a *heteroglossian* 'principle of deniability' (literally so, in the case of *WALL-E* director Andrew Stanton, who publicly denied that the film is a climate change allegory).[114] In such cases, disambiguation is rarely offered; instead, audiences are left to interpret what 'messages' films are attempting to disseminate. This type of ambiguity is less a failure of resolve on the filmmakers' part than a deliberate textual strategy that responds to Hollywood's need to accommodate the heterogeneity of the global market. It is inherent in the multivalent appeal of these films (supported by complex, ambivalent modes of address) that a plurality of interpretive possibilities remains open to the viewer. Consequently, by their very nature, they are 'open' texts – ones that invite and that are able to sustain multiple interpretations – to a far greater degree than the comparatively 'closed' fantasies that characterised animated features of the classical period. As a result, the 'cynical' reading does not necessarily negate the 'idealistic' one, or vice versa.

Broadly speaking, post-1990s Hollywood animation is built on the regular updating of traditional textual strategies for a modern, cross-demographic audience. One word that is often used by producers and audiences (though less so by critics) is 'relatability', which is used to describe the ability of viewers to engage with a text on a profound emotional level – or even to interpret a character or situation, on some level, as an analogue of themselves and their own lives.[115] The term 'relatable' has permeated everyday language in Western popular culture. A search on Google Ngram reveals that English-language usage of it skyrocketed just after the turn of the millennium, coinciding with the sharp increase of references to 'relatability' in popular discourses, where it is has become one of the most common registers of cultural value. A cursory internet search reveals hundreds of articles devoted to 'relatable' situations and characters in Hollywood animated features; many of them fall into the category of 'clickbait', but there are comparatively serious and developed pieces published by major media outlets such as the Huffington Post and BuzzFeed.[116] Notably, Jennifer Lee, co-director of *Frozen*, suggests that the quality of 'relatability' is essential 'if you wanna do a film where you have a big scope'.[117] Equally, of course, for a fictional work to be labelled as 'non-relatable' is to condemn it to the dustbin of irrelevancy. US broadcaster Ira Glass attracted a measure of ridicule when he tweeted that Shakespeare is 'not relatable, unemotional'.[118] Nonetheless, such discourses reflect a perception, shared by producers and movie-goers alike, that mass audiences will only attend films in which they can find strong resemblances to their own lives.

In order to consider how this idea might work in practice, let us imagine a 'typical' North American nuclear family of the kind that Hollywood studios envisage and cater for during a film's production process. Each member of this family can probably identify, on some level, with a classical-era Disney character such as Cinderella: even if her behaviour and the situations she finds herself in are not exactly familiar, we can like her, sympathise with her miserable home life and hope she finds eventual happiness and fulfilment. But the physical and moral conformism of characters like Snow White, Cinderella and Sleeping Beauty might also be alienating to modern audiences, particularly when measured against the protagonists of a film such as *Frozen*, where 'human' imperfections are not only celebrated, but actively undergird the narrative. Whereas the Manichean binaries that Zipes identifies as a *sina qua non* of the classical Disney formula still proliferate, many post-1990s productions also exhibit greater degrees of moral complexity. As Pallant points out, Disney films of the late 1990s began to introduce 'characters exhibiting both "good" and "bad" qualities'.[119] The tendency in subsequent films has been for flawed – albeit ultimately heroic – protagonists who do not look or act like classical heroes, sometimes pitted against villains whose motivations are understandable or even sympathetic. Our hypothetical family will be expected to identify more profoundly with contemporary films of this type because the characters, and many of the situations, are engineered to resemble their everyday lives. This is not to say that individual viewers cannot make an interpretive leap and empathise with classical-era Disney princesses, merely that, for the majority of modern spectators across the globe, there is a greater gap between those fictional representations and lived reality.

Writing in the 1940s with specific reference to Disney's early films, the Russian filmmaker and theorist, Sergei Eisenstein, claimed that animation's elasticity of form ('plasmaticness') has the capacity to elicit 'pure ecstasy' in its audiences.[120] He suggested that this feeling results from animation's 'prelogical attractiveness', which is 'not yet shackled by logic, reason or experience', and thus engenders, through the form's inherent mutability, a sense of a space 'from which *everything* can arise'.[121] It is probably true that animation arouses pre-social pleasures less accessible to live-action cinema (especially the socialist realism that dominated Russian screens when Eisenstein was writing), thereby underpinning its aesthetic appeal to children and adults alike. Nevertheless, this hypothesis cannot fully explain the popular attraction of Hollywood animation, which appears to stem at least as much from its adherence to hyper-realism. A transparent visual style with its own established conventions (many of which are familiarising because they approximate laws of nature), hyper-realism is an implicit rejection of unfettered abstractionism. The more 'realist' – though still hardly mimetic – mode of post-1990s animation (and particularly films such as *Toy Story* and *The Incredibles*) bridges the gap between the abstraction of the animated medium and the comforting assurance of the everyday world even further.

This 'realism' is idiomatic as much as visual. As Oliver Lindman argues, the gradual evolution of Disney's musical tradition from what he describes as the 'operatic uniformity' of its classical period to the 'upbeat eclecticism' of its post-1990s productions is at least partly underpinned by the need to promote audiences' emotional identification with the films and their protagonists.[122] Whereas the musical structures and composers of the early features were associated with 'high' culture (most obviously in *Fantasia*, in which animation is set to pieces of classical music conducted by the world-renowned Leopold Stokowski), post-1990s Disney films feature scores written and performed by world-famous, populist musicians such as Elton John and Phil Collins; a number of original songs featured in these films have even become top-ten hits in the US Billboard Hot 100 charts.[123] By the same token, the central characters in contemporary films are far removed from the remoteness of classical-era Disney protagonists, whose background, cod-Shakespearean linguistic idiom and appearance are all fundamentally strange to most modern audiences (which, of course, is not to say that strangeness is always and necessarily unappealing). Indeed, the perceived 'weirdness' of the classical-era princess is acknowledged and satirised by one of Disney's own films, *Ralph Breaks the Internet* (Rich Moore and Phil Johnston, 2018), in which the quirkily non-conformist but 'relatable' Princess Vanellope (Sarah Silverman) finds herself in a gathering of Disney princesses who challenge her to prove she is one of them:

POCAHONTAS: What kind of princess are you?
VANELLOPE: What *kind*?
RAPUNZEL: Do you have magic hair?
VANELLOPE: No.
ELSA: Magic hands?
VANELLOPE: No.
CINDERELLA: Do animals talk to you?
VANELLOPE: No.
SNOW WHITE: Were you poisoned?
VANELLOPE: No!
SLEEPING BEAUTY/TIANA: Cursed?
VANELLOPE: No!
BELLE/RAPUNZEL: Kidnapped or enslaved?
VANELLOPE: No! Are you guys ok? Should I call the police?!
ARIEL: Then I have to assume you made a deal with an underwater
    sea witch, who took your voice in exchange for a pair of human
    legs?
VANELLOPE: No! Good lord, who would do that?!
SNOW WHITE: Have you ever had true love's kiss?
VANELLOPE: Ooh, barf!
JASMINE: Do you have daddy issues?
VANELLOPE: I don't even have a mom!
ALL, IN UNISON: Neither do we!

> RAPUNZEL: And now for the million-dollar question: Do people assume all your problems got solved because a big, strong man showed up?
> VANELLOPE: Yes! What is up with that?
> ALL, IN UNISON: She *is* a princess!

This sequence underlines just how far removed the narrative aesthetic of contemporary animation is from the classical style, both in terms of gender politics and the milieux inhabited by the main characters. Whereas most Disney fairy tale characters are archetypes, the motivations of their post-1990s counterparts are drawn much more emphatically. We can see this in the convention in Disney films since *The Little Mermaid* to include a Broadway-style 'I want' musical number in which the protagonist expresses their inner desire, as well as in the provision of what I term 'origin stories' for the central characters in films such as *Up* (Pete Docter, 2009) and *Frozen*.[124] As Christopher Finch observes, another key difference between Ariel (Jodi Benson) from *The Little Mermaid* and previous Disney heroines is that she 'talked the language of today's teenagers' and 'expressed herself in ways that post-Beatles adolescents could identify with'.[125] Even in cases where a film's situation and setting are alien, such as *Frozen* (which is set in a distant fairy tale kingdom, albeit one drawn loosely from Sámi mythology), the principal characters of Anna (Kristen Bell) and Elsa (Idina Menzel) talk and act more or less like twenty-first century North Americans. Put another way, they converse in the demotic register of everyday language, rather than the hieratic register of 'high culture', authority and officialdom.

Sometimes, the introduction of modern speech patterns creates inconsistencies in the film's diegesis. Finch argues that 'the directors perhaps tried *too* hard' to make the title character in *Aladdin* (Ron Clements and John Musker, 1992) appear 'contemporary', with the result that he seems 'jarringly American in the Middle Eastern context of the movie'.[126] Of course, appearance and speech patterns are not the only factors involved. In the age of transnational cinema, it is more important that films should be seen to evoke recognisable situations, and be able to elicit in their audiences universal (or near-universal) responses to them. Elsa, who chooses to isolate herself from wider society when she discovers that she has potentially dangerous magical powers, is assumed to be 'relatable' to anyone who has wilfully repressed a fundamental aspect of themselves because of social taboo, such as their sexuality. Equally, Dory (Ellen DeGeneres) from *Finding Nemo* (Andrew Stanton, 2003) and *Finding Dory* (Andrew Stanton, 2016) may be 'relatable' because she, like many viewers, has a disability and is not outwardly heroic, but nonetheless succeeds against the odds.

Such characterisations still accord with the traditional Disney 'coming of age' narrative and Campbell's 'hero's journey' structure, and thus represent the continuation of much older story tropes that transcend local cultural specificities. The familiar and accessible aesthetics, the pleasingly 'transparent' narrative structures, and the 'relatable' idiom of contemporary Hollywood animation are all strategies of proximation intended to forge deep and personal emotional connections between text and spectator. Indeed, as I will argue throughout the book, this degree of proximation is one of the primary points of difference between post-1990s Hollywood animation and earlier forms. Yet the intimacy that such texts attempt to foster with their audiences remains universalistic in its intent: mainstream Hollywood films tap basic affective and emotional responses in the pursuit of a pluralistic, international mass audience.

CRITICAL APPROACH

In recent years, scholars have shown substantial interest in post-classical Hollywood animation. In addition to several peer-reviewed journals specifically addressing animation as a medium, the past decade or so has seen the publication of book-length investigations of the changing aesthetics of Disney animation;[127] of animated film as a medium;[128] of the 'hidden messages' of Hollywood animated children's films;[129] of Hollywood's historical tradition of family films;[130] of the mythic, cultural and psychoanalytic dimensions of Pixar as a studio;[131] of the narrative ideology of DreamWorks animation;[132] of how films embody values of diversity and identity;[133] of major auteurist figures in the industry;[134] and of highly significant individual films.[135] This is not a thorough list, but it does give a sense of the vibrancy of the field as it currently stands. What has *not* yet emerged – and what this book aims to provide – is a comprehensive introduction to Hollywood animation since the 1990s that encompasses cel-animated, computer-animated and stop-motion traditions of filmmaking, examines major formal, ideological and industrial trends, and relates films to social and cultural developments in the United States. In its relation to prior scholarship in this area, my approach is perhaps closest to Paul Wells's indispensible *Animation and America* (2002). More generally, though, this book reflects my belief that a cinematic form as broad and substantial as Hollywood animation cannot fully be understood solely through the individual lenses of genre, aesthetics, industrial contexts or narrative ideology, but rather requires a methodology that synthesises these different approaches.

Having established some of the industrial, stylistic and narrative contexts that inform post-1990s Hollywood animation in this opening chapter, the remainder of this book will focus on a select, but broad-ranging, group of films as case studies within a thematic, rather than chronological, structural approach. Chapter 2 will explore the predominance of family and kinship structures since the early 1990s, the point at which the majority of films began to centre on the reconstruction of damaged or incomplete families, or on the formation of surrogate families. At the same time, it will examine how mainstream Hollywood animation utilises a variety of textual strategies to attract a mixed, cross-demographic global audience. Chapter 3 will discuss the ways in which contemporary animation reflects aspects of North American culture and society, with a particular focus on what I describe as the 'embedding' of contemporaneousness in a form previously associated primarily with fantastical or fairy tale landscapes. Chapter 4 will consider how individual and shared identities are represented, and particularly the ways in which Hollywood animation attempts to accommodate 'difference' through highly visible strategies of inclusivity, diversity and multiculturalism. Finally, Chapter 5 will concentrate on films which reside on the margins of the mainstream and simultaneously target a mass market while addressing audiences that might reject Hollywood animation in its more conventional forms.

2. CROSSING BOUNDARIES: FAMILIES, AUDIENCES AND THE MAINSTREAM AESTHETIC

This chapter explores two overarching and interrelated themes. The first is the narrative centrality of family and friendship in post-1990s Hollywood animation, and how this relates to broader social practices in contemporary America. The second is the intended universalism of the films, which are exemplary instances of Hollywood family entertainment in their simultaneous embodiment of quintessential US mythologies and their recapitulation of more universalistic norms, values, fantasies and fears. As I suggested in Chapter 1, it is central to the commercial logic of Hollywood animation that it possesses a broad, cross-demographic, transnational appeal. Consequently, in order to mobilise a pluralistic, global mass audience, it must utilise a range of textual strategies to ensure that films are able to cross boundaries of age, gender, class, race, religion, language and culture.

The greater visibility of the family unit in post-1990s Hollywood animation is closely related to behind-the-scenes efforts to broaden the audience base beyond the (presumed) core demographic of pre-teenage children. To this extent, animation has followed the trend of post-1970s live-action family movies such as *Close Encounters of the Third Kind* (Steven Spielberg, 1977), *E.T. The Extra-Terrestrial* (Spielberg, 1982), *Back to the Future* (Robert Zemeckis, 1985), *Home Alone* (Chris Columbus, 1990), *Hook* (Spielberg, 1991) and *Mrs Doubtfire* (Columbus, 1993). All of these films present multi-generational American families but emphasise adult subjectivities and fantasies at least as much as those of children.

By the late 1970s, there was growing awareness at Disney that its films were failing to attract the teenage and adult audiences that had made George Lucas's *Star Wars* (1977) the biggest box office attraction of the decade. In fact, few Disney releases, including the much-lauded live-action sci-fi blockbuster *The Black Hole* (Gary Nelson, 1979), escaped what Peter Krämer has called 'the children's ghetto'.[1] It was *The Little Mermaid* (Ron Clements and John Musker, 1989) that re-established Disney's credentials among older viewers; Tino Balio has called it 'Disney's first open attempt to court baby boomers and their children'.[2] Concerned that *The Little Mermaid* would appeal primarily to young girls, executives arranged rigorous audience testing with adult audiences. Encouraged by the positive feedback, Disney ensured that the film's marketing strategy emphasised its appeal to older viewers as well as children.[3]

Mainstream Hollywood animated features have always been regarded as 'family films' that address so-called 'family audiences'. However, it was not until the release of *The Lion King* (Rob Minkoff and Roger Allers, 1994) and Pixar's *Toy Story* (John Lasseter, 1995) that family relations consistently became a central theme.[4] In a recent survey of representations of family in Disney animated features, Jessica D. Zurcher, Sarah M. Webb and Tom Robinson note that families in some configuration – ranging from single-parent, nuclear, guardian and extended families to several other permutations – are present in the majority of releases.[5] However, a large proportion of Disney animated features prior to the mid 1990s centre on orphaned children (or childlike figures) and their processes of maturation outside the family environment. In several other cases, such as in *Peter Pan* (Clyde Geronimi et al., 1953) or *The Rescuers* (Wolfgang Reitherman et al., 1977), family remains a tangential presence, or an implied future that is heralded by the climactic romantic coupling, as in fairy tale films like *Sleeping Beauty* (Geronimi et al., 1959). However, the heightened importance of family in post-1990s animation cannot simply be reduced to questions of representation. Contemporary animated features explore the dynamics of family life much more acutely than their classical-era counterparts; the individual characters are more developed, and, as this chapter will argue, a new emphasis on psychological realism and relatability emerges.

In some regards, post-1990s Hollywood animation adopts the successful strategies of the live-action family-centred films cited above, which work on a similar presumption to classical Hollywood family films such as *Meet Me in St. Louis* (Vincente Minnelli, 1944) and *The Sound of Music* (Robert Wise, 1965) that child and adult spectators each require on-screen identification figures. As the press book for *Meet Me in St. Louis* proudly claimed, '[it] is one of those rare pictures which is everyone's dish, from grandpa to little sister, because that's exactly whom it's about'.[6] Even in the majority of pre-1990s Disney features where parental figures appear, such as *Pinocchio* (Ben Sharpsteen and Hamilton Luske et al., 1940), the narrative focalisation largely remains with the child and young adult protagonists, with the characterisation of adults rarely transcending the level of archetype. In contrast, in the films discussed in this chapter – *The Lion King*, *Toy Story*, *Monsters, Inc.* (Pete Docter, 2001) *Finding Nemo* (Andrew Stanton, 2003), *The Incredibles* (Brad Bird, 2004), *The Simpsons Movie* (David Silverman, 2007), *Up* (Docter, 2009), *Despicable Me* (Pierre Coffin and Chris Renaud, 2010), *Inside Out* (Docter, 2015), *Finding Dory* (Stanton, 2016), *Coco* (Lee Unkrich, 2017) and *The Incredibles 2* (Bird, 2018) – the focalisation is shared by child and adult figures. The greater emphasis on family relations in post-1990s Hollywood animation, I argue, reflects the acknowledged commercial importance of adult demographics. This chapter will analyse the films' representations of family in context of their programmed strategies of dual (child–adult) address, and – more widely – their transnational and transcultural appeal.

The Family Audience

Discussing commercial mass media in terms of meeting a cultural need may appear precarious. Unquestionably, however, family films perform social functions. Besides their obvious textual modes of appeal – e.g. escapism, sensory stimulation, emotional uplift – they also fulfil a ritual imperative: bringing families (in their multiple configurations) together and engendering kinship through a shared viewing experience. The close relationship between Hollywood animation and family audiences is further heightened by distribution and exhibition strategies intended to facilitate the films reaching the largest possible demographic cross-section. Family films are often released during ritualised periods of family togetherness, such as during school and public holidays. In the United States, the most popular release slots are summer, Easter, Christmas and Thanksgiving. Internationally, family films often buck the pervasive trend of simultaneous release in multiple territories in order to coincide with public holiday periods in each respective country.[7] The same is true of television broadcasts of family-oriented films, which occur with much greater regularity during periods where the potential family audience is maximised, and in time slots where all members of the family are liable to be watching (e.g. afternoon and early evening).[8] This is not a recent phenomenon; since its beginnings as a mass medium, Hollywood has been eager to emphasise its identity as a leading purveyor of family entertainment.[9] Although the classical-era conception of the movie-going public as a unified mass entity has long since given way to the recognition of a pluralistic, divided market predominantly driven by the interests of teenagers and young adults, the perceived importance of the so-called 'family audience' remains apparent. A recent publication of the industry's trade agency, the Motion Picture Association of America (MPAA), proudly detailed the relative cheapness of movie-going compared to that of other popular 'family' recreational activities, such as attending theme parks and football matches.[10]

Both live-action and animated Hollywood family films employ a broad range of textual strategies to attract a sizable cross-demographic audience base. A large proportion of Disney animation (as with classic children's literature) is predicated on a belief in the overlapping entertainment requirements of adults and children. One enduring source of pleasure for adults in children's fiction is that of nostalgia for one's own childhood, coupled with a fascination for the symbolic potentiality of childhood. In *The German Ideology*, Karl Marx wrote, 'an adult cannot become a child again, or he becomes childish. But does the naiveté of the child not give him pleasure, and does he himself not endeavour to reproduce the child's veracity on a higher level?'[11] Walt Disney expressed a similar belief in claiming that his films addressed children of all ages, recuperating 'that fine, clean, unspoiled spot down deep in every one of us that maybe the world has made us forget and that maybe our pictures can help us recall'.[12] The idea expressed in these quotations – that close engagement with children and, by extension, children's culture, serves a therapeutic function for adults – has been articulated in various quarters. Sociologist Talcott Parsons, writing in the 1950s, suggested that 'children are important to adults because it is important to the latter to express what are essentially the "childish" elements of their own personalities'.[13] Indeed, even though adult consumption of texts intended primarily for children is subject to considerable social stigma, the practice does not necessarily connote imbecility or cultural illiteracy. Rather, it could reflect a desire or a need for temporary escape from the social and interpretive bounds of adulthood. The pleasure of such texts for adults, we might surmise, derives in part from the exchange of what Freud called the 'debt to life with which we are burdened from our birth' for a pre-sexual world of friendship, adventure and lack of affectation.[14]

Those modes of adult appeal might be seen as resting on the claim to recuperate a lapsed or dormant 'inner child'. However, the commercial need in the family film to mobilise cross-demographic audiences has also led to Hollywood's employing multilayered modes of address. What is generally termed 'dual address' rests on a conceptualisation of children and adults as *separate entities*, each with their own requirements.[15] As we have seen, sometimes this simply takes the form of adult identification figures, such as Mr and Mrs Banks, Mary and Bert in *Mary Poppins* (Robert Stevenson, 1964). Such films feature episodic vignettes – micronarratives – that elaborate on the concerns and motivations of the adult figures and which provide a counterpoint to the films' ostensible primary focus on child and/or young adult protagonists. Another common form of dual address is the provision of materials that only adults will fully grasp but are unlikely to alienate children, such as jokes, wordplay, and allusions to extra-textual issues or other artefacts of popular culture. Many of these forms of dual address are highly visible in the contemporary Hollywood animated feature.

In post-1970s Hollywood family entertainment, what is clearly distinct from classical Hollywood animation is the degree to which adult subjectivities have come to the fore. Spielberg's early-period family films – *Close Encounters of the Third Kind*, *E.T.* and *Hook* – are most radical in the degree to which the fantasies and neuroses of the parental figures underpin the narrative. Themes of social alienation and family disintegration become appropriate subjects, not merely as a supplement to the primary storyline, but as intrinsic to it. Roy Neary's existential crisis, Mary's borderline nervous breakdown, and Peter Banning's yuppie guilt at being a largely absentee father all point to a profound reconfiguration of attitudes to selfhood and family in productions that, up to this point, were regarded almost universally as artefacts of children's culture (and thus possessing scant social significance). As Krämer correctly observes, these narratives – as with the majority of Hollywood's biggest post-1970s hits, including the *Star Wars*, *Superman* and *Indiana Jones* franchises – are essentially 'children's films for the whole family and for teenagers, too'.[16] They are constructed around the recapitulation of adult fantasies, combined with many of the traditional pleasures of family entertainment. Indeed, all of these films offer considerable appeal for children, regardless of whatever 'adult' modes of appeal they might develop. As a child, I had little cognisance of the 'adult' aspects of *Mrs Doubtfire*: its depictions of a married couple falling out of love, their attempts to balance their family obligations and their own happiness, and the guilt and fear of failing as parents. I was concerned only with the film as a locus of play, whimsy, humour and adventure.

Since the mid 1990s, Hollywood animated features have drawn on similar strategies of dual or multivalent audience address. As I suggested in Chapter 1, the phenomenal cross-demographic popularity of *Who Framed Roger Rabbit* (Robert Zemeckis, 1988) was a turning point in Hollywood's conceptualisation of animation's potential market, convincing studio executives such as Disney's chairman, Jeffrey Katzenberg, that films must contain substantial, programmed adult appeal in order to transcend the children's audience. Films such as *Toy Story* and *Rango* (Gore Verbinsky, 2011) employ recognisable adult stars with proven box office appeal for the benefit of mature audiences, while many others – especially those produced by DreamWorks in its early-to-mid period – are replete with adult-coded intertextual allusions (see Chapter 3). Furthermore, as Ellen Scott correctly argues, Pixar's films utilise an updated version of the Production Code-era 'principle of deniability', in which complex themes – and sometimes difficult and traumatic issues – are mediated by a mode of address that, because it operates through what Scott calls the 'guise of animation', does not register as censorious, nor as especially adult-coded.[17]

In addition to these multi-demographic modes of appeal, Pixar's emergence brought with it a greater emphasis on comedy and a de-emphasising of fairy tale tropes and musical numbers. Hollywood animation began to explore modernity (and postmodernity) in more direct and complex ways. The industry's movement away from the fairy tale film brought with it a reorientation from the largely displaced ('once upon a time'), female-centred princess narrative to the recognisable, contemporary domestic relationships foregrounded in *The Lion King* and *Toy Story*. According to *Toy Story* director John Lasseter, Katzenberg 'very much wanted' the film 'to be hip, adult'.[18] To ensure this cross-demographic appeal, all of the major Hollywood producers of family films preview their films with a range of different demographics. Walt Disney's deliberately homespun, almost antediluvian claim in 1938 that '[at Disney] we don't think of grown-ups and we don't think of children' no longer applies; rather, the process of strategically and simultaneously targeting multiple audience demographics has been codified virtually to a fine art.[19]

The statistical evidence we have at our disposal confirms the extent to which Hollywood animation is a multi-demographic phenomenon. At the time of writing, a list of the top 50 highest-grossing films in North America includes 12 post-1990s Hollywood animated features: *Incredibles 2*; *The Lion King* (Jon Favreau, 2019); *Finding Dory*; *Frozen II* (Chris Buck and Jennifer Lee, 2019); *Shrek 2* (Andrew Adamson, Kelly Asbury and Conrad Vernon, 2004); *Toy Story 4* (Josh Cooley, 2019); *The Lion King* (1994); *Toy Story 3* (Lee Unkrich, 2010); *Frozen* (Chris Buck and Jennifer Lee, 2013); *Finding Nemo*; *The Secret Life of Pets* (Chris Renaud, 2016); and *Despicable Me 2* (Pierre Coffin and Chris Renaud, 2013). The huge popularity of these films raises important questions regarding their audience, particularly in light of MPAA box office statistics revealing that children under the age of 12 accounted for only 10 per cent of all tickets sold in the United States in 2017 and 2018.[20]

ComScore's PostTrak exit polling service provides valuable insights on the composition of audiences during films' initial theatrical run. PostTrak data consistently registers that adults – people over the age of 18 – make up around half of all attendees during the opening weekend of major animated features in the United States. Even taking into consideration the fact that parents are often required to accompany young children the theatre, this is a striking statistic. Given the films' acknowledged appeal to adults, it may not be surprising that children aged 2–11 made up only 31 per cent of audiences for *Up*, and 26 per cent for *Incredibles 2*.[21] Interestingly, however, only 40 per cent of audiences during the opening weekend of *Cars* (John Lasseter, 2006) were under the age of 18, which might appear hard to reconcile with the film's reputation as one of Pixar's most child-oriented releases.[22] Increasingly, millennials have emerged as a pivotal audience group, particularly in relation to sequels to much older films. The 18–24 demographic accounted for 40 per cent of movie-goers for *Finding*

Dory, the sequel to *Finding Nemo*, which might be attributed to the fact that many individuals in this age bracket would first have experienced the original film in childhood.[23] Conversely, 51 per cent of audiences for DreamWorks' *How to Train Your Dragon* (Chris Sanders and Dean DeBlois, 2010) were over the age of 25.[24] Non-child audiences clearly play a major role in driving the box office potential of contemporary animated films to levels that – in previous generations – would have been unimaginable. These figures, while confirming the boundary-breaking reach of the films in question, also reveal the inherent heterogeneity of the so-called 'family audience'. What emerges is a mutable entity rather than the stable, clearly delineated demographic section that the term itself might imply.

REPOSITIONING THE FAMILY: *THE LION KING* AND *TOY STORY*

At the turn of the 1990s, Disney was the only significant presence in the field of feature animation within Hollywood. While surveys have shown that Disney is widely seen by the general public as being synonymous with 'family values', its films were largely divorced from the daily realities of family life.[25] *The Lion King* and *Toy Story*, by contrast, brought intra-family relationships to the centre of the narrative. Furthermore, both films are more overtly adult-oriented than any mainstream Hollywood animated feature to that point, with the notable exception of *Who Framed Roger Rabbit* (which was distributed via Touchstone, a label reserved for Disney's more 'adult' fare).

The basic plot of *The Lion King*, it has often been observed, bears resemblance to *Hamlet*: a lion cub named Simba (voiced by Jonathan Taylor Thomas and Matthew Broderick) must avenge the murder of his father, the great lion king Mufasa (James Earl Jones), by his cowardly and duplicitous uncle, Scar (Jeremy Irons). The death of the father facilitates a primary narrative strategy in Disney animated features, namely the individuation, maturation and eventual victory of the child protagonist. Jeffrey Katzenberg seems to have internalised this specific element of the Disney narrative ideology; according to James B. Stewart's account of the initial conversation between Katzenberg and Peter Schneider, the former outlined the basic premise as follows: 'A child loses a parent, goes out into the world, tries to avoid responsibility, then faces it [. . .] the animal kingdom is a metaphor.'[26]

Although *The Lion King* may be located within a wider tradition of Disney orphaned child narratives, there is an important point of difference. Whereas the absent parents in earlier films such as *Snow White and the Seven Dwarfs* (David Hand et al., 1937) and *Cinderella* (Clyde Geronimi et al., 1950) died long ago – or long enough, at least, that their death is not emotionally disturbing for the orphaned child or for movie-goers – Mufasa's death occurs roughly one-third of the way into the film, by which point he is firmly established as a figure of strength, courage and benevolence on whom Simba relies for protection and moral guidance. *The Lion King* further divagates from most previous Disney orphaned-child narratives in that the means by which Mufasa is killed (and Simba orphaned) is graphically depicted: Scar ruthlessly drops Mufasa from a cliff-top and watches as he is trampled to death by stampeding wildebeest. According to story consultant Christopher Vogler, this sequence was the subject of considerable debate amongst Disney animators, many of whom considered it potentially traumatic for children and therefore untenable. Eventually, it was decided to proceed on the basis that the film was being made 'for the entire spectrum of the audience, not just for infants'.[27]

The shooting of Bambi's mother is an obvious point of reference here, but the comparison is only partially valid, as her killing takes place off-screen and her corpse is never seen. In *The Lion King*, the emotional impact of the father's death is brought to the centre of the narrative; indeed, the moment of Mufasa's death is framed in slow-motion from Scar's point of view, implicating the viewer in the violent act and emphasising its horror (Figure 2.1). In this sense, the quest narrative is given new dramatic impetus: Simba is defined by his perceived need to live up to the legacy of his father and his forebears. It is his adolescent existential confusion, coupled with his fears of inferiority when compared to his venerable father, which are the central problems the narrative must resolve.

Adult male fantasies and anxieties are pre-eminent. Some critics observed that, unlike *The Little Mermaid* and *Beauty and the Beast* (Gary Trousdale and

Figure 2.1   Scar's POV shot of Mufasa's death (*The Lion King*, Disney, 1994). Frame grab.

Kirk Wise, 1991), *The Lion King* is more clearly a boys' film than a girls' film. Mufasa's influence looms large over the maturing Simba throughout the narrative, but it is also shown that the transmission of strength, courage and wisdom from father to son forms part of a larger patrilineal structure. Indeed, Simba's learning of these virtues occurs wholly independently of the mother, who largely recedes into the background for long passages of the film and reappears only fleetingly at the end. It is also pertinent – in terms of the film's prospective appeal to adult men – that the events of the film are not shown solely from Simba's point of view. Instead, we are presented with sequences that reveal Mufasa's own preoccupations (e.g. his dismay over his ongoing rivalry with his treacherous brother, his fear that his son will come to harm when he learns that Simba has ventured outside the Pride Lands and into the hyenas' territory). The film thus offers avenues of address for adult viewers that are distinct from the more comic, intertextual mechanisms employed in *Who Framed Roger Rabbit* or *Aladdin* (Ron Clements and John Musker, 1992), and which are rooted in the same parental neuroses that frame Robin Williams' *patres familias* in *Hook* and *Mrs Doubtfire*. The presence of such themes should not be very surprising, given both the ever-increasing realisation in the studio that such films must contain appeal to older children and to adults, and the desire on the part of Jeffrey Katzenberg to draw story elements, semi-autobiographically, from his own formative years. More than any other protagonist in the 'Disney Renaissance', Katzenberg worked to embed 'adult' textual elements in these films.

The Lion King continually emphasises the cyclicality of life. This can be seen, primarily, in its narrative structure. The lion cub Simba does not merely replace his dead father, but effectively becomes a re-embodiment of him. The lyrics of the opening musical number, 'The Circle of Life', is explicit in the view that time is not linear, but rather is governed by patterns of continuity: birth, life, death and renewal. As Mufasa tells Simba, 'A king's time as ruler rises and falls like the sun. One day, Simba, the sun will set on my time here, and will rise with you as the new king'. The theme is again reaffirmed when Mufasa, in response to Simba asking if they will always be together, replies: 'Let me tell you something my father told me. Look at the stars. The great kings of the past look down on us from those stars . . . So whenever you feel alone, just remember that those kings will always be there to guide you – and so will I.' The 'Circle of Life', as Martin Barker points out, is 'both natural and moral'; it 'is how things are but therefore tells the characters what they have to do'.[28] Simba cannot become king until he meets his responsibilities, but these responsibilities are part of a larger, transcendent, natural order. Like all Disney films, *The Lion King* is inherently didactic, but the moral lessons it attempts to impart are not presented as such; rather, as Barker argues, they are 'emotional truths'.[29] This point applies to the overwhelming majority of Hollywood family films. The ideological naturalness of the moral structures and behavioural patterns that undergird them is repeatedly emphasised, so that the films appear to be fundamentally innocent and non-political, but with the implicit corollary that any substantive deviation from these natural laws is aberrant.

The child's learning of responsibility and subsequent coming of age – a metanarrative of children's fiction – is fulfilled by Simba's eventual return to the plains to overthrow Scar. Though the sequence in which his friend, Nala (Moira Kelly), persuades him to return is framed as a moral choice that will ensure the survival of the pack, what is truly at stake is Simba's eschewal of the indulgent self-absorption of his life in the forest with his friends Timon (Nathan Lane), a meerkat, and Pumbaa (Ernie Sabella), a warthog. The trio's way of life is emblematised by their catchphrase, 'Hakuna Matata', which translates literally in Swahili as 'no worries'. The term suggests a negation of duty and responsibility that the Disney ideology – with its valorisation of Calvinist ideals of hard work and productivity – implicitly rejects. In his position as ancestral ruler, it behoves Simba to restore order, marry Nala, and father the next generation of lion cubs. Ultimately, the much-vaunted 'Circle of Life' is localised in the climactic vision of Simba presenting his cub to the pack, just as Mufasa had done at the outset of the film. Having successfully established Simba's masculine prowess – his successful restoration as literal and symbolic father – the film's coda serves an important additional function, reaffirming the continuation of family, kinship and heritage.

In this sense, *The Lion King* can be seen in context of the Hollywood trope of 'the restoration of the Father', which Robin Wood has called

> the dominant project, ad infinitum and post nauseam, of the contemporary Hollywood cinema, a veritable metasystem embracing all the available genres and all the current cycles, from realist drama to pure fantasy.[30]

The Father, as Wood has it, must be understood 'in all senses, symbolic, literal, potential: patriarchal authority (the Law), which assigns all other elements to their correct, subordinate, allotted roles'.[31] According to Wood, the *Star Wars* films are a paradigmatic example: they work to 'put everyone back in his/her place', reassert the ideological legitimacy of patriarchal authority (represented here by Obi-Wan and Yoda), and 'reconstruct' audiences as children who must obey the Law of the Father. The final scenes of *The Lion King*, according to Wood's thesis, fulfils Simba's 'Oedipal trajectory': he becomes, essentially, a reincarnation of his forefathers. Tellingly, in the trade press Katzenberg described the film as 'a love story between a father and son'.[32] Yet in its restoration of the patriarchal order, this climax seemingly disallows the possibility that change (individual, social) is desirable or even possible. Although a high proportion of earlier Hollywood animated features might be said to function in a similar manner in a symbolic sense, relations between fathers and sons assumed far greater narrative centrality from the mid 1990s onwards, following in the wake of live-action family films such as *Back to the Future*, *Hook* and *Mrs Doubtfire*.

If *The Lion King* constituted a notable shift from earlier traditions of mainstream Hollywood animation in reasserting the centrality of family relationships, then *Toy Story* goes even further in rooting these preoccupations within a clearly recognisable, modern domestic setting. This reorientation from the fantastic milieu of the fairy tale film to the domestic environment is more significant than it may appear. As Hollywood's first computer-generated animated feature, the storyline – according to Disney executive Thomas Schumacher – 'was highly dependent on the computerised technique, which gave the characters a three-dimensional quality and thereby provided greater emotional weight'.[33] Since the mid 1990s, emotional realism – the source of what is commonly known as 'relatability' – has attained particular centrality. *Close Encounters of the Third Kind* and *E.T.* were key precursors in their focus on the emotional subjectivities of their protagonists and the psychological impact of family breakdown. As with the children in those two films, *Toy Story*'s central child figure, Andy (John Morris), is forced to grow up in a single-parent household with an absentee father. However, while all three films acknowledge changing definitions of family, *Toy Story* follows *Mrs Doubtfire* in normalising the single-parent family, rather than characterising it as a form of social malfunction. *Mrs Doubtfire*, released more than a decade after *E.T.*, is able to forecast a possible future for 'family' *after* the divorce of the parents. *Toy Story* presents a functional domestic environment in which the absence of Andy's father is never even remarked on. Essentially, in their attempt to engage with and assuage anxieties surrounding family breakdown, these films are participating in a form of social work.

Toy Story presents a dual family dynamic: the literal family, as noted above, but also the symbolic family, composed of the toys, and led by a surrogate father – the 1950s cowboy doll Woody (Tom Hanks). As with the literal family, the toys' symbolic family structure outwardly appears precarious. They live under constant fear of being usurped by newer, more technologically advanced iterations of themselves. They are relieved when Andy unwraps his birthday presents to discover a lunchbox, bed sheets and a board game, but are horrified when Buzz Lightyear (Tim Allen) – who possesses 'more gadgets that a Swiss army knife' – is revealed as Andy's new toy. While Andy's other toys are impressed by Buzz, the newcomer elicits violent jealousy in Woody, who is terrified that his status as 'Andy's favourite' is being usurped. These anxieties are borne out when Andy is seen literally weighing his two favourite toys in each hand, and then when he chooses to take Buzz, not Woody, out on a play date. Possessively, Woody warns Buzz to 'Stay away from Andy – he's mine, and no one is taking him away from me', and then attempts to push his rival out of the window. Their mutual antagonism is the central problematic that the narrative must resolve. The film adopts the narrative ideology of the 'buddy movie' genre as a mechanism through which quasi-familial (platonic, fraternal) love can eventually flourish. Thus the film's much-lauded 'emotional realism' is firmly embedded within the larger conventions of the family film, in which kinship ties are ultimately reaffirmed, whatever obstacles the film puts in their way.

But *Toy Story* goes further in its strategies of cross-demographic address. Animation historian Leonard Maltin points out that:

> Disney's audience was always parents taking kids [. . .] Now they're going after young moviegoers, the same audience every other studio is going after. If you can expand your audience without excluding the one you already have, then you've hit paydirt.[34]

Although the film's 'adult' modes of address require close analysis, they are never a vital component of the scenes in which they are placed. As such, they do not exclude children (or any other faction) who are unable to understand them. Indeed, much of the film's comedy is doubly coded: either equally accessible to children and adults (e.g. slapstick and sight gags), or operating on more than one interpretive level. One example of the latter occurs when baby Molly misaligns Mr Potato Head's face. He then turns to another character and quips, 'I'm Picasso!' In order to comprehend this reference, the spectator must know of Picasso's abstract paintings of human heads with their misaligned facial features. This level of cultural literacy is beyond most young children (and many adults too), and this is both acknowledged and diffused by Hamm's response: 'I don't get it.' But the joke operates on a simpler level: the incongruity of the misaligned face still works as a sight gag.[35] Similarly, the aforementioned scene in which a depressed Buzz is discovered by Woody drinking tea also functions as comic absurdity. Even fairly young children will understand that it is impossible to become intoxicated by drinking imaginary Darjeeling tea, so his slurred speech is a non sequitur. The image of the exaggeratedly masculine Buzz wearing a flowery apron and drinking tea (with their feminine, maternal coding), meanwhile, is a comical *visual* incongruity that is accessible to all types of audiences.

The film's strategy of tapping adult desires is also visible in its deliberately cultivated modes of nostalgia. Randy Newman's music is part of this: despite his success with Disney, he came to prominence as a singer-songwriter in the 1970s. The film's non-diegetic musical moments, sung by Newman in his idiosyncratically homespun, sardonic drawl, bespeak authenticity, negating the ingratiating professionalism of some of Disney's earlier musical numbers. As Jack Zipes has observed, most of Disney animated features from *Snow White* to *Aladdin* adhere to the conventions of the 1930s Hollywood musical.[36] However, director John Lasseter made a conscious decision to move away from diegetic songs, believing that characters spontaneously bursting into song would detract from the film's 'realist' credentials.[37] Diegetic musical numbers largely fell out of favour in live-action Hollywood family films during the 1970s, but non-diegetic songs had been used to memorable effect in such films as *Back to the Future*, where 'The Power of Love' by Huey Lewis and the News underlines the film's youth and adult sensibilities. Newman's songs verbally express the inner thoughts and emotions of the characters in the usual fashion, but their more up-tempo and ironic style adds a further layer of adult appeal.

Moreover, many of the toys are old enough to be familiar to adult audiences from their own childhoods: Mr Potato Head and Slinky Dog first retailed in the United States during the early 1950s. Evoking adult nostalgia for childhood in this fashion is a constant of the Hollywood family film. Relatedly, *Toy Story* is preoccupied with the transience of childhood. The toys' omnipresent fear of Andy's growing up is rooted in the sure knowledge that his maturation portends their symbolic death: a future in which they are never played with, shelved, or destroyed. The films look wistfully on childhood as an Arcadian realm of boundless imagination and uninhibited play that, once left, can never be regained. Whilst most children in the 'real world' actively look forward to adulthood for its supposed liberation from overbearing authority, the film's interpretation of childhood is rooted to adult subjectivities. Bert's (Dick Van Dyke) portrait of childhood slipping 'like sand through a sieve' in *Mary Poppins* is typical of a broader trope in post-twentieth-century adult-generated children's fiction, in which the celebration of childhood's spontaneity and unaffectedness is clouded by a regretful, nostalgic preoccupation with its evanescence.

In a sense, the film's obsession with growing up – and 'growing out' of childhood – reasserts the binary social distinction between 'childhood' and 'adulthood' that contemporary Western culture, and post-*Star Wars* live-action family films in particular, have worked to erode. Cultural critics such as Benjamin Barber have spoken against the 'infantilising' effects of neo-liberal economics and consumer capitalism, arguing that Western popular culture constructs and maintains a permanent childhood in adults in which reason and thought give way to the instant desires of the Freudian pleasure principle.[38] Barber would probably see *Toy Story* as a cog in this machine, but the film actually disavows his 'infantilist ethos' in two key regards. Firstly, as we have seen, it clearly addresses child and adult audiences as *separate entities*, recognising that their partially discrete interests stem from differing levels of cognitive development, knowledge and experience. Secondly, all of the *Toy Story* films actively repudiate the 'kidulthood' that Barber now sees as coterminous with Western society. There is no forecasting of lifelong play in their vision of Andy's adult life. Rather, the imminent threat of abandonment (or, in the case of Jessie, Stinky Pete and Lotso in the second and third films, the traumatic memory of it) hangs heavy over every toy in the series.

Disney's animated films had always proven phenomenally successful in addressing not just real children, but also 'the child within the adult', presenting narrative pleasures designed to 'regress' adult spectators to symbolic childhood. While this form of 'undifferentiated address' is clearly present in *Toy Story*, the film presents a more diverse range of attractions – popular adult stars, verbal and visual puns, intertextual allusions, heightened emotional realism, and social commentary – to appeal directly to more sophisticated sensibilities, including those of 'tweens' and teenagers. This was widely acknowledged by critics on release. The *New York Times* called it 'a parent-tickling delight [. . .] a work of incredible cleverness in the best two-tiered Disney tradition. Children will enjoy a new take on the irresistible idea of toys coming to life. Adults will marvel at a witty script and utterly brilliant anthropomorphism'; *Newsweek* thought it had 'something for everyone on the age spectrum'; and *Variety* called it 'a clever mix of simplicity and sophistication that cuts across all age barriers with essential themes'.[39]

This kind of cross-demographic appeal underpins the enormous popularity of studios such as Pixar, DreamWorks and Disney itself. In turn, the boundary-breaking appeal of *The Lion King* and *Toy Story* corresponds with an interesting phenomenon where, according to user-generated IMDb ratings and aggregated review sites such as Rotten Tomatoes and Metacritic, a number of post-1990s Hollywood family-oriented animated features rank amongst the best films ever made. At the time of writing, the IMDb user-generated ranking of the top 100 films of all time includes *The Lion King* (1994) (#44), *Spider-Man: Into the Spider-Verse* (#59), *Coco* (#61), *WALL-E* (#66), *Toy Story 3* (#86), and *Toy Story* (#96).[40] This level of esteem reflects the effectiveness of the repackaging of Hollywood feature animation from inconsequential children's fare to what is now widely viewed as a serious and legitimate art form operating on multiple interpretive levels. This 'tradition of quality' is supported by the Hollywood studios' machineries of promotion and distribution, as well as unparalleled resources in terms of funding, production personnel, and equipment. Nevertheless, in its broad-appeal narrative strategies, *Toy Story* has served as a template for the subsequent tradition of 'quality' animated family films distributed by most of the major Hollywood studios since the turn of the century.

Family and Kinship

Contemporary Hollywood animated features have tended to follow *The Lion King* and *Toy Story* in weighing the predominance of family as a social system with awareness of its changing structures. The bourgeois Victorian conception of the family as a 'tent pitch'd in a world not right' – or, as John Ruskin characterised it, 'the place of peace; the shelter, not only from all injury, but from all terror, doubt, and division' – still holds considerable sway, but post-1970s films also concede the possibility of family itself as a locus of conflict and division.[41] In productions such as *Monsters, Inc.*, *Finding Nemo*, *Up*, *Despicable Me*, and *Finding Dory*, the mostly unproblematic nuclear and extended families of classical (live-action) Hollywood family entertainment are displaced by depictions of single-parent or surrogate families, representations of disability, and various other permutations that deviate from traditional family structures. To this extent, Hollywood is merely reflecting clear and measurable changes in the composition of families in the United States. Between 1970 and 1998, the proportion of households comprising a married couple with at least one child declined from 40 per cent to 26 per cent.[42] Equally, by the mid 1990s, the number of babies born outside marriage had risen to 25 per cent amongst white mothers, 41 per cent amongst Hispanic mothers, and 70 per cent amongst African American mothers.[43]

Popular definitions of the word 'family' have also evolved. Although the US census continues to define it as 'a group of two persons or more (one of whom is a householder) related by birth, marriage or adoption and residing together', a survey conducted in 1992 by the Massachusetts Mutual Life Company found that almost three-quarters of the respondents wished to widen the definition to include any 'group of people who love and care for each other'.[44] Films such as *Frozen II* advance non-traditional models of family that reflect these attitudinal changes: the quintet comprising sisters Elsa (Idina Menzel) and Anna (Kristen Bell), Anna's boyfriend (later fiancé) Kristoff (Jonathan Groff), Sven the reindeer and Olaf (Josh Gadd) the anthropomorphised snowman is explicitly presented as a family unit made up of people who live together and love and support one another, and whose individual differences are celebrated. Nevertheless, representations of 'alternative' family structures have only gone so far; at the time of writing, gay and lesbian families remain invisible in contemporary Hollywood animation, reflecting deep-set ideological tensions regarding changes to accepted codes of social normalcy.

Each of the films discussed in this section deals with a mature, single man who unexpectedly finds himself the lone father (or surrogate father) to a child and who must quickly learn to cope with this new arrangement. In the process, the father's own neuroses and insecurities are laid bare in a fashion that, once again, is reminiscent of the adult-oriented live-action family films of the late 1980s and early 1990s. Admittedly, part of the attraction of these films derives from a familiar comic trope: that of the incompetent, fish-out-of-water patriarch, incongruously forced to engage in domestic duties. Nevertheless, the recurrence of this specific narrative pattern also reflects attitudes to adulthood, parenthood, and the ongoing social function of the family in twenty-first-century America. As Shawn Haley has noted, 'the bonds between the essential members of the family group (Husband–Wife, Mother–Child, Father–Child, and Sibling–Sibling) are becoming weaker', underpinned by the broader perception of 'family arrangements as temporary'.[45] At the start of this chapter, I suggested that family films serve instrumental functions; one of these may be a revanchist claim to the desirability, if not the perceived necessity, of family, which has long been construed as the bedrock of the socialisation process.

Monsters, Inc., despite its surface quirkiness, ultimately reaffirms the primacy of family and friendship and suggests ways they might be kept in balance. Pixar's third feature, following *Toy Story* and *A Bug's Life* (John Lasseter, 1998), it centres on the character of James P. Sullivan (John Goodman), known as Sulley, a supposedly fearsome but actually gentle and cuddly 'monster' whose job is to scare and elicit screams from children. At the start of the film, Sulley knows nothing of children or family life. Indeed, he is admonished by his best friend, the fellow 'monster' Mike Wazowski (Billy Crystal) – another comically incongruous 'ordinary' name – for spending his entire time outside work attempting to hone his ability to scare children. Unlike Mike, who pursues a relationship with a gorgon-like receptionist called Celia (Jennifer Tilly), Sulley appears uninterested in the possibility of family. This changes when he meets, and is entranced by, the three-year-old human girl, Boo (Mary Gibbs). Unlike other human children (which the monsters believe to be toxic), she is not frightened of him, and his latent paternal instincts are brought to the fore.

Much of the dramatic substance of the film is contained within Sulley's attempts to defeat his rival, the reptilian Randall (Steve Buscemi), who intends to use a dastardly device called 'The Scream Extractor' to forcibly extract the children's screams that power the city of Monstropolis. However, the darkest point in the narrative occurs when Sulley, compelled by his boss to produce a monstrous roar, inadvertently makes Boo frightened of him. The shot/reverse shot editing pattern emphasises this fundamental shift in their relationship: a point-of-view shot shows Boo's perspective of Sulley's enormous, threatening face bellowing at her; the reverse angle frames his vision of her terrified face. This momentary switching from 'objective' to 'subjective' camera reveals the moment of crisis from the viewpoint of both characters. However, the fact that the film's single child figure is too young to talk, or even to express herself beyond gestures and facial expressions, inevitably serves to direct audience attention and engagement towards Sulley. His subsequent, anguished remark to Mike – 'Did you see the way she looked at me . . .?' – brings forth adult fears of failure, rejection and abandonment. (It also anticipates the father's similarly horrified reaction to his son's exclamation of 'I hate you' in *Finding Nemo*.) These are momentary crises that are quickly overcome, but the insecurities they embody are more abiding, addressing real-world perceived anxieties on the part of the substantial adult male audience. In this regard, the figure of Sulley perhaps deliberately inhabits a kind of liminal identity between childhood (cuddliness, naivety) and adulthood (symbolic father to Boo).

This central child–adult relationship reasserts a widely held belief in the transformative powers of parenthood to rehabilitate self-absorbed adults. At the same time, however, the father–daughter bond threatens Sulley's close friendship with Mike, whose fierce resentment precipitates what appears to be an intractable breakdown in the relationship. Mike's earnest attempt at reconciliation is rendered comical as it is accompanied (and punctuated) by the invisible Randall attacking Sulley, but the sentiment is worth reproducing:

> Look, it's not that I don't care about the kid . . . I was just mad, that's all. I needed some time to think . . . You and I are a team. Nothing is more important than our friendship . . . I'm sorry I wasn't there for you, but I am now.

The sequence is explicitly double-voiced, presenting a (child-coded) humorous action sequence of comic misunderstanding and slapstick absurdity, while reasserting a more earnest (and perhaps more adult-coded) reconciliation between the estranged friends. The need to balance the perceived emotional and cognitive requirements of audiences of all ages is clearly apparent here. Moreover, while it may be interpreted as asserting the primacy of Sulley and Boo's relationship, the film ultimately posits a compromise. In the final act, Sulley and Mike are again inseparable, and although Boo is returned to the human world, the last scene implies that Sulley is to be allowed visiting rights (allegorising the part-time presence of divorced parents in the lives of their children in the 'real world'). Randy Newman's closing title song contains the suggestive lyric, 'I wouldn't have nothing if I didn't have you.' The lyrics refuse to specify the subject of the song, and the fact that both Goodman and Crystal sing sections of it allows us to surmise that it is a paean jointly to family and to friendship.

As with *Toy Story*, *Monsters, Inc.* appropriates generic elements of the 'buddy movie', foregrounding the friendship between two adult male figures. In this sense, male platonic relationships fulfil a similar role to that of the heterosexual romances that are usually the ultimate narrative goal in the classical-era Disney fairy tale. Another similarity between the two films is that both take a potentially uncanny premise – that of inanimate objects brought monstrously to life – and impose on it broadly 'relatable' themes of individual and group identity. Although the neuroses of the characters are mined for comedy, anxieties surrounding the individual's place in the world – the need to measure one's accomplishments against those of others, and the role of interpersonal relationships as support mechanisms – are highly prominent. For children, the protagonists of these films can be taken at face value as loveable, empathetic figures that exhibit elements of the childlike and of benign adulthood, divorced from the outward associations of adult identity (e.g. size and shape, physiognomy). For older spectators, they are more recognisable as simulacra of adults, with all the responsibilities and anxieties that entails. The CG rendering, therefore, operates as a veneer, beneath which the familiar voices of actors such as John Goodman and Billy Crystal – performers known predominantly for their work in mainstream, non-children's media – anchor the film to adult preoccupations. These performances also function intertextually, with Crystal's characters in, say, *When Harry Met Sally. . .* (Rob Reiner, 1989) or Goodman's various screen *patres familias* informing our understanding of the characters they portray here.[46] Certainly, viewers familiar with Goodman's quintessential American patriarch in the sitcom *Roseanne* (1988–2018) and the 1990s live-action adaptation of *The Flintstones* (Brian Levant, 1994) might well be primed for James P. Sullivan's transformation from work-obsessed monster to sentimental surrogate father.

Whereas *Monsters, Inc.* centres on an outwardly monstrous character that has to learn the qualities of the nurturing parent, *Finding Nemo* is concerned with the potentially infantilising effects on the child of over-zealous parenting. As Roger Ebert pointed out in his contemporary review of the film, *Finding Nemo* is a relatively rare animation about fatherhood.[47] Allegedly inspired by a trip to the zoo in which it dawned on director Andrew Stanton that his over-protectiveness was inhibiting a potential moment of father–son bonding, the film invests in the figure of an anxious, neurotic single father, the clownfish Marlin (Albert Brooks) single-handedly raising his son, Nemo (Alexander Gould), after his wife and their eggs are eaten by a barracuda. Male parent anxiety is signposted at the start, as the expectant father Marlin nervously asks of his children, 'What if they don't *like* me?' *Finding Nemo* follows *Toy Story* in viewing single parenthood as a quotidian reality of modern life, but nonetheless probes the psychological implications of this family structure on the father and the child. In some regards, the fact that the protagonists are rendered as tropical fish emphasises rather than obscures this dynamic: the allegory invites identification, but without the self-consciousness that might be present in live-action with human performers. Although the dazzling colours and fluid oceanic movements make *Finding Nemo* perhaps Pixar's most aesthetically pleasing release, there is a serious parable of modern parenting barely beneath the surface.

Much of the film concerns Marlin's attempts to recover Nemo after the child, frustrated and ashamed by his father's excessive caution, disobeys Marlin's exhortations not to swim into open water and is subsequently carried away by the currents. Whereas *Toy Story* and *Monsters, Inc.* have widely been seen as buddy movies, *Finding Nemo* appropriates the structure of the quest narrative, eschewing Disneyesque fairy tale in favour of a set of generic tropes more recognisable to adult viewers while still operating within the family-adventure framework. The obvious subtext is that Marlin, by rescuing Nemo, must also earn his son's respect. It is clear that Nemo holds an extremely low opinion of his father's abilities: when a fish remarks to Nemo, 'You're lucky to have someone out there who's looking for you', he replies, 'He's not looking for me. He's scared of the ocean.' Marlin's eventual rescue of Nemo presents a valedictory and cathartic experience, not just for the on-screen father but perhaps for fathers watching the film as well.

The final line of the film, Marlin's happy yet melancholic 'Bye, son', as Nemo swims off to new adventures (albeit within the relative security of his school class), addresses adult emotions rather than those of the child. The pleasure of seeing one's offspring successfully individuated – no longer emotionally or physically dependent on the parent and able to think and behave with self-sufficiency – is weighed against the inevitable sadness that this formative period is over. Yet it also marks a psychological breakthrough for Marlin: as for director Stanton, the moment of epiphany liberates him from the paralysing fear of failing as a parent. The film's belated sequel, *Finding Dory*, builds on this theme, repeatedly emphasising the value of impetuous action over caution and logic. Spontaneity is framed as a means of accomplishing goals that appear, outwardly, to be highly dangerous if not impossible. It is presumably no coincidence that this quality is usually associated with children: people yet to learn adult conservatism and – judging by the two films' repeated mockery of Marlin – should aim to avoid doing so, because rationalism and caution are viewed as paralysing vices of adulthood.

Finding Nemo is one of several Pixar films that advance a fluid definition of family in which orphaned or isolated protagonists are ultimately reintegrated within surrogate family structures; other examples include *Toy Story*, *Monsters, Inc.*, and *WALL-E*. The lost and hapless Dory (Ellen DeGeneres), a blue tang suffering from short-term memory loss, is effectively adopted into Marlin and Nemo's similarly incomplete family in a quasi-maternal role. *Finding Dory* takes this trope further still, uniting Dory's surrogate and biological family (her long-lost parents) in an all-inclusive kinship network that also includes the recalcitrant octopus, Hank (Ed O'Neill). In the process, Dory finally explicitly acknowledges Marlin and Nemo as her 'family'; she places the same importance on rediscovering them, after they are accidentally separated, as she did on finding her own parents.

Another obvious link between *Finding Nemo* and *Finding Dory* is their portrayal of disability. The films' three central characters (Marlin, Nemo and Dory) are all disabled in some way. Nemo was born with a deformed fin on his right side, limiting his ability to swim. As such, he has to overcome not just his father's over-protectiveness but also his own self-doubt. In one scene, he becomes trapped in the fish-tank filter and cries for help from the other fish. Gill (Willem Dafoe), another fish with the same disability, refuses to help him and insists that Nemo frees himself. Marlin and Dory have less visible but still highly debilitating afflictions. While Marlin clearly suffers from a form of post-traumatic stress disorder linked to his failure to protect his wife and children at the outset of *Finding Nemo*,

Dory's short-term memory loss, mined for comedy in the first film, is brought to the centre of the narrative in *Finding Dory*. Her periodic flashes of recollection, in tandem with her qualities of goodness and tenacity, allow her to overcome her disability and succeed against the odds. At the end of the film, having successfully found her parents and liberated the entire piscine inhabitants of an aquarium, Dory recalls words spoken to her by her mother in childhood: 'You can do whatever you put your mind to, Dory.' Both films, essentially, are inspiring parables of self-empowerment against the odds. Historically, physical and mental disabilities have not featured prominently in Hollywood family entertainment (indeed, if they are present at all, they have tended to be markers of perversity). However, their presence in these films reflects a paradigm shift in attitudes to diversity in the United States, and the greater opportunity (if not the need) to engage with serious issues in more explicit ways.

Whereas the Pixar films discussed in this section work to build or reconstruct a 'complete' family from an incomplete one, Illumination Entertainment's lucrative *Despicable Me* series (2010–) is, at heart, a parable on the challenges and rewards of single parenthood. The films centre on the figure of Gru (Steve Carell), a supposed international super-criminal whose tough veneer crumbles after he adopts three orphaned girls. Given the instrumental functions of the family film in reaffirming law and order, of course, even Gru's initial nefariousness is a form of pantomime villainy that is free of malice or lasting harm. His crimes include stealing miniature replicas of the Statue of Liberty and the Eiffel Tower from Las Vegas, and jokingly threatening to kill a neighbour's dog when it relieves itself on his front lawn. Hunchbacked and sporting an outrageous Eastern European accent, Gru is an obvious comic parody of a bad guy whose villainy merely serves to emphasise his softening into kindliness and domesticity. Inevitably, many of the scenes of Gru learning the responsibilities of parenthood are mined for comic value. In one sequence, we see him doing housework, incongruously wearing a gingham apron, and the girls' clothes have accidentally dyed his super-villain outfit an unmanly shade of pink; in the following scene, his mother is showing the girls pictures of Gru as a child with shoulder-length hair that moves one of them to observe, 'He looks like a girl!' to his obvious discomfort.

The joke, obviously, is that of Gru's unwilling effeminisation, which plays incongruously against his hyper-masculine image. Yet there is a serious undercurrent in such scenes. Gru's unfeeling exterior is clearly established as a direct consequence of his feelings of rejection as a child: whenever he is rebuked by another character, he has flashbacks to his unsuccessful attempts to impress his mother; even launching his fully functional rocket ship in the back garden merely elicits from her an apathetic 'meh'. Good parenthood, the film suggests, requires kindness, attentiveness and encouragement; a failure to follow these basic tenets of child-rearing has direct consequences in terms of the child's character formation. Gru's three adopted children, Margot, Edith and Agnes (all dyed-in-the-wool all-American girls' names), are well-adjusted and sweet-natured – perfect simulacra, indeed, of the Romantics' image of incorruptible childhood. Their innocence also brings into sharp relief the necessity of Gru's rehabilitation: he must change not just for his own salvation (nor even that of society), but in order to be the good dad that they need and deserve. Although he disappoints the children by missing their dance performance, he redeems himself from rescuing them from the clutches of his nemesis, Vector (Jason Segel). In the process, he displays hitherto unseen physical capabilities, such as dodging an arsenal of heat-seeking missiles and defeating a shark in hand-to-hand combat. It is an important aspect of such films that the personal sacrifices made by adults when they assume domestic responsibilities are seen ultimately as empowering, not enfeebling. Indeed, rather like *The Incredibles*, *Despicable Me* disavows what is presumed to be an oppressive fear amongst American adult men, namely that fatherhood entails an irreversible negation of masculine potency; instead, both films repositioned it as a source of strength. The fact that the pleasures and the comforts of parenthood are able to reform even an unregenerate malefactor like Gru is the ultimate proof of the sanctity of family.

Perhaps no sequence in *any* film more underlines the importance of adult demographics in contemporary family-oriented animation than the opening scenes of *Up*. The film begins with a pastiche of a 1930s newsreel relating the attempts of explorer Charles Muntz (Christopher Plummer) to chart the 'lost world' of South American wilderness Paradise Falls. Footage of the newsreel – which documents Muntz's heroic voyage and subsequent disgrace when

Figure 2.2   The reformed Gru with his adopted family (*Despicable Me*, Illumination, 2010). Frame grab.

he is accused of fabricating evidence of a giant bird discovered in Paradise Falls – is intercut with reaction shots of the nine-year-old Carl Fredericksen (played as a child by Jeremy Leary, and as an adult by Ed Asner), a fanatical young admirer of the explorer. Subsequent shots of Fredericksen playing on the streets, imagining himself as Muntz while the voice of the newsreel narrator describes his adventures, lead him to fellow Muntz fanatic Ellie (Elizabeth Docter), with whom he immediately forms a close bond. Ellie shows Carl her secret 'adventure book' that begins with a pictorial fantasy of living in a house on top of Paradise Falls, and makes him promise that he will take her there; the empty pages of the book are reserved for future adventures in South America. With carefully signalled, rhythmical shifts forward in time, a musical montage sequence comprising 23 short scenes (each wholly devoid of dialogue) goes on to chronicle their lives together:

1. The sequence begins with their marriage ceremony: Ellie's side of the family, like her, is exuberant and extroverted; his side is reserved, like him;
2. Carl is seen carrying Ellie over the threshold of their new home (recognisably the dilapidated house in which they first met);
3. They work together to repair the house;
4. They add furniture to the now-repaired and refurbished living room;
5. They put up a mailbox in the front garden; she puts the finishing touches to a hand-painted sign on it reading 'Carl & Ellie', and both of them add their handprints to it;
6. We see the couple on a summer picnic, Ellie points out a tortoise pattern in the clouds overhead;
7. Initially it appears that they are on holiday in South America, but later we infer that they both work in a zoo; Ellie (presumably a keeper) enters the frame with a tame parrot on her arm, and Carl is seen as a vendor of helium balloons;
8. The couple are seen reading side-by-side in their living room; their hands reach out to touch one another;
9. Again, the couple are seen laying on their backs at the top of a grassy hill; Ellie points out a cloud that looks like a flying elephant; Carl points to a cloud that looks like a baby, and Ellie then imagines every cloud in the sky as a baby;
10. The couple paint and decorate a nursery in their house;
11. A tearful Ellie, comforted by Carl, apparently being told by a doctor that she is unable to have children;
12. Carl solemnly looks out of the window as Ellie sits outside, alone, facing the other way (the first time we see them apart); he comforts her by presenting her childhood 'Adventure Book';

13. Ellie, assisted by Carl, paints their house on top of Paradise Falls, and Carl puts the first coin into a collection jar labelled 'Paradise Falls';

14. They suffer a tire blow-out in their car, forcing them to raid the collection jar; this is followed by a succession of minor mishaps – including a tree falling on their roof during a storm – that repeatedly consume their savings;

15. There is a rapid succession of almost identical shots in which Ellie fixes Carl's tie, signalling the passage of time; by the end the couple are grey-haired;

16. Carl is again seen selling helium balloons to children;

17. The couple waltz privately in their living room, the collection jar sits, apparently forgotten, on a shelf in the background;

18. The couple are seen cleaning the house; Carl notices a picture of himself as a child with his Muntz-inspired aviation goggles and hat, then looks wistfully at Ellie's forgotten painting of their house on top of Paradise Falls;

19. Carl buys plane tickets to South America;

20. The couple return to their favourite picnic spot, but Ellie is clearly ailing and in unable to reach the summit of the hill and collapses repeatedly; Carl rushes to help her, framed by the setting sun;

21. Ellie is in a hospital bed; a sombre Carl goes to her bedside to comfort her, but she passes him her adventure book in tacit admission that she is incapable of realising their fantasy; he kisses her on the forehead;

22. Carl sits alone in a darkened church, holding one of his balloons;

23. Carl returns to the house alone; as he walks through the front door, the screen fades to black.

The four-minute sequence relates the entire married life of Carl and Ellie. This form of compressed narrative has several uses here. In terms of character motivation, it establishes the reasons for Carl's otherwise unfathomable obsession with journeying to Paradise Falls later in the film. It also builds sympathy and empathy with the character, rationalising his grumpiness as a response to the trauma of losing his wife, and paves the way for an important new relationship in his life: the paternal bond he comes to share with the pre-adolescent boy Russell (Jordan Nagai), a 'wilderness explorer' trying to win a badge for assisting the elderly, and who comes to represent the child he and Ellie never had. The montage sequence is not exclusively adult-oriented; young audiences are able to see Carl's progression from child to maturity to old age, and empathise with his motivations and actions as a child (adventure, play, mimicry of adult heroes, a deep friendship with another child with similar interests). However, its adult resonances are particularly profound. The popularity of this sequence has found expression in some rather grandiose critical testimonials that point to its adherence to conventions of the adult-oriented romantic drama. The sequence invites a range of emotional responses: the early scenes, which emphasise the couple's strength as a unit and their ability build for future plenitude, evoke misty-eyed idealism; the middle scenes see the couple reconciled to the impossibility of children and the indefinite deferment of their hopes of adventure and are much more plangent, epitomised by the blank, prosaic repetition of Ellie fixing Carl's tie; the later scenes initially evoke an autumnal contentment but build progressively towards the desolation of Ellie's death.

In each case, the *mise-en-scène* and cinematography reflect the subjectivities of the characters. The picnic scenes are initially joyous, brightly lit with warm colours as Carl and Ellie segue from romantic play to the potentialities of immanent parenthood. The middle and later scenes are lit less exuberantly and coloured in comparatively neutral tones; Carl's repeated smashing of the collection jar and anxious glance at Ellie's largely forgotten painting of Paradise Falls reflect his mounting anxiety that their youthful ambitions will remain unfulfilled. The larger pattern to this montage sequence suggests the ways in which the ageing process – or, more precisely, the social (as opposed to biological) process of maturation – necessitates many small compromises of the unbounded idealism of childhood. Carl and Ellie's dreams of adventure never go away; they are not negotiated, rationalised or dismissed – life simply intrudes. Unlike the coda of Lewis Carroll's *Alice's Adventures in Wonderland* (1865), in which the child's graduation from childhood and the onset of a settled, pragmatic maturity is actively celebrated, contemporary children's fiction typically perceives a tragic dimension to the transformations of childhood innocence and unaffectedness into the knowing cynicism of adulthood.

In this sense, the aged, widowed Carl's insistence on transporting himself, and his home, to Paradise Falls, can be interpreted in several ways. The first and most obvious is as a quixotic but meaningful gesture that honours his memory of Ellie and their shared fantasy. The second possibility is that it represents regression to symbolic childhood; Carl, essentially, giving himself over to the Freudian pleasure principle, casting aside the responsibilities of civilisation and rejecting the pragmatism, restraint and sobriety that Plato, Aristotle and Freud viewed as essential to the functioning of an ordered society. We can understand this impulse in context of a wider cultural turn to 'kidult' values in Western society, representing a philosophical belief – one that has taken hold particularly since the 1960s – that it is both unhealthy and unnecessary to repress the conceptual 'inner child' that exists, notionally, as a latent force inside every adult. Of course, the fact that young and old often have a special kind of bond, both in reality and in fiction, has widely been observed,[48] and we may recall that the senescence of the last of Shakespeare's 'Seven Ages of Man' is described as 'second childishness'.[49] This final aspect gestures towards the explicitly child-oriented modes developed in the remainder of the film. Indeed, even if we interpret this initial montage sequence as particularly adult-oriented (though nothing in it is actively unsuitable for children), then the film's 'adult' markers are still largely contained within it; the remainder of the narrative operates through familiar forms of double address.

Like the earlier films discussed in this chapter, at various points the film draws attention to changing family structures, particularly the normalisation of divorce and weakening kinship ties of the kind that are commonplace in contemporary US society but less common – and subject to much greater degrees of social stigma – when Carl was growing up. One exchange between Carl and Russell regarding the boy's family is especially notable:

> CARL: You've been camping before, haven't you?
> RUSSELL: Well, never outside.
> CARL: Well, why didn't you ask your dad how to build a tent?
> RUSSELL: I don't think he wants to talk about this stuff.
> CARL: Why don't you try him sometimes? Maybe he'll surprise you.
> RUSSELL: Well, he's away a lot. I don't see him much.
> CARL: He's got to be home some time.
> RUSSELL: Well, I call, but Phyllis told me I bug him too much.
> CARL: *Phyllis*? You call your own mother by her first name?
> RUSSELL: Phyllis isn't my mom!
> CARL: [long pause] Oh.

Initially, Carl is oblivious to the possibility that Russell might not live in a traditional nuclear family, and he is surprised to discover that the boy's father does not live with his mother, but rather a woman called Phyllis who seems to regard Russell as an intolerable nuisance. Again, this positions Carl as a man out of time; his age and belief systems continually mark him out as a social outsider. This has mostly positive rather than negative effects: his slightly passé values regarding the sanctity of family and the responsibilities of parenthood are pitted, nostalgically, against modern individualism and its attendant elevation of the self above the collective. For his part, Russell comes to perceive Carl as a figure on to whom he can project his own fantasies of ideal fatherhood: presence, solidarity, trustworthiness, and protectiveness, all qualities lacking in his own father, but which are evident when Carl insists 'I don't want your help, I want you *safe*!' when the boy tries to assist him in a dangerous task. Russell recounts a story about the ways in which he and his father would engage in trivial ways of passing their time together; after a while, Russell admits that these activities might sound boring, but 'the boring stuff is the stuff I remember the most'. Tellingly, the child holds these mundane activities as possessing greater significance than the material goods – such as the expensive GPS system – that the absentee father apparently showers him with.

The turning point in the film occurs after Carl alienates Russell when he prioritises saving his house from destruction over the welfare of Kevin, the priceless exotic bird obsessively hunted by Muntz. He turns to Ellie's adventure book, and is surprised to discover it filled with pictures of their life together. As he turns to the final picture of them (sitting side-by-side in old age), he reads a handwritten note from Ellie: 'Thanks for the adventure – now go have a new one! Love, Ellie'. In essence, what is at stake is the belated realisation that their life together is as rich as any that might have taken place in Paradise Falls, and that Carl must now move on with his life, relinquishing his narrow-minded pursuit of their shared childhood fantasy. Seeing Russell embark on an ill-advised attempt to rescue Kevin by himself, Carl is only able to pursue by emptying his house of a lifetime's worth of possessions in order to lighten its weight so that the depleted helium balloons will lift it.

Up, as with *Finding Nemo* and *Finding Dory*, makes a strenuous case for the pursuance of adventure and idealism (qualities usually invested in youth) in older people. After the end of the opening montage sequence, a depressed Carl is seen being intimidated by a construction firm that wishes to demolish his house and move him into a dubious-sounding retirement home called Shady Pines. Having been charged with assault (he accidentally injures a man who damages his post box) and faced with the seeming inevitability of having to leave his home, Carl is able to liberate himself from the final vestiges of his integration in society. In some ways, this makes his act of apparent recklessness – attaching thousands of helium balloons to his house to take him to Paradise Falls – a logical one. However, having appeared to endorse the individualist's fantasy of regression to a world of childlike indulgence with the wonderfully surreal image of Carl's house floating away from civilisation, the film here reverses course and reasserts the responsibilities of adulthood and (surrogate) parenthood: Carl is morally obliged to look after Russell and help liberate Kevin. Of course, the relationship between Carl and Russell is mutually beneficial. Just as the transformative powers of freshness, innocence and optimism embodied by the child engenders in Carl a symbolic regression to childlike spontaneity (albeit one leavened by responsibility), so the film forecasts the future transmission of Carl's wisdom and experience to Russell.

Nevertheless, the film directly addresses the adult sections of the audience in its contention that the death of a spouse or partner need not (or *should* not) mark the effective end of life itself. Having embarked on this journey in deference to his memory of Ellie and their unfulfilled fantasy, Carl's ultimate narrative victory is his ability to form and to fulfil new ambitions. Indeed, he also seems to regress *physically*; by the end of the film he no longer needs his walking cane and is able to engage in impossible acrobatic feats in his final battle with Muntz. Initially a portrait of staid, emotionally repressed twentieth-century masculinity, Carl Fredericksen thus re-establishes himself as an ideal simulacrum of the twenty-first-century patriarch: a man of substance imbued with the qualities of moral strength and awareness of his responsibilities that the filmmakers appear to see as lamentably lacking in the current generation of father figures.

Family and Individualism

In contemporary Hollywood animation, the centrality of family is constantly weighed against individualist desires. That this is the case is unsurprising when we consider the broader shift in family structures away from the collectivist goals of the traditional family and towards an acknowledgement of the some-times conflicting needs of its individual members. Sociological perspectives on the North American nuclear family have noted a progressive re-emphasis, since the mid twentieth century, from the 'family of procreation' (husband, wife, children) to the 'family of orientation' (father, mother, *self*). As Haley argues, 'this subtle shift in focus alters the dynamics of family life by giving the "self" precedence. This in turn reduces the commitment the self has to the survival of the family as a unit', with the result that the bonds between individual fam-ily members are 'becoming weaker'.[50] Landon Jones, in a book exploring the socio-political dimensions of the US baby boom generation, goes further:

> The Good Times Generation never doubted its priorities: first family, then marriage, and finally self. But the baby boomers turned it upside down: their first priority was the self. Then came marriage, if it worked. And finally family, if that worked, too.[51]

In the 1970s and 1980s, Jones argues, 'the cult of the child [became] the cult of the adult'.[52] I have already discussed how these shifting social currents have privileged adult-male desires in many post-1990s Hollywood animated films. However, this section is concerned with the tensions between individualist and family desires, and how these narratives attempt to resolve them.

Like several Pixar films, *The Incredibles* refines and updates a classical Hollywood-era genre, in this case the domestic comedy, as typified by studio-era films such as *Little Women* (George Cukor, 1933), *Ah, Wilderness!* (Clarence Brown, 1935) and *Meet Me in St. Louis*. The comic spin here is that every mem-ber of the central family has superpowers. Indeed, parents Bob and Helen Parr (Craig T. Nelson and Helen Hunt) are former superheroes who have been forced into retirement by a government relocation programme and are now living with their children, Violet (Sarah Vowell) and Dash (Spencer Fox), in dreary subur-ban obscurity. Much of the early sections of the film chronicles the frustration held by Bob, the former 'Mr Incredible', at what he considers a dull, mediocre life, a perception evident from his frequent visits to his private study, a shrine to former glories, where the walls are covered in newspaper and magazine tributes dating from his time as a superhero: a front page of *Life* magazine proclaiming him 'Superhero of the Year'; a bronze statue; an action figure; a record cover; thank-you letters from children; the keys to the city. His psychological malaise is matched by an evident physical decline: since being forced to relinquish his superhero identity and assume a sedate white-collar job he has gone to seed (at one point he is referred to as a 'fat guy').

On one level, *The Incredibles* functions as a meditation on ageing, particularly the mounting realisation in middle-age that one's best days may be gone and that past feats are no longer possible. Yet Bob still cannot resist playing out his fantasies of rejuvenated phallic omnipotence by moonlighting as a vigilante superhero on weeknights without his family's knowledge. The film presents this as a midlife crisis. However, having completed a black ops mission for an as-yet-unknown employer, Bob is revitalised; a montage sequence relates his bounding around the house with renewed vigour, playing with his children, passionately kissing Helen and engaging in playful sexual behaviour with her around the house. In short, Bob's sense of self-worth is directly linked to his preferred image of self-reliant masculinity. Interestingly, although Helen rebukes Bob for his vigilantism, she is sexually attracted by his re-emergence from drab middle-aged conformism; shots of Bob working out (bench-pressing freight trains and so on) and measuring his reduction in waist size are interspersed with him leaving the house on a morning – ostensibly to go to work – and Helen pulling him back into the house for an implied sexual interlude. The inescapable subtext is that the wife and mother is aroused by Bob's display of exaggerated masculinity; the further inference is that she is as dissatisfied as Bob is by his ossifying and emasculating desk job.

Nevertheless, Bob's desire to regress to pre-domestic individualism is presented as deeply misguided. The film mines various jokes from Helen's misreading of Bob's malaise. When another character tells Helen that 'men at Robert's age are often unstable, prone to weakness', the remark chimes with Helen's as-yet-unarticulated fear that Bob is having an affair. She later observes, 'I'm such an idiot! I let this happen, you know. The sports car, the getting in shape, the blond hair, the lies! I'm losing him!' However, there are more serious implications at play. In an exchange of dialogue reminiscent of *Hook*'s treatise on the work–life balance, Helen berates her husband for continuing to place his work above the needs of his family. Helen insists: 'This – our family – is what's happening now, Bob. And you're missing this.' It is not until the entire family has been captured by the super-villain, Syndrome (Jason Lee), that Bob admits that his selfishness and egotism is at the root of their problems. He confesses: 'This is my fault. I've been a lousy father. Blind to what I have. I was so obsessed by being under-valued I under-valued all of you. So caught up in the past I . . . You are my greatest adventure – and I almost missed it.'

As in *Hook*, the beleaguered middle-aged patriarch ultimately succeeds in balancing the demands of work and family (and, in the process, restoring his own fragile sense of self-worth). Inevitably, although the primarily narrative focalisation is on Bob, the family rally round him and together, using their respective powers, they succeed in overcoming the misanthropic Syndrome, whose primary weakness, as a sociopathic individualist, is that he has no one to support him – or come to his rescue – in the film's final moments. The narrative thus advances several moral and ideological positions, the three most obvious of which are: (1) family life is sacrosanct; (2) all members of the family possess their own individual talents, but they are stronger as a collective when those abilities are channelled to common goals; and (3) the pursuance of individual accomplishment, if it is at the expense of cultivating and maintaining close family ties, is an act of self-annihilation. All of these positions are locatable within broader, long-held US ideologies, but the preoccupation with the father and his internal conflict between the desire for social (and possibly sexual) freedom and professional accomplishment, on the one hand, and domestic fulfilment, on the other, hearken back to late-1980s and early-1990s anxieties regarding changing gender roles and attitudes towards male parenthood.[53]

Again, male anxieties take clear precedence over those of females. Helen seems to have accepted post-careerist domesticity with little or no sign of the self-pitying identity crisis that bedevils Bob. Although she chastises him when she learns of his benign vigilantism, the real source of her displeasure seems to be Bob's missing Dash's 'graduation' from fourth to fifth grade rather than his dishonesty. At times, she threatens to approach the buzz-killing antipathy of Sally Field's working mother in *Mrs Doubtfire*, who persistently throws cold water on the wacky antics of Robin Williams' patriarch in a manner that not only threatens the audience's sense of fun, but implies the impending obsolescence of the nuclear family. Yet Helen's loyalty and love for Bob ultimately wins out – she chooses to return to her renounced identity as a superhero in order to save him, and the end of the film makes it fairly clear that the couple are not simply going to return to the prosaic 'normal' life that Bob finds unendurable. Rather, the entire family emerge as superheroes in their own right.

Incredibles 2 is set shortly after the end of the first film (belying the near 15-year gap between their releases), and similarly deals with the tensions between individualism and domestic life. More specifically, Bob's neuroses regarding his dual identity as family man and 'Mr Incredible' recur once more, but in this case it is the fact that Helen – and not himself – is selected to spearhead a new project aimed at restoring the public's trust in superheroes that punctures his sense of masculine entitlement. Eventually, despite their mutual reluctance, he endorses her for the role, but a speech announcing his support

Figure 2.3   Mr Incredible's malaise when Helen supersedes him in the action stakes (*Incredibles 2*, Pixar, 2018). Frame grab.

is punctuated by a series of comically grotesque, agonised facial expressions that signal his ambivalence. Such sequences demonstrate that competitive individualism clearly flourishes even within the confines of Bob and Helen's happy marriage. Rather than being buoyed by Helen's spectacular success on the job after she saves a runaway train from destruction, Bob is deflated by it; he is seen, dressed in his pyjamas, miserably flicking from one news report detailing her rescue of the runaway train to another (Figure 2.3).

Subsequent scenes of Helen (in her 'Elastigirl' persona) engaged in the stereotypically 'masculine' activity of crime-fighting in the big city are repeatedly intercut with scenes of Bob – having been stripped of his 'Mr Incredible' persona – increasingly bored and frustrated, engaging in stereotypically 'feminine' household activities, such as looking after the baby and attempting to help Dash with his homework. Bob fails in each of his domestic duties: Violet's date does not turn up, leaving her heartbroken and resentful of Bob's clumsy attempts to comfort her; Dash falls asleep without completing his homework; and the baby, Jack-Jack, uses his powers to escape the house and engage in violent battle with a racoon in the garden. In contrast, Helen's first day as a crime fighter involves her saving a runaway bullet train. Significantly, she achieves her mission without a single casualty, further depressing Bob, who was rejected in favour of Helen because of his reputation for causing collateral damage in the line of his work. Helen's competency is not merely a nod to gender equality, but serves to emphasise male anxieties of obsolescence: Bob, presumably, is not especially concerned that he is an incompetent homemaker, but as a muscle-bound hero whose phallic omnipotence is at the very core of his being, he is wounded greatly by the possibility that Helen can trump him in the action stakes as well.

Such scenes satirically pressurise the pious hope of emancipated mothers and fathers who are equally comfortable and adept in the domestic sphere as the professional one. Comedy is derived from how ill-at-ease Bob is in this way of life, and it is a measure of how much traditional forms of gender stratification endure in the twenty-first century that the film's absurdist representation of the fish-out-of-water patriarch vainly attempting everyday domestic duties is scarcely different from near-identical situations in much older films, such as *Father's Doing Fine* (Henry Cass, 1952) or *Uncle Buck* (John Hughes, 1989). In each case, the father is hopelessly out of his depth, suggesting that Frank F. Furstenberg's 1988 claim that 'the good provider role is on its way out [. . .] but its legitimate successor has not yet appeared on the scene' remains true today.[54] The subtext to such representations (if one can even call it a subtext) is that 'traditional' gender roles are more conducive to a happy, fully functional domestic environment than the topsy-turvy dynamic essayed here. Despite her claims to the contrary, Helen clearly intuits that Bob is not up to being a house-husband. His very mention of Jack-Jack's name during a telephone call when she is engaged on a mission sends her into an almost hysterical announcement that she is 'coming home right now'; she later attempts, unconvincingly, to reassure him that she has faith in his ability.

Bob's increasingly frazzled, eccentric performance in the domestic sphere leads his friend Lucius (Samuel L. Jackson) to observe that he requires 'a major life realignment'. It is implied that it is Bob's act of self-abnegation – eschewing his superpowers for lacklustre everyday domesticity – that has led to this existential crisis. Although Bob apologises to Violet for his failures and admits, 'I just want to be a good dad', Violet responds: 'You're not good – you're super.' The words assume a double meaning, outwardly alluding to his superior ability, but also hinting that it is his (masculine) powers that truly define him. Some surveys have shown that married men tended to be happier in the 'good provider' role, but often this desire cannot be realised, since – as Russell Duncan and Joseph Godard observe – 'a return to that model would require women to give up the gains of the past 30 years and return to patriarchal models, something not many are willing to consider'.[55] This narrative problematic is not definitively resolved. Although Bob and the children leave the domestic environment to help Helen win the day, the film stops short of showing who (if anyone) will go on to assume primary child-rearing duties. Ultimately, then, the film is unable or unwilling to offer a convincing alternative to traditional modes of gender stratification.

Although much of the focus of these films is on the adult characters, the increasing emphasis on the whole-family-as-superhero dynamic refocuses attention on the ongoing desirability of the family as a coherent and mutually supporting unit. As we have seen, some sociologists of the late-industrial American family have come close to characterising family as merely a group of individuals who happen to share the same space, but both films ultimately reject this inference. The ongoing desirability of the nuclear family is under-lined early in the film, when Violet observes: 'I just thought it was kind of cool . . . Fighting crime as a family.' Indeed, as in the first film, the equilibrium of the family is only restored when the banality of the domestic environment is set aside and the family comes together to defeat the villainous 'Screenslaver'. In the process, each member of the family makes an important contribution using their own special powers (a metonymy for their uniqueness and individu-ality). Crucially, these special abilities serve the common cause of the family. Individualism and family life, therefore, do not need to be positioned antitheti-cally in relation to one another (as Bob fears they will), but may be mutually supporting – a comforting conclusion for many adult viewers, no doubt.

Coco operates in a similar fashion to *The Incredibles* films, weighing desires for self-fulfilment against the individual's responsibility to others, specifically close family. However, the social commentary is even more pronounced here. The film centres on a music-obsessed Mexican boy, Miguel (Anthony Gonza-lez), who dreams of becoming a professional musician but is forbidden by his family because a maternal ancestor was abandoned by her husband to pursue a career in music. Defying his family, Miguel steals a guitar belonging to his idol, a legendary but now-deceased musician called Ernesto de la Cruz (Benja-min Bratt), and is accidentally transported into the mythical Land of the Dead, where the spirits of the dead reside. There he meets the down-at-heel Héctor (Gael García Bernal), who is eventually revealed as the would-be musician who was thought to have abandoned the family several generations ago. It is important to the narrative's recuperation of the family that Héctor turns out to be innocent of this misdeed – he was murdered by de la Cruz, who then stole his songs. However, while Miguel and Héctor repeatedly prove themselves to be brilliant musicians, they only achieve genuine self-actualisation when they repudiate the credo espoused by the villainous de la Cruz, who sacrifices everything to the altar of personal ambition: 'Seize your moment.' In their suc-cessful, climactic reintegration within the family network, Miguel and Héctor ultimately eschew the egoism of their all-consuming commitment to music and reassess their initial view of family as anathema to self-expression.

Fox's animated sitcom, *The Simpsons* (1989–), remains one the most influ-ential and enduring depictions of contemporary family life in the United States. Centring on a supposedly dysfunctional (but actually mostly typical) nuclear family, the show develops a satirical, often self-referential narrational mode that nevertheless lays bare the many facets of the modern American family. The series' eventual big-screen adaptation, *The Simpsons Movie*, concentrates to a much greater degree on the dull-witted family patriarch, Homer (Dan Castel-laneta), and his relationship with his long-suffering family. The true point of narrative crisis is not the family's expulsion from their hometown, Springfield, after Homer foolishly dumps a silo of toxic waste into the town's lake, but

Homer's refusal to join his wife, Marge (Julie Kavner), and their children in returning to the town to save its inhabitants from destruction. Marge's subsequent video message to Homer, in which she appears irreconcilably to end their marriage due to his selfishness (taping over their wedding tape in the process) triggers Homer's epiphany, in which he finally sublimates his own egoism to the needs of his friends and family.

These films seem to suggest that individualism, one of the core ideological tenets of US society, can only carry so far. The needs of the individual must be balanced against those of family and community – although Homer, in response to a question regarding his motivation in saving the town, can only manage an exclamation of bemusement that acknowledges an unwanted moral compunction ('Risking my life to save people I hate for reasons I don't quite understand'). The narrative resolution allows Homer to play the hero, but two codas cut to the core of the film's valorisation for the family. The first is the tender reconciliation between Marge and Homer, with her earlier, apparently deep-seated, misgivings about the marriage suddenly forgotten. The second is the more macho rapprochement between Homer and son Bart (Nancy Cartwright), founded on their shared predilection for anarchic adventure and the realisation that their differences are outweighed by their similarities. The more traditional *paterfamilias*, the upstanding Christian next-door-neighbour Ned (Harry Shearer), is eventually rejected by Bart, for while he may offer stability, he lacks the oafish but essentially benign spontaneity embodied by Homer.

The compromise made by post-millennial films such as *The Incredibles*, *Coco* and *The Simpsons Movie* allows for an idealised rapprochement between self and family. All three films instantiate Wood's metanarrative of the Restoration of the Father. In *The Incredibles*, Bob must be allowed to retain his sense of masculine potency. In *Coco*, Miguel and Héctor return to the family home and apparently promise to remain there, come what may, but only when their families forgive their abandonment and agree not to curtail their musical ambitions. And in *The Simpsons Movie*, an isolated act of community-spirited heroism allows Homer to reintegrate into the nuclear family while escaping any meaningful character development. While these films reject the selfish absolutism that Tom Wolfe famously identified as the keynote of the 1970s (the 'Me' decade), they appear to view enforced self-repression on the father's part – even in the service of the common good – as an imposition equally pernicious as family abandonment.[56] This is a tension that these narratives cannot easily revolve. What is ultimately required is self-actualisation with restrictions that are entered into *voluntarily*, along the same lines as Peter Banning's heroic reinvention as high-flying corporate lawyer and devoted family man in *Hook*. Hollywood family-oriented narratives in both live-action and animated media continue to emphasise adult anxieties regarding the need to balance personal and professional ambition in a society that still valorises strong and stable domestic structures while, at the same time, maintaining unrealistically high expectations of accomplishment in the workplace.

CHILD–ADULT CROSSOVERS

As we have seen, many post-1990s films are predicated on the recognition of biological and cultural distinctions between childhood and adulthood, a recognition that is reflected in the provision of multilayered textual strategies intended to appeal to them as discrete demographic entities. However, a parallel tradition also asserts the essential continuities and likenesses between children and adults, or even – in some respects – their fundamental *sameness*. In one highly suggestive sequence in Pixar's *Inside Out*, the increasingly depressed adolescent protagonist, Riley (Kaitlyn Dias), angrily repels questions from her parents about the first day in her new school in San Francisco, to which the family has recently relocated. This is the only point in the film at which the subjectivity shifts momentarily from Riley to one of the adult characters. Uncertain as how best to respond, but feeling obliged to react in the 'appropriate' (i.e. conventional, socially prescribed) manner, her father (Kyle MacLachlan) panics and 'puts his foot down', ordering her to her bedroom and leaving Riley's mother (Diane Lane) to observe to herself, 'Well, that was a disaster.' This implies that the moral responsibility assumed by parents is largely affectation or bluff, and divagates markedly from the portrayal of the strong, resolute patriarchs of the classical-era Hollywood family film, who had long since evolved beyond the primitive emotional and behavioural conditions of childhood. Riley's father, by contrast, is shown to be equally as hesitant and at the mercy of his emotions as Riley herself. As child psychologist Lisa Damour observed at the time of release, the film shows the outwardly 'immature' adolescent and her seemingly 'mature' father as possessing the same 'basic mental equipment' so that 'his feelings operate no more harmoniously than hers do'.[57]

In other words, the film works to question, if not altogether break down, the barriers between childhood and adulthood. The final credits sequence seems to reinforce this point; it features a series of vignettes in which minor characters in the film are seen with their own versions of Riley's 'command centre', the film's narrative representation of the brain's cognitive and neural processes. Each character possesses variations of the same five core emotions that she does. The sentiment is broadly humanistic: everyone, regardless of their age, background or vocation is motivated by common impulses. While growing up entails its own complex processes of cognitive and emotional development, childhood and adulthood are not construed as fundamentally different orders of being, but rather as a continuum. The final scene's allusion to Riley's ongoing maturation (the new command centre has a large red button marked 'Puberty') is significant in this regard: as she continues her development towards adulthood, new behaviours and preoccupations assert themselves. Yet while additional nuances in emotional response will be evident, she is still recognisably the same person.

Pixar's first production featuring a non-princess female protagonist, *Inside Out* follows less mainstream animated films such as *Coraline* (Henry Selick, 2009), both in focusing on the adolescent girl in a contemporary everyday context, and in its emphasis on emotional realism. *Inside Out* is Hollywood's most overt attempt at representing the subjectivity of children, and thus implicitly challenges one of the most persistent charges levelled at children's fiction: that it does not address real children, but only constructs an imaginary audience – a 'preferred reader' – predicated on socio-cultural conceptions of childhood. Furthermore, such texts inevitably reproduce the desires and the preoccupations of its (usually) adult creators; it is this fact that leads Jacqueline Rose to speak of the 'impossibility' of children's literature.[58] This argument could easily be extended to children's films. Generally, children's films have attempted to reflect children's subjectivities in other ways, particularly through narrative focalisation (e.g. the story is told from the perspective of youth) and the use of specific filmic techniques, such as the subjective point-of-view shots and low-level camera positioning in films such as *E.T.* and *ParaNorman* (Chris Butler and Sam Fell, 2012). *Inside Out* works in a different way, by actualising children's emotional states. This is still 'impossible', in Rose's rather puritanical terms, since the film only offers *adult conceptions* of children's psychological make-up, but the film's significance perhaps lies more in its simultaneous disavowal and reassertion of the distinctions between childhood and adulthood in psychology, cognitive ability and emotional maturity. Although it shows how the fears, insecurities and fantasies of pre-adolescence persist in teenagers and grown-ups, *Inside Out* also functions as a metonymy for the maturation process, which is marked by new desires and the partial leaving behind of the psychological and cultural worlds of childhood. These complexities of 'growing up' are often denied or overlooked by modes of children's fiction which work upon an undifferentiated address to the 'inner child'.

As with many recent animated features, *Inside Out* features a short prologue that introduces a pre-adolescent child protagonist who then graduates to adolescence within the first act. It is the difficult transition from the unaffectedness of childhood (here marked predominantly by carefree happiness) to the emotional difficulties of puberty that is at the film's centre. The trauma of the family moving to a different city, Riley leaving behind her friends, and the pressures associated with her father's problems at work represent the first real period of difficulty in the 11-year-old's life. She quickly relinquishes the comforting accoutrements of childish play, represented by imaginary spaces such as 'Princess Dream World' and 'Sparkle Pony Mountain' and, most poignantly, by the eventual fading to nothingness of her forgotten childhood imaginary friend, Bing Bong (Richard Kind). When the characters of Joy (Amy Poehler) and Sadness (Phyllis Smith) accidentally get lost in Riley's subconscious, it coincides with a new stage in the girl's psychological development: her temporary inability to feel either emotion, with each of her 'personality islands' – the remnants of her child persona – shut down one by one. The dismantling of Riley's childhood identity is confirmed at the end of the film, when new 'personality islands' more befitting young adulthood (such as 'Tragic Vampire Romance Island' and 'Boy Band Island') have formed.

The figure of Joy, with her irrepressible drive for positivity and fun in every situation, could easily be a metaphor for the crude emotional cadences of the family film in its most sentimental iterations, in which pensiveness or sadness are seen as anathema. Films such as *E.T.* and *Mrs Doubtfire* added layers of nuance and ambivalence to the presentation of family in Hollywood child-centred films. *Inside Out* works in a similar way; its embrace of Sadness as a central character rests on a recognition – both psychological and generic – that childhood is a complex and multifaceted development stage requiring modes of filmic representation commensurate with that complexity. Joy's limitations (as a character and as a state of being) become clearer as the film unfolds. She finds herself unable to comprehend Riley's depression, and her single-minded insistence on always seeking the positives in every situation is repeatedly shown to be misguided. Sadness, a peripheral (if not superfluous) character at the outset of the film, becomes increasingly central as the psychological necessity of the emotion is made clear. It is she who comforts Bing Bong by commiserating with him but not attempting to deceive him by sugar-coating the truth of his obsolescence; in contrast, Joy appears emotionally tone-deaf, fruitlessly attempting to cheer him up with childish tomfoolery. The subtext is that relentless optimism is not only grating and simple-minded, but also psychologically unhealthy. (A similar sentiment can be discerned in the character of Princess Unikitty in *The Lego Movie* [Phil Lord and Christopher Miller, 2014], a unicorn–cat hybrid who represses all negativity until her resentment erupts in a destructive fit of rage.) As Joy eventually comes to realise, many moments in life are marked by emotional ambivalence.

A more common feature in post-millennial Hollywood animation is what might be termed the 'origin story', a short prologue that establishes the background of the central characters and makes an explicit connection between child and adult desires. This narrative strategy recurs in a number of Disney/ Pixar films, including *The Princess and the Frog* (Ron Clements and John Musker, 2009), *Brave* (Mark Andrews and Brenda Chapman, 2012), *Frozen*, *Inside Out*, *Moana* (Ron Clements and John Musker, 2016), *Finding Dory* and *Zootopia*. The agenda appears to be twofold. Firstly, such prologues serve the instrumental function of supplying films with both a child and a young adult protagonist, thus offering identification figures to multiple audience demographics. Secondly, and relatedly, this form of narrative structure establishes what is commonly known as a 'character arc' – a set of goals that explicitly link the child and adult iterations of the same figure. The substance of the film consists of an exploration and resolution of these motivations, deepening the audience's emotional engagement and reaffirming the idea that foundational experiences in childhood carry over into, and shape, adulthood (another important tenet of children's fiction).

Hollywood's fixation with 'relatability' is at the forefront of this approach to storytelling: just as 'kidult' media is widely seen as attempting to regress adults to symbolic childhood, so these films remind grown-ups that they never really graduated from it. Equally, younger viewers are invited to accept the young adult protagonists of *Frozen* and *Moana* as larger but still-recognisable versions of the pre-adolescent children encountered in the prologue. The old axiom of 'putting away childish things' cannot apply here: these Disney and Pixar protagonists are permanently rooted in the events, traumas and preoccupations of their childish selves.[59] Contrary to the implications of Shakespeare's 'Seven Ages of Man', what happens in childhood has a direct bearing on how we turn out as adults (and we might recall Freud's postulation that our desires and neuroses can be traced back to pre-adolescent experiences).

The textual strategy of opening a film with a short section set during the protagonist's childhood, and then focusing primarily on the development of the characters in young adulthood, is designed to make these characters intelligible to a number of different audience demographics. Carl Fredricksen's obsession with reaching Paradise Falls in *Up* and Dory's need to reunite with her parents in *Finding Dory* represent the fulfilling of latent, suppressed, but potent, childhood desires that, through narrative strategies of focalisation, are shared by spectators. This aspect of storytelling further extends the structural conventions of character-centred experience and character-centred causality. It is not simply that the protagonists are presented with problems they must overcome, but that this problematic is embedded as their core, unalterable and insuppressible characteristic. To put it another way, these characters must fulfil their childhood fantasies in order to become fully actualised grown-ups.

In some respects (and as the following chapter will show), these films are highly determined artefacts of late-industrial civilisation; their deliberate blurring of the cultural-behavioural distinctions between childhood and adulthood reflects much broader social and cultural changes in Western nations (and in the United States in particular). In other ways, of course, the motivations that underpin these films are intended to be comprehensible to audiences of all ages and backgrounds, since they are rooted in experiences that approach universality: family, friendship and adventure.

3. HOLLYWOOD ANIMATION, LATE MODERNITY AND CONTEMPORARY AMERICA

One of the primary distinguishing features of post-1990s Hollywood animation is its foregrounding of contemporary culture and society. While many of the 'classic' Disney films are set in fantastical or fairy tale landscapes geographically and temporally removed from everyday life ('once upon a time . . .'), most animated features from the early 1990s onwards are self-conscious artefacts of late modernity. Indeed, this contemporaneousness is central to their aesthetic. There are two primary manifestations of the foregrounding of contemporary culture in post-1990s Hollywood animation. The first, and most immediately visible, is (a usually comic) intertextuality that takes the form of an intensified referentiality to other works of popular culture and to modern life more broadly. In common parlance, these allusions are widely described as 'cultural references' and, in isolation, they are rarely an essential component to the story or narrative; instead, they take the form of isolated, punctuating moments of comic self-reflexivity within the diegesis. The second form is that of social commentary, which is often satirical in nature and tends to be a more abiding thematic focus than the intertextual allusion. Nevertheless, as this chapter will argue, both forms serve a similar function: they are strategies of proximation that anchor films to recognisable and identifiable situations and events.[1]

POSTMODERN IRONY: DREAMWORKS AND BEYOND

The strategies of comic intertextuality that suffuse post-1990s Hollywood feature animation are widely seen as products of late modernity and 'postmodern' culture. However, many of them are rooted in familiar comic mechanisms of irony and self-reflexivity. 'In the beginning was the gag', writes Geoff King of the foundational years of commercial cinema in the United States (c.1896–1905), a period dominated by single-reel comedy shorts.[2] Raymond Durgnat refers to gag-based comedy as 'sharp, rapid, cynical, often cruel, reflecting a faster, quicker-witted world', and early animation was built on similar narrative principles, often foregrounding the anarchistic potentiality of the cartoon form, which Paul Wells sees as occupying a liminal position between modernity and postmodernity.[3] Although Disney cartoon shorts became known for their hyper-realist aesthetic, sentimentality and overt moralism, those produced by Warner Bros. after about 1935 adopted a far more adult-oriented mode associated with irony and anarchism. As Wells observes, Tex Avery, the renowned Warner Bros. animator, particularly 'understood that children would be appeased by physical slapstick while adults required a more knowing, *self-conscious* approach, which would engage with more mature themes'.[4]

In part, this approach was predicated on logical and necessary product differentiation, in much the same way as DreamWorks and Laika have deliberately pursued a different aesthetic to that of Disney and Pixar. For instance, Daffy Duck, the madcap Warner Bros. animated 'star', was a blatant variation on Disney's Donald Duck, but inhabited a Saturnalian world of logical impossibilities in which little truck was given to ingratiating cuteness or sentiment. Furthermore, some of the Warner's shorts exhibit clearly 'postmodern' strategies of irony and self-reflexivity. For instance, in *Screwball Squirrel* (Tex Avery, 1944) a Disneyesque bunny rabbit is beaten up by Screwy Squirrel, who then turns to the camera and expresses cynical relief (which the viewer is expected to share) that this unbearably cutesy animal has been dispensed with. It is important to acknowledge, then, that irony, parody, pastiche and self-reflexivity are neither specifically 'modern' nor 'postmodern'. Indeed, David Bordwell makes a strenuous case for the prevalence of intertextual mechanisms in studio-era Hollywood, pointing out that the classical Hollywood system 'has room for citation, reflexivity, pastiche, parody', and suggesting that the critical tendency to view these as 'recent inventions' is misguided.[5]

Classical-era Disney features do contain the odd allusion to contemporary culture. Cruella de Vil in *One Hundred and One Dalmatians* (Wolfgang Reitherman et al., 1961) is said to have been modelled on Bette Davis and Tallulah Bankhead, the four vultures in *The Jungle Book* (Wolfgang Reitherman, 1967) are caricatures of The Beatles, and sections of *The Rescuers* (Wolfgang Reitherman et al.,

1977) take place against the backdrop of contemporary metropolitan life. Yet such examples stand out because of their relative scarcity. Since the 1990s, 'postmodern' textual elements have become a dominant feature. As we saw in Chapter 2, their deployment is entirely deliberate, and must be viewed in context of a programmed strategy of providing multiple avenues of access for a pluralistic, cross-demographic movie-going public, with the explicit intention of moving beyond the supposed core demographic of pre-teen children. The self-conscious referentiality that suffuses post-1990s Hollywood animation has been termed 'authorial intertextuality' by Sam Summers.[6] Summers describes authorial intertextuality as an 'aesthetic tool deployed by authors to create a specific meaning, to encourage a certain reading, and to engage an audience'.[7] As such, the category is distinct from the conventional definition of intertextuality (developed by Julia Kristeva and others) as encompassing all linguistic structures. Rather, 'it has more in common with metaphor and other rhetorical devices than it does with the post-structuralist notion of an intertextual web connecting all texts'.[8]

The cachet of authorial intertextuality for adult spectators is fairly clear. The ability to recognise and 'decode' intertextual allusions is a marker of cultural literacy, and therefore – remembering Pierre Bourdieu's arguments in *Distinction: A Social Critique of the Judgement of Taste* (1979) – a perceived reflection of 'the quality of the person'.[9] Indeed, as Noël Carroll argues, intertextual allusions are prominent in the adult-oriented 1970s output of 'Hollywood Renaissance' filmmakers such as Peter Bogdanovich, Francis Ford Coppola, Terence Malick, Brian DePalma and Martin Scorsese (some of whom were educated in film schools and thus highly knowledgeable in the field of cinema history).[10] The various practices of textual allusion that Carroll delineates – 'quotations, the memorialisation of past genres, the reworking of past genres, *homages*, and the recreation of "classic" scenes, shots, plot motifs, lines of dialogue, themes, [and] gestures' – are all highly visible in contemporary Hollywood animation.[11]

Furthermore, many of the films Carroll identifies as quintessential examples of this narrative approach combine critical acclaim with a reputation for being 'hip' and 'edgy'. A selective list includes *The French Connection* (William Friedkin, 1971), *The Long Goodbye* (Robert Altman, 1973), *The Conversation* (Francis Ford Coppola, 1974), *Assault on Precinct 13* (John Carpenter, 1976), *Carrie* (Brian DePalma, 1976), *New York, New York* (Martin Scorsese, 1977), and *American Gigolo* (Paul Schrader, 1979). These films are viewed as serious artistic accomplishments but also appeal, crucially, to the sensibilities of young adults. According to Gary R. Edgerton, by 1976, 62 per cent of the movie-going public in the United States was aged 16–29.[12] This was precisely the demographic that tended to denigrate children's films and that would need to be won over if animated features were to return to the levels of profitability and mass popularity that met the early Disney releases.[13]

Nonetheless, the postmodern turn was part of a wider trend in contemporary US popular culture. Intertextuality, as David Buckingham observes, 'has become a dominant characteristic of contemporary media' that transcends formal and generic boundaries.[14] Timothy Shary argues that 'a distinct postmodern operation' can be discerned in 'virtually all of Hollywood's young adult movies' from *Fast Times at Ridgemont High* (Amy Heckerling, 1982) onwards, and while the contemporary Hollywood animated feature remains one of the most visible vehicles for authorial intertextuality, it is also a recurrent and often highly self-conscious feature of post-1990s US indie cinema.[15] Bordwell himself acknowledges that contemporary Hollywood cinema in general 'would seem to ask its spectators to take a high degree of narrational self-consciousness for granted', and that 'by the 1990s allusionism had expanded into a general recognition that popular media constituted the shared culture of movie consumers'.[16] However, he is also correct in pointing out that self-consciousness in contemporary Hollywood is primarily aesthetic rather than narrational; many films revel in 'displays of technique – all the while surrendering to the pull of a tale constructed on more or less traditional lines'.[17]

North American television of the 1980s was a perfect vehicle for postmodern impulses. David Weinstein identifies *The Simpsons* (1989–), *Seinfeld* (1989–98), and the characters Pee-wee Herman, Max Headroom and Beavis and Butt-Head as all belonging to 'the wave of self-reflexive television programmes which, since the mid-1980s, have offered viewers new ways of watching and understanding television'.[18] These television shows and characters are recognisable, to some degree, as popularist descendants of the comparatively highbrow postmodern turn in post-war US art and literature. The key difference here is that 'postmodern' elements are used not as alienating devices, but as a further layer of aesthetic attraction. Part of this, as I will argue below, is the cognitive pleasure of decoding extra-textual allusions. However, such devices in contemporary film and television are typically predicated on the topicality of the allusions. The whole premise of 'once upon a time' fairy tale or fantasy narratives is that while they *may* be taken as parables or allegories of contemporary society, they are outwardly unrecognisable as such. Conversely, authorial intertextuality foregrounds (if not flaunts) the currencies of late modernity; the politics, the culture, the idiom, and the discourses of the 'now'.

What we are talking about here is a programmed insertion of *contemporary* reference points in a medium that often appeared to be (and presented itself as) largely ahistorical. But even though post-1990s Hollywood animation enters into close engagement with aspects of modern society, this extreme allusiveness also represents a resolutely 'safe', non-controversial way of embedding contemporaneousness without committing to potentially compromising political standpoints. Discussing a similar tendency in 1980s Hollywood cinema, Andrew Britton argues, 'Reaganite entertainment refers to itself in order to persuade us that it doesn't refer outwards at all. It is, purely and simply, "entertainment" – and we all know what that is.'[19] In its strongest manifestation, this is a form of textual solipsism. While many animated features are, indeed, predicated on allusionism, their terms of reference are largely confined to the associative world of contemporary popular culture – an inwards-looking culture that appears to be (even if it isn't really) hermetically cut off from broader socio-political issues. Nevertheless, this reconfiguration of Hollywood animation was a gradual process. As Summers observes, by the late 1980s Disney's animated features were evidencing increasing engagement with contemporary culture. In *Oliver & Company* (George Scribner, 1988), one of the studio's lesser-known productions, Disney 'pepper[ed] the voice cast and soundtrack [. . .] with well-known pop stars, and its visual landscape with advertisements for real-life products'.[20] While *Who Framed Roger Rabbit* (Robert Zemeckis, 1988) – which is often invoked as a turning point in contemporary Hollywood animation – certainly captures the madcap anarchism and self-reflexivity of the Warner Bros. classical-era shorts, its parodic, *film noir* setting disavows associations with contemporary culture, and is more reminiscent of the 1940s crime-film homage, *Dead Men Don't Wear Plaid* (Carl Reiner, 1982).

The character of the Genie in *Aladdin* (Ron Clements and John Musker, 1992), as played by Robin Williams, signalled a more substantive shift towards cultural allusion. Wells observes that the Genie functions in a similar way to *Who Framed Roger Rabbit* in that both operate as 'a compendium of comic cartoon expression'.[21] The crucial difference is that the Genie is a deliberate incongruity within the film's diegesis; his contemporary vocabulary and idiom, and the topicality of the manifold allusions to contemporary Western civilisation in his (partly improvised) dialogue, separates the character from the film's otherwise largely conventional, hyper-realist aesthetic. As Marwan M. Kraidy observes, the Genie brings 'chaotic streams of intertextual references' to the film, 'harnessing signs from a variety of popular culture domains such as Hollywood's film industry, American (U.S.) political life, the music industry, and more mundane consumer items'.[22] It is equally important to recognise, as Summers does, that the film's 'contra-diegetic inclusions' are entirely confined to the character of the Genie, so that the 'laughs', as Wells puts it, occur 'outside the context of the narrative'.[23]

Pixar's first release, *Toy Story* (John Lasseter, 1995), was the keynote film; it embedded itself fully within the 'contemporary culture' that earlier films merely gestured towards. This was widely recognised by critics on initial theatrical release, with the *New York Daily News* calling *Toy Story* 'Disney's [sic] neatest film ever' and quipping that it 'makes other Disney flicks look as cutting edge as a bound volume of Reader's Digest'.[24] The review's reference to the film's 'belonging' to Disney is notable since, at this point in its history, Pixar had relatively little creative leverage. Rather, it was Disney – and particularly studio chairman Jeffrey Katzenberg, who insisted on the film being 'hip, adult' – that drove the agenda of cultural topicality.[25] The strategies of multivalent address in *Toy Story* (as discussed in Chapter 2) underpin the film's status as a paradigmatic postmodern cultural artefact. David Denby, in his *New York* magazine review, wryly observed that:

> The postmodernist jokes give the movie a spark [. . .] Have the filmmakers (too many of them to list) been reading Guy Debord, Jean Baudrillard, or some of the other French theorists of illusion and representation? It's possible. It's also possible they just picked up on an idea floating around everywhere: In our world, nature is dead, and everything is now a representation of one sort or another; we're all lost in the forest of simulacra.[26]

Toy Story, like many of the post-1970s films and TV shows referenced above, draw freely on the 'postmodern' traits of irony, parody, pastiche, satire and self-reflexivity. Such texts are further characterised by what Mike Featherstone calls 'stylistic promiscuity': an open-handed *bricolage* that works to assemble and order a disparate set of images, iconography, story elements and tropes gathered from multiple sources.[27]

It may also be said that intertextuality constitutes an intertext in its own right. Fredric Jameson coined the term 'blank parody' to describe the postmodern pastiches that he sees as endemic to the culture of late-industrial society: highly allusive, self-reflexive texts that appropriate indiscriminately, without any pretensions to artistry or social comment.[28] Since *Toy Story*, 'postmodern' narrative strategies have become closely associated with family-oriented animation, and by the early 2000s were viewed as integral to the medium's cachet with teenagers and adults. Post-1990s features that engage heavily in authorial intertextuality are often celebrated for their ingenuity, providing multiple layers of narrative appeal that reward recognition of current trends, memes and representational elements in contemporary Western popular culture. Textual allusions of this kind may appear to be throwaway, but they should not be seen as extraneous: in animation, everything on the screen carries performative functions. Foregrounding intertextuality has thus served an important role in Hollywood animation retaining its narrative distinctiveness from non-animated family films, where postmodern narrative strategies have rarely been as pronounced.

One of the primary pleasures in such texts is cognitive play of the kind associated with puzzle-solving.[29] Intertextual allusions must be identified and interpreted as such, and this is not an autonomic process: it requires knowledge and some degree of effort. This has significant implications for the relationship between text and spectator. It is generally assumed that the appreciation of intertextuality is largely confined to adult (or certainly post-adolescent) audiences. In a helpful content analysis of 'adult humour' in post-1990s Hollywood 'children's films', Chelsie Lynn Akers takes it as read that extra-textual allusions appeal solely to mature audiences.[30] Furthermore, while Christine Wilkie-Stibbs concedes that children are able to 'take ownership' of texts in a fashion that precludes 'the imperialism of the text and the author', she also argues – in relation to intertextuality in fiction intended for young audiences – that adults have an advantage, since 'children's intersubjective knowledge cannot be assured'.[31] That is to say, intertextuality has the capacity to disrupt children's engagement with the text or alienate them entirely. However, empirical studies of children's humour development have revealed a more complex situation. Although young children often prefer slapstick comedy, after the age of eight they tend to find 'more cognitively challenging' humour – that which requires 'work' to understand it – to be funnier than simpler forms such as visual incongruity or nonsense wordplay.[32] By the pre-adolescent (age 9–12) stage there also tends to be greater pleasure derived from 'inside jokes' or 'metahumour'.[33] The inclusion of such comic forms strengthens appeal not only to adults, but also to older children seeking to graduate from the fantasies of the child's world.

With the foundation of DreamWorks SKG in October 1994, Disney was faced with a significant competitor in the field of Hollywood feature animation for the first time. DreamWorks, a co-initiative between Steven Spielberg, Jeffrey Katzenberg and David Geffen, received approximately $500 million from Microsoft co-founder Paul Allen, and eventually expanded into live-action filmmaking, television and music distribution. Katzenberg's major interest, however, was in building an animation studio to rival Disney. He took the patented brand of multivalent narrative he had introduced at Disney in the early 1990s – a narrative style marked by irony, referentiality and self-reflexivity – with him to DreamWorks. Although intertextual strategies are evident in a wide range of post-1990s Hollywood animated features, it is in DreamWorks films that they find their fullest expression. This was part of a concerted programme of product differentiation. David Geffen articulated this most succinctly, admitting: 'What we're doing is making animated movies that aren't like Disney.'[34] Indeed, as Summers notes, authorial intertextuality is not a prominent feature of the so-called 'Disney Renaissance' films of the mid-to-late 1990s.[35] After Katzenberg's departure, Disney (and Pixar) largely eschewed the extreme self-reflexiveness that he had promoted during his tenure as chairman of Walt Disney Studios.

DreamWorks' policy of product differentiation is strongly evident in its first two films, the computer-animated *Antz* (Eric Darnell and Tim Johnson, 1998) and the traditionally animated *The Prince of Egypt* (Brenda Chapman et al., 1998). Reflecting on this initial period, Katzenberg later admitted, 'We were experimenting [. . .] That was our R&D [research and development] period.'[36] In late 1998, DreamWorks executive Ann Daly acknowledged, 'There has been a growing recognition that animation can have direct appeal to adults [. . .] The transition that we would like to see happen is that an adult could hear about an animated movie and not think that they need to have a child with them in order to go.'[37] *Antz* co-director Tim Johnson made similar remarks to the press, claiming, 'We didn't want to turn off the family audience but we didn't want to make a movie for really young kids, either.'[38]

It is well documented that executives at Disney and Pixar were incensed at the strong resemblance between *Antz* and Pixar's second feature, *A Bug's Life* (John Lasseter, 1998), on which Katzenberg had worked before his departure. Both films centre on anthropomorphised insects; allegedly, Lasseter felt personally betrayed that Katzenberg not only appropriated the basic premise of Pixar's production, but attempted to undermine the studio by rushing *Antz* into theatres so that it premiered first. In the event, while both films were highly profitable, *A Bug's Life* was the clear winner at the box office: it grossed approximately $350 million, compared to *Antz*'s $170 million. And indeed, despite the obvious similarity in premise, the films are substantially different. Whereas *A Bug's Life* is whimsical and primarily child-oriented, *Antz* is self-consciously 'adult', a fact immediately announced by Woody Allen's opening voice-over narration, which parodies the neurotic intellectual persona he embodies in his 1970s 'nervous romances', *Annie Hall* (1977) and *Manhattan* (1979). The opening sequence begins with what appears to be a shot of the Manhattan skyline which then fades into a graphically similar shot of blades of grass; the camera then pans down into an ant's nest, where Allen's Z, a feeble worker ant, is recounting his fears of inadequacy, confinement, and abandonment by his father to a therapist (in much the same way Alvy Singer does in *Annie Hall*).

Much of the humour in *Antz* is derived from the fact that, conceptually, it is a fairly conventional romantic comedy, albeit one suffused with comic irony. Whereas *A Bug's Life* (and many other Hollywood animated films) works largely through metonymy – the ant colony is a human society in disguise – *Antz* comically examines the disjuncture between the characters' humanlike inclinations and their insect proclivities. Z's inferiority complex is comprehensible within a culture in which, as one of thousands of worker ants, he really *is* insignificant; and although these ants inhabit a society we can identify with (they are intelligent, speak English, and value friendship and family), their difference is emphasised at strategic points, such as when Z declines to drink an 'aphid beer' on the grounds that 'I have a thing about drinking from the anus of another creature', or when two insects are seen eating around a camp fire and one of them observes, 'This stuff tastes like crap'; another asks to taste it, and adds: 'Hey, it *is* crap. Not bad.'

While many children might appreciate scatological humour of this type, there are more explicit instances of self-consciously 'adult' dialogue. Several of the verbal exchanges between Z and the princess of the colony, Bala (Sharon Stone), are characterised by a sexual directness unusual in family-oriented films. The princess tells Z that she was 'slumming it' when she initially approached him in the workers' bar; stung, he replies, 'You know, I was going to let you become part of my most erotic fantasies, but now you can just forget that.' This is a stark contrast with the conventional, chaste expressions of romantic ardour that characterise the traditional Disney princess movie. On one level, this kind of dialogue continues the trend in post-1990s Hollywood animation such as *Aladdin* and *Toy Story* of evoking everyday situations and relationships (and late modernity more broadly), but it is not the level of verbal sophistication, rather the clear intent to address an older audience, that most clearly demarcates *Antz* from the Disney oeuvre. Even in *Toy Story*, the 'adult' jokes are subtle or doubly coded (e.g. Potato Head miming 'kiss my ass' by bumping a pair of plastic lips against his bottom) so that young children may not notice them, or they are brief enough not to disturb their engagement, or they are able to appreciate them in another way. But in *Antz*, extended passages are wholly given over to lewd verbal exchanges and existential wrangling.

The film is also a satire of the class system. Z, besotted with the princess, manages to convince his soldier friend, Weaver (Christopher Walken), to exchange places with him so that Z can take part in a military parade in which the princess will be participating. When Z is erroneously hailed as a hero after he is the only ant to survive a suicidal attack on a termite nest, the workers begin to recognise the social stratification to which they have been subject since birth (when, as larvae, they are divided into soldiers and workers) and begin a revolution, fuelled by pseudo-Marxist slogans such as 'It's the workers that control the means of production!' Just as the worker ants come to realise that there is more to life than hard work and productivity, so the princess must come to terms with her own relative cosmic insignificance when two haughty wasps recognise no hierarchical difference between her and Z, both of them 'crawling insects' who are 'dirty and smelly'. The mindless conformity of the colony – represented by the tyrannical soldier ant, General Mandible (Gene Hackman), who insists that independent thought and action 'makes us vulnerable' – is disavowed late in the film by a familiar expression of individualism when the princess tells Z, 'You're pretty strange', and cuts off his objection by adding: 'I like it – you're not like anyone else.' As Martin Barker suggests, if we were to apply a commutation test to the film, imagining its dialogue and situations occurring in a non-animated production, we would perceive a much more radical, adult-oriented work.[39] In this sense, the animated medium – widely seen in the West as purely or primarily child-oriented – forms a protective layer of irony and self-consciousness that disavows potentially subversive content.

DreamWorks' next computer-generated feature, *Shrek* (Andrew Adamson and Vicky Jenson, 2001), marks the apotheosis of Katzenberg's policy of producing highly self-conscious, contemporary-inflected animated films that explicitly challenge Disney formulae. Katzenberg told the press that the film was 'supposed to be subversive', but unlike *Antz*, the target of its subversion is not contemporary society, but increasingly clichéd genre conventions.[40] The idiom of the Disney fairy tale film, in particular, is subject to such persistent, deconstructive lampooning that it is hard to see how fairy tale films built on 'traditional' principles would be viable without substantial revisionism – a fact that Disney was eventually forced to confront with productions such as *Tangled* (Nathan Greno and Byron Howard, 2010) and *Frozen* (Chris Buck and Jennifer Lee, 2013). In some ways, however, the conventional categorisation of *Shrek* as a 'postmodern' text is misleading. Although it is replete with irony, intertextual allusion, parody and pastiche, it ultimately presents what it appears to disavow: a broadly appealing family movie with the usual conventions of the genre, including a goal-oriented protagonist, moralistic overtones, the victory of 'good' over 'evil', heterosexual romantic union, and emotive uplift. A more radical postmodernism might have involved strategies of political subversion and/or distantiation (as in, say, the fiction of William S. Burroughs), but *Shrek*'s ironic credentials form part of a larger programme of multilayered narrative and aesthetic attractions. The normative modes of mainstream Hollywood animation and children's fiction remain firmly in place, but the double text offers a parallel set of pleasures: the intertextual gag, the sardonic quip, the double entendre, and the perpetually raised eyebrow.

Shrek attempts to revitalise the moribund fairy tale mode in two specific ways. First, it rewrites conventions that can no longer be presented 'straight'; the film trades in their familiarity but playfully acknowledges their outmodedness. Second, relatedly, it persistently alludes to contemporary issues and objects. The film's deconstructive agenda is signalled in the opening sequence, which begins with the time-worn conceit of a storybook prologue:

> Once upon a time there was a lovely princess. But she had an enchantment upon her of a fearful sort which could only be broken by love's first kiss. She was locked away in a castle guarded by a terrible fire-breathing dragon. Many brave knights had attempted to free her from this dreadful prison, but none prevailed. She waited in the dragon's keep in the highest room of the tallest tower for her true love and true love's first kiss.

At this point, the swell of orchestral music suddenly cuts out, and an enlarged, green hand – which we learn belongs to Shrek (Mike Myers), the eponymous ogre – rips out the offending page with a dismissive 'Like that's *ever* gonna happen!' A further note of vulgarity is added when the next shot reveals Shrek to be sitting on the toilet; his profane 'What a load of c—' is drowned out by the sound of a toilet flushing. The ahistorical, 'once upon a time' overtones of the prologue, already contemptuously dismissed by Shrek, is disavowed altogether by the credits sequence, which sees Shrek washing and farting in a dirty swamp in tune to the grungy rock number, 'All Star' (performed by the band Smash

Mouth). Anecdotally, it is worth noting that animation historian Jerry Beck watched the film in the company of teens and twenty-somethings on initial release, and reported that the audience 'went berserk' at this point.[41]

Despite the broadness of its terms of reference, then, *Shrek* clearly asserts itself as a product of millennial-era US culture. The 'hipness' of the screenplay, and its occasional vulgar excesses, are indebted to MTV-era shows like *The Simpsons* and *Beavis and Butt-head* (the writers of which co-wrote *Shrek*'s screenplay). When Eddie Murphy's talking donkey observes that Shrek 'definitely need[s] some Tic Tacs or something cause your breath stinks', when Cinderella is described as enjoying sushi in the magic mirror's take-off of *The Dating Game*, when Shrek dispatches hordes of medieval knights with wrestling moves, and – most notably – when the outwardly demure Princess Fiona (Cameron Diaz) dispatches an annoying troupe of Merrie Men-like characters with kung fu, freezing in mid-air before delivering the knockout move in conscious aesthetic homage to *The Matrix* (The Wachowski Brothers, 1999), the film invokes familiar accoutrements of late modernity (and epitomises contemporary popular cinema's obsession with 'relatability') in an arena where disbelief is usually willingly suspended. Sequences like the kung-fu parody – which *Variety* called 'a sop to tastes of the moment and [. . .] the element that will first appear to date the film in years to come' – serve a further function, namely, expanding the aesthetic possibilities of the medium beyond the cartoon-like hyper-realism popularised by Disney.[42]

The film also contains intertextual references to Disney fairy tales and to Hollywood family films more broadly. Characters in the film are themselves familiar with fairy tale conventions and either aspire to them or pointedly reject them. Princess Fiona initially presents herself as a classical fairy tale heroine in the Sleeping Beauty mould who desires to be rescued by a handsome prince (her 'true love') and talks in an exaggerated burlesque of Shakespearean English. When the fantasy breaks down and her rescuer proves to be an ogre, the pretence is dropped and the princess reveals herself as a feisty, somewhat brittle character who converses in a modern idiom. The notion of 'fairy tale creatures' being hunted allows for several intertextual jokes. In one scene, a Pinocchio-like wooden boy protests that he is a 'real boy', whereupon his nose grows to extreme length; later, a group of iconic fairy tale figures, including Snow White accompanied by seven dwarfs and a wolf dressed up as a grandmother, invade Shrek's house. Other visual and/or verbal gags include the ruined castle in which Fiona is imprisoned vaguely resembling a dilapidated iteration of Disney's 'magic kingdom'; the three pigs chorusing, 'He can fly, he can fly' when Tinker Bell temporarily imbues the donkey with the powers of flight (*Peter Pan*); Donkey being told, 'That'll do, donkey. That'll do' (*Babe*); and the crippled gingerbread man remarking at the end of the film, 'God bless us, every one' (*A Christmas Carol*).

All of these intertextual references are potentially cross-demographic in that they invoke texts that are widely accessible to children. However, in keeping with the more adult humour in *Antz*, there are several jokes intended largely for older viewers. When Shrek, Fiona and Donkey approach the enormous castle belonging to the villainous Lord Farquaad (John Lithgow), Donkey observes that Farquaad 'is compensating for something, which I think means he has a really—'. Shrek wallops Donkey before he can complete the innuendo about the villain's presumably inadequate penis, but the joke remains comprehensible to everyone except very young children. A more obscure (and hence adult-coded) comic reference is the decrepit priest who marries Fiona and Farquaad bearing a noticeable resemblance to the priest played by Peter Cook in identical circumstances in *The Princess Bride* (Rob Reiner, 1987). A final representative example of the film's deconstructive impulse is its disavowal of Disneyesque sentimentality towards nature. There is a decidedly non-cutesy sequence when Princess Fiona, singing in duet with a songbird, raises her pitch to such an extent that the bird explodes. The next shot is of three unattended eggs in the bird's nest; the shot after this shows the three eggs frying for breakfast. This kind of cynicism in relation to animals evokes memories of Tex Avery's repudiations of cutesy anthropomorphism, and foreshadows manifold sequences in a similar vein in adult-oriented animated TV shows such as *Family Guy* (2000–) and *BoJack Horseman* (2014–20).

Shrek's narrative strategies are not entirely deconstructive. On the contrary, it presents the kind of double-voiced endorsement and ironic disavowal of sincerity that characterises several self-consciously 'postmodern' examples of contemporary Hollywood animation, such as *Fantastic Mr. Fox* (Wes Anderson, 2009) and *Rango* (Gore Verbinsky, 2011).[43] For all his cynicism, gross-out behaviour and superficial obnoxiousness, Shrek is a heroic character that embodies virtues of tolerance, gentleness, friendship and love. His physical unattractiveness avails another homily that recurs across countless children's texts: do not judge by appearances. This is implicit when Shrek, looking at the night sky, points out patterns in the constellation of Orion and observes, 'You know, Donkey, things are sometimes more than they appear,' developing his earlier insistence that ogres are like onions, possessing several layers beneath the surface. Princess Fiona later tells Shrek, 'Maybe you shouldn't judge people before you get to know them.' Yet it is a mark of the film's apparent discomfort with overt moralising that this moment of earnestness is immediately leavened by the princess delivering a comically unladylike belch. *Shrek* is no less didactic than the majority of Hollywood animated features, but the form in which didacticism is presented – smuggled in via the Trojan horse of postmodernist irony – implies a degree of discomfort, or perhaps a tacit acknowledgement that the time for drawing moral lessons in a more earnest fashion has passed. A similar point can be made of Donkey's line, 'I was hoping this would be a happy ending', after Fiona and Shrek share their first kiss. The convention is recognised and, to some degree, longed for, but it is so familiar that self-consciousness cannot be avoided.

The achingly trendy, compiled soundtrack also demands some consideration. As we have seen, *Shrek* largely eschews the nostalgic inflections that suffuse *Toy Story* in favour of an insistent 'hipness' that is localised in its parodic treatment of its multiple sources, its occasionally risqué humour, and its plethora of throwaway intertextual allusions. Equally important, however, is the filmmakers' rejection of the aesthetic style of symphonic German Romanticism that plays a substantial part in traditional Hollywood animated features, instead offering a soundtrack that privileges contemporary trends in popular music. While Randy Newman's songs in the first few Pixar releases are clear concessions to adult viewers (many of whom will recall Newman's sardonic compositions from the 1970s), *Shrek*'s soundtrack also takes aim squarely at teenagers, with Smash Mouth's 'All Star' and the band's newly recorded cover of Neil Diamond's 'I'm a Believer' alongside songs from more established, adult-associated artists, such as John Cale's rendition of Leonard Cohen's 'Hallelujah' and The Proclaimers' karaoke standard 'I'm on My Way'. Other artists featured on the film's commercially released soundtrack include Rufus Wainwright and Eels, both of whom possessed an international cult following mostly made up of teenagers and young adults.

As Stan Beeler argues, the synchronisation of these primarily teen- and adult-oriented songs with more child-oriented visuals maintains the equilibrium of the film's strategies of dual address. The overtly juvenile toilet humour of the opening scene (Shrek on the toilet and bathing in mud) is counterpointed by the lyrics to 'All Star', which emphasise the more 'adult' sentiment of 'the need to enjoy life while you have it'.[44] Furthermore, Beeler is correct in noting that 'children's films regularly use popular music from an earlier generation to superimpose a more complex psychological narrative upon the more direct diegetic pleasures of a children's animated feature film'.[45] That is to say, the use of compiled soundtracks in *Shrek* and other films functions intertextually: a song such as 'Hallelujah' possesses nostalgic appeal for adult audiences (recollections of past times, particularly childhood and youth), but also embodies psychological complexities that would appear incongruous as part of the film's diegesis. At the same time, the films contain these 'adult' markers within isolated musical moments so that they do not suffuse the wider narrative, while juxtaposing them with overtly child-oriented pratfalls and sight gags. This strategy is reused in the majority of subsequent DreamWorks films. As Summers notes, of DreamWorks' 24 computer-generated features released between 1998 and 2015, 18 utilised well-known, pre-existing songs.[46]

Figure 3.1   Shrek bathing in mud: the child-oriented pictorial counterpoint to the youth-centred soundtrack (*Shrek*, DreamWorks, 2001). Frame grab.

Upon its theatrical release in May 2001, *Shrek* was widely received by critics as a turning point in the field of Hollywood animation. Todd McCarthy's *Variety* review is not unrepresentative:

> 'Shrek' is an instant animated classic. Rudely sending up even the most beloved fairy tale traditions while at the same time effectively embodying them, this spirited and often very funny lark accomplishes something that most films in the bygone Hollywood studio era used to do but is remarkably rare in today's world of niche markets: It offers entertainment equally to viewers from 4 to 104. This story of an ogre's odyssey from contented oblivion to unexpected love will make out like a Prince Charming wherever it plays, repping a bonanza for DreamWorks theatrically and forever after in home-viewing markets.[47]

Elvis Mitchell, writing in the *New York Times*, noted that 'The cycle of kiddie musicals typified by "Aladdin" seems to be drawing to a close'; instead, *Shrek* was seen as 'a blistering race through pop culture', bringing 'the brash slob comedy of "The Simpsons" and "South Park", as well as the institutional irreverence of "Saturday Night Live", to a very young audience'.[48] Much like *Toy Story*, the film's status as iconic text in contemporary popular culture obscures its impressive but by no means stratospheric box office gross of just under $500 million (much less than the year's Pixar release, *Monsters, Inc.* [Pete Docter,

2001], which brought in more than $600 million). However, *Shrek*'s influence on Hollywood animation of the 2000s can hardly be overestimated. As Summers argues, in popularising a mode of 'narrative-cartoonalism' characterised by absurdity, self-reflexiveness and fourth-wall-breaking intertextual strategies,

> DreamWorks triggered a shift away from what had been the dominant mode of feature animation in America since the form's inception with Disney's *Snow White* in 1937; a mode characterised by a dedication to realism, sustained as the industry standard due to Disney's consistent commercial success.[49]

The success of the 'narrative-cartoonal' mode, Summers suggests, partly reflects the medium-specific requirements of computer-generated animation, which is 'uniquely suited to intertextual contra-diegesis and comedy, and less suited to other aspects of cartoonalism' due to 'the medium's ability to convincingly replicate three-dimensional sets and live-action cinematography'.[50] Yet *Shrek* is also the natural culmination of the increasing, strategic injection of allusions to contemporary culture and society into Hollywood animated features over the course of the 1990s. Its phenomenal popularity established something of a blueprint for other studios to follow in films such as Blue Sky's *Robots* (Chris Wedge, 2005), Disney's *Chicken Little* (Mark Dindal, 2005), and Sony's *Surf's Up* (Chris Buck and Ash Brannon, 2007). Consequently, the 2000s can legitimately be described as the 'DreamWorks Decade'.[51]

SOCIAL COMMENT AND CONTEMPORARY AMERICA

Although authorial intertextuality remains an important feature of contemporary Hollywood animated features, there was a broad but noticeable retreat from pop-culture referentiality at the turn of the 2010s. In part, this may be a response to consumer fatigue; the later *Shrek* films were met by an increasingly lukewarm critical reception and declining box office grosses, and the term 'Shrekification' emerged as a contemptuous description of this narrative style.[52] In 2011, *The Hollywood Reporter* noted that 'There seems to have been backlash against the pop-culture references and topical humour that the Shrek films brought to the forefront', and Christopher Miller – director of Sony's *Cloudy with a Chance of Meatballs* (Phil Lord and Christopher Miller, 2009) and Warner's *The Lego Movie* (Lord and Miller, 2014) – remarked, 'I prefer that any kind of comedy come from the situations, the character and the story. For me, those pop-culture moments snap me out of the movie. They also date a film.'[53] Subsequently, DreamWorks repositioned itself within a more realist aesthetic with the *How to Train Your Dragon* series (2010–) and *The Croods* (Chris Sanders and Kirk DeMicco, 2013), perhaps sensing that persistent parodies of generic conventions eventually weaken the very foundations on which Hollywood family-oriented animation is built. Hollywood animation in the 2010s has also been marked by proliferation of different aesthetic styles (a subject explored in depth in Chapter 5); as Summers observes, 'The Pixar/DreamWorks stylistic binary which characterised the CG landscape in the 2000s has been effectively dissolved by [a] plurality of modes and aesthetics.'[54]

Other forms of intertextuality – particularly the social satire – have come to the fore. Although the combination is evident in earlier films such as *Toy Story*, perhaps the most notable example of the hybridisation of postmodern stylings and social commentary is *The Lego Movie*. The first instalment in a lucrative film franchise, which also comprises *The Lego Batman Movie* (Chris McKay, 2017), *The Lego Ninjago Movie* (Charlie Bean et al., 2017) and *The Lego Movie 2: The Second Part* (Mike Mitchell, 2019), it builds a coherent fictional universe around Lego, the globally successful Denmark-based toy manufacturer of interlocking plastic bricks. *The Lego Movie* centres on Emmet Brickowski (Chris Pratt), an 'everyman' construction worker living in a hyper-consumerist state built entirely of Lego, and presided over by the totalitarian uber-capitalist Lord Business (Will Ferrell). Emmet, like everyone else in the city, is indoctrinated to believe that 'everything is awesome', but lives a dull, conformist life built solely on hard work and mindless consumption. Towards the end of the film, it transpires that this entire world is the invention of a human boy, Finn (Jadon Sand), who is secretly playing with an expensive Lego collection owned by his neurotic father (also played by Ferrell). Finn has invented the tyrannical Lord Business as an embodiment of his father's joyless perfectionism, which demands that entire contents of the Lego city must be glued down to prevent it from being played with. Finn and his father reconcile once the latter realises how his son regards him, and the Lego universe section of the film ends with a peaceful rapprochement between Lord Business and the residents of the city.

The Lego Movie is a self-consciously 'open' text in that its discourse is able to sustain multiple interpretations (*heteroglossia*, in the Bakhtinian sense). There are at least three readings of the film's relationship with contemporary culture that appear equally plausible. The first is that it ingeniously disguises the fact that it is both a product and a reification of advanced capitalism by presenting a seemingly explicit anti-capitalist, anti-materialist narrative. This would implicate the film within the ideological structures it appears to disavow. The second is that *The Lego Movie* presents a deliberate, satirical critique of the very institutions that produced it, introducing audiences to Marxist concepts of false consciousness in an age of mechanical reproduction. The third is that the film is a self-consciously incoherent text – and therefore quintessentially postmodern – that is content to have its cake and eat it, not even attempting to reconcile the inherently paradoxical representations at its centre. Indeed, the film deliberately invites ambiguity; it is not in its interests to resolve the paradox of its double-voiced repudiation and reaffirmation of advanced capitalism, since that ambiguity is imperative to its ability to appeal simultaneously to different ideological positions.

The proposition that postmodernism *itself* has become an intertext is fully manifested here; not only does *The Lego Movie* self-consciously parody other cultural forms in wide currency, but it actively invokes the very *idea* of the postmodern. This is taken to *reductio-near-absurdist* levels when Will Ferrell, that modern hero of mainstream-alternative US comedy, unexpectedly breaks into the diegesis in a live-action segment that comments on the artifice of the surrounding narrative. On one level, this interlude tips the wink to adult spectators that the film is not taking itself particularly seriously. Yet the live-action sequence is merely part of a wider strategy of asserting the film's fundamental good-humouredness, its embrace of absurdity (implicit even in the very concept of a film built around the Lego brand) and disavowal of seriousness at almost all levels of textuality, as if to pre-empt and diffuse the inevitable accusations that the film is merely another symptom of the corporatisation of Hollywood that offers up further proof of the industry's creative bankruptcy.

The obvious disjuncture here is the fact that, however subversive *The Lego Movie* may present itself as being, from a corporate perspective it is very serious business indeed. Grossing almost $500 million at the global box office, it provided Lego with an exceptionally 'toyetic' product, justifying the time spent by the filmmakers in the company of Lego's 'brand designers' in Denmark in translating 'the principles of the brand into a story'.[55] Lego sales in the first half of 2014 rose by 15 per cent in the wake of the film's success, making it the biggest toy firm in the world ahead of California-based Mattel.[56] There is a clear link here with other recent transmedia franchises, particularly the hugely profitable *Transformers* film series (2007–). While the *Transformers* films have been regarded generally as shameless, artistically negligible exploitation releases, *The Lego Movie* was received much more favourably. The *Los Angeles Times* attributed its 'postmodern' virtues to a rare case of executive 'latitude' in keeping the production free from 'corporate interests'.[57] The *New York Times*' Heather Havrilesky also noted the 'brilliance' of its 'surface-level subversion', despite the fact that, as she pointedly observes, the film actually perfectly embodies the value of 'creative play' that Lego insists is at the heart of its brand.[58]

Nonetheless, *The Lego Movie* and *Toy Story*, both nominally 'postmodern' films, enter into commentary on aspects of Western late modernity. This is particularly visible in their critique of play, consumption and waste. For instance, the *Toy Story* films implicitly lament the wastefulness and greed generated by advanced capitalism and its strategies of inbuilt obsolescence. All of the anthropomorphised toys owned by their human owner, Andy, live in constant fear of being superseded by the next, putatively 'better', toy off the production line. In empathising with the fate of inanimate toys, and asserting the value of the old and apparently obsolete and the importance of recycling, the film takes aim at the Western society's fetishisation of the new and its endless cycle of production, consumption and wastage. In so doing, it also allegorises contemporary green debates surrounding sustainability and emphasises the need to raise ecological awareness.

The Lego Movie is strikingly similar in this regard. Whilst the ordered, regimented society in which Emmet lives might put one in mind of totalitarian regimes, it also evokes the conformist plasticity of contemporary Western consumer culture. The soulless music, $37 cups of branded sugary coffee, and inescapable culture of positivity embody some of the negative corollaries of advanced capitalism. The latter characteristics invoke the brand identity of Silicon Valley conglomerates with their fraudulent ethos of collectivism under a tyrannical leader – here personified by Lord Business, a seemingly benevolent executive whose villainy is centred on his obsessive pursuit of 'order and precision'. The film's portrayal of the artificial positivity of the corporate workplace, a near-dystopia populated by a literal two-faced employee called Bad Cop/Good Cop and monstrous, transformer-like machines called 'Micromanagers', will be recognisable to a high proportion of the film's adult viewers. The 'immaculately coiffured' Emmet – an identikit Lego everyman – is an ideal citizen for a totalitarian regime (nation state or workplace) in his unquestioning acceptance of authority and his adherence to a manual that contains 'instructions on how to fit in, have everyone like you and always be happy'. His contented daily repetition of the propagandist, muzak jingle 'Everything is Awesome', when it is anything but, underlines the magnitude of his condition of false consciousness. Emmet's awakening from this state is both a satire of the metanarrative of individualism and the little man coming out on top and an uplifting rehearsal of it.

The film's anterior plotline concerns the fastidious 'real-world' adult toy collector joylessly maintaining his perfect but untouched basement Lego city. This vision lampoons a particular iteration of modern kidulthood: the grown man who has never really left behind childish things, but cannot comfortably reconcile the desire to preserve his childlike self with social expectations that adults should conduct themselves with responsibility and sobriety. Will Ferrell's 'Man Upstairs' prizes and maintains the artefacts of his childhood but no longer engages (plays) with them, as a child would do. Rendered in his son's play-space as a villain obsessed with neatness and conformity, he is a redeemable version of the stereotypically geeky toy collector in *Toy Story 2* (John Lasseter, 1999) who steals the rare, 1950s cowboy doll Woody (Tom Hanks), restores him, and promptly puts him on display on his shelf as a fetishised but unloved object. The collector is presented, unambiguously, as perverse, and cannot really be seen as anything but a satirical comment on the practice of adults – crudely reified in the figure of a small, fat, balding, middle-aged, socially inept loner – actively partaking of a children's culture that, by normative conventions of adult society, they should have left behind. Tellingly, there is no forecasting of lifelong play in the vision of Andy's adult life at the end of *Toy Story 3* (Lee Unkrich, 2010), when the college-bound teenager donates all of his toys to a pre-adolescent girl.

In contrast, *The Lego Movie* sees nothing inherently wrong with adult obsession with toys. Indeed, because the film operates as a brand ambassador for Lego, and since adults are now a vital consumer group for the toy industry, the *Toy Story* films' implicit hostility to 'kidulthood' would be untenable here. Finn's father's transgression is of a different kind: he uses the toys to create a microcosm of a perfectly ordered society, precluding the spontaneity, tactility and active enjoyment that should be a vital part of toy ownership. Owning toys, we are told, ought to be *fun*. Not only does the father pompously describe his model city as 'a highly sophisticated interlocking brick system', but he forbids Finn from playing with it, much to the bemusement of the boy, who points out, 'But we bought it at a *toy store*.' The warning stickers he adds to the model ('Do not touch', 'Hands off', 'Off limits') inhibit the values of play and creativity at the centre of the film and the brand ethos of the production company. The final scene's envisioning of the entire family – father, pre-adolescent son and younger sister – all happily partaking of Lego products is not simply a blatant example of corporate sponsorship of the media industries. It also reaffirms the centrality of play in contemporary Western society as a fulfilling, lifelong activity rather than a frivolous or perverse pursuit. *The Lego Movie* exploits this shift in attitudes towards play and reasserts its social value as a recreational activity in which all members of the family can partake, and be brought together by the experience.

Figure 3.2   Father and son engage in brand-based play (*The Lego Movie*, Warner Bros., 2014). Frame grab.

Toy Story and *The Lego Movie* blend the postmodern strategies discussed earlier in this chapter with social commentary. However, the foregrounding of self-conscious irony and parody disavows seriousness, and thus insulates them from the charge of excessive politicising. Cultural allusions can be seen as a form of representing contemporary culture and society in primarily *non-political* and hence non-sensitive, non-controversial ways. This aligns with the overarching commercial project of Hollywood family entertainment: that of pleasing as many, and offending as few, consumers as possible. Admittedly, some viewers may be mildly irritated by the self-conscious intertextuality at play in a high proportion of contemporary animated features, but the practice is unlikely to provoke the kind of moral outrage liable to cause longer-term damage to the major studios' bottom line. Even when engaging in critique of consumer culture, films such as *Toy Story* and *The Lego Movie* mostly pick low-hanging fruit, since even hawkish conservatives would be hard pressed to argue that burning up the planet is a desirable goal. Furthermore, because their social commentary tends towards satire or overt comedy, the assault on late modernity has no particular sting. Such films, therefore, walk something of a tightrope between the need to avoid offending the sensibilities of any large audience group and the need to remain relevant – current, 'real', 'relatable'.

While social commentary has emerged as a useful authorial strategy in post-1990s animation, films that engage in more explicit and serious forms of it remain open to accusations of impropriety. Partly, this is because the practice contravenes Hollywood's well-cultivated reputation for non-activist modes of discourse, and partly it is because the idea of politicising the classroom is highly sensitive. It is impossible for any cultural text to be entirely value-free, of course, so what we are really talking about are films that *appear* to advocate political standpoints widely seen as contentious or partisan. Perhaps the clearest example is *The Iron Giant* (Brad Bird, 1999), Warner Bros.' adaptation of Ted Hughes's children's novel, *The Iron Man* (1968). The film is located in 1950s Rockwell, where a nine-year-old boy, Hogarth Hughes (Eli Marenthal), investigates the site of an apparent meteor crash and discovers the arrival of a strange but benevolent giant alien robot (Vin Diesel). Set at the height of the Cold War, just after the launch of the Soviet Union's satellite *Sputnik* heralded the beginning of the US–Soviet space race, the film is an explicit anti-war parable. The film's primary antagonist, the rampantly paranoid government agent Kent Mansley (Christopher McDonald), hates foreigners and irrationally desires to obliterate the Iron Giant. Alluding to *Sputnik* in conversation with Hogarth, Mansley refers to the 'dark side' of the atomic age, emphasising that the Soviet satellite is 'foreign, and all that that implies', a piece of dialogue that establishes him as a hawkish conservative. In contrast, the smart, curious, hyperactive and friendless Hogarth Hughes is perhaps the first in a relatively long line of misfit child protagonists in contemporary Hollywood animation (a topic discussed in greater depth in Chapter 5).

On one level, *The Iron Giant* is a product of the enormous popularity of the early-1990s 'Disney Renaissance' features, which led to a minor gold-rush as rival studios (including Sony and Twentieth Century Fox) attempted to cash in on the renewed profitability of feature animation. Like DreamWorks' *The Prince of Egypt*, *The Iron Giant* was marketed as sophisticated, high-quality fare that utilised the potential of animation – largely untapped by Disney – as a medium of artistic experimentation. Moreover, Warner Bros.' marketing campaign emphasised the film's moral advocacy. The studio sent copies of the film to each member of the US Congress and Senate, and organised an event on Washington's Capitol Hill that was attended by several members of the House, including Edward Markey, author of the Children's Television Act, and Mark Foley, chairman of the House Entertainment Industry Caucus, as well as lobbyist Peggy Charren, founder of Action for Children's Television.[59] Markey claimed that the film demonstrated 'that Hollywood's capacity for great children's cinema is still immense', while Charren approvingly observed that it marked 'a giant step forward in the production by a major studio of a nifty film for kids and families [. . .] Parents, teachers and everyone who cares about young audiences should make sure that children everywhere over seven get a chance to see this classic film.'[60] Warner Bros.' Warren Lieberfarb explained that 'a movie like "The Iron Giant" comes around once in a lifetime', while fellow studio executive Thomas Lesinski added that 'There are very few movies with such high quality and such a strong moral perspective'.[61]

Despite this initial enthusiasm, *The Iron Giant* bombed at the box office, returning little more than $30 million from its estimated outlay of $70 million. As *USA Today* put it, 'Much of Hollywood has spent the past few weeks trying to explain the failure of a movie that, by most accounts, was one of the most anticipated of the year.'[62] Warner Bros.' president of production, Lorenzo Di Bonaventura, grimly observed: 'People always say to me, "Why don't you make smarter movies?" The lesson is: Every time you do, you get slaughtered.'[63] The film also polarised critical opinion. On the one hand, *The Iron Giant* was held by many as a superbly animated production with a true moral centre – a rare instance of a Hollywood family film engaging thoughtfully and imaginatively with important issues. The film won numerous awards on initial release, such as the BAFTA Children's Award for 'Best Feature Film' and nine Annie Awards, including 'Outstanding Achievement in an Animated Theatrical Feature'. On the other hand, several critics appeared mildly affronted by its perceived liberal moralising. Although Lawrence Van Gelder, writing in the *New York Times*, noted that 'Many adults, including parents eager to have their children absorb lessons about the perils of guns and the merits of peace and tolerance, will doubtless approve of the film's messages', Steve Persall of the *St. Petersburg*

Times predicted, '*The Iron Giant* is going to surprise some moviegoers, especially card-carrying members of the National Rifle Association.'[64] The *Washington Post*'s Stephen Hunter was more direct in his view: 'At a certain point "The Iron Giant", without missing a beat in charm or artistry, skews off into TULWC. And that would be The Usual Left-Wing Crap.'[65]

The film's commercial underperformance is more likely a result of its incongruity with the dominant narrative aesthetic of 1990s Hollywood animation than its vaguely leftist politics. *The Iron Giant* can be seen as a forerunner to post-millennial social comment films, such as *Happy Feet* (George Miller, 2006), *WALL-E* (Andrew Stanton, 2008), *Zootopia* (Byron Howard and Rich Moore, 2016) and *Isle of Dogs* (Wes Anderson, 2018). Viewed alongside them, it appears far less radical. The primary point of distinction is that these later films – not unlike *Toy Story* and *The Lego Movie* – operate through a double-voiced assertion and disavowal of seriousness that blends sincerity with overt comedy. In this way, any apparent ideological position is ameliorated or diffused through a principle of plausible deniability, whereby the filmmakers can claim (as did many of the Production Code violators of the Hollywood studio era) that censoriousness is present only in the imagination of the prurient spectator, not encoded on to the text itself. In part, as Ellen Scott argues, this practice operates through the 'digitised circumlocution of the "real" through animation', a mode that involves an 'abstraction from reality' and thus facilitates ambivalence and ambiguity.[66] These films address some of the most important issues of the time: waste and consumption; bigotry and fundamentalism; war; climate change and environmentalism; and, ultimately, the threat of planetary extinction. However, they do so via a narrative mode that, even when it is not inflected with humour and irony, can be defended as essentially innocent.

Three films that exemplify this narrative ideology are *Happy Feet*, *WALL-E* and *Zootopia*. Of the three films, *Happy Feet* is closest to the liberal earnestness of *The Iron Giant*. Co-written and directed by George Miller, whose career has included such diverse and acclaimed projects as the *Mad Max* series (1979–), *The Witches of Eastwick* (1987), and *Babe* (1995), the film centres on an anthropomorphised colony of emperor penguins in Antarctica. It develops two primary narrative lines, one of them a story of individual self-actualisation, the other an allegory of ecological conservation. The primary character, the young adult emperor penguin Mumble (Elijah Wood), cannot sing like his compatriots and has to resort to dancing to communicate, much to the disapproval of his comparatively conservative colony. In the process, he discovers the existence of humans (which the fellow animal citizens of Antarctica refer to as 'aliens') and their increasingly destructive interventions into the natural world. The film's final scenes, which depict Mumble's return to the penguin colony after being exiled for his non-conformism, see him fully accepted; even the conservative elders of the colony become convinced that tap dancing is a valid form of self-expression. Moreover, he is able to prove the existence of humans, whose combined governments ultimately agree to a cessation of the practice of intensive fishing in the region when faced with evidence of the soon-to-be-irreversible damage to the local ecology.

The film opens with an expansive shot of the Milky Way galaxy; as the camera rapidly zooms in, first the Earth, then Antarctica, and finally a colony of singing penguins come into view. The soundtrack to this establishing shot is a medley of familiar pop numbers, each representing the Emperor Penguins' respective mating songs. The medley thus makes diegetic sense within the film's internal logic, but, like *Shrek*, uses the strategy of imposing psychologically complex, adult meanings over more child-oriented visuals. Throughout the film, music and dance are presented as universal channels of inter-species communication, and form the basis on which the penguins and humans come to a rudimentary mutual understanding. Yet dance and music also serve an important instrumental function in the film's multilayered mode of audience address, presenting points of identification and appeal in what might seem a somewhat remote (i.e. non-relatable) setting. While Miller brings a live-action filmmaker's sensibility to the production, with a preponderance of expansive tracking shots, the film's most obvious aestheticisation is its soundtrack. Like *Shrek*, the film uses a compiled soundtrack made up of previously released tracks (e.g. 'Do it Again' by the Beach Boys) and covers of songs by contemporary artists (e.g. Pink, Brittany Murphy and K. D. Lang), alongside a newly composed song by Prince.

Happy Feet, in common with Miller's primarily live-action film, *Babe*, champions human ethical awareness of animals and the natural world. In *Babe*, a simpatico relationship is developed between the pig and the human farmer, one that is based on non-verbal communication. In *Happy Feet*, the humans only become aware of the threat to the penguins through kinesics; a human child is the first to make contact with Mumble by tapping out a basic rhythm on a glass window, which he later mimics. (The specialness of his peculiar talent is thus finally reaffirmed; Mumble emerges as the potential saviour of his entire civilisation.) Here, as in classic children's texts such as Henry Williamson's *Tarka the Otter* (1927), the childlike subjectivity of the animal is emphasised and humans (or, rather, human adults) are figured as an unfathomable, destructive force. The low fishing stocks, which put the penguins at risk of starvation, result from industrial harvesting: vast trawlers sweep the oceans entirely indiscriminately. But the wastefulness of post-industrial society is also observed (as it is in a different way in the *Toy Story* films) when non-biodegradable plastics wash up on to the Antarctic glaciers, threatening local wildlife; in once sequence, the penguin Lovelace (Robin Williams) catches a plastic six-pack ring round his throat, almost choking him. The penguins' later co-ordinated dancing forces the human explorers to take notice of their plight, leading to an impassioned appeal by several conservationists, who recognise: 'We are messing with their food chain.' As the debate escalates, a montage sequence conveys a number of contrary opinions being voiced (including passing references to 'money' and 'jobs'), before a United Nations summit finally agrees a ban on industrial fishing. The occasional shots that punctuate the narrative of the Earth viewed at distance in space imply awareness of larger concerns, and a need to transcend a cultural and ethical parochialism.

As with *The Iron Giant*, it is possible to interpret *Happy Feet* as an assault on the dominant ideology. The eventual validation of the non-conformism Mumble represents portends the overthrowing of the old, illiberal order. His cultural leanings are themselves vaguely counter-cultural; his tap-dancing not only physically resembles contemporary dance moves but can stand as a metaphor for almost any major cultural intervention. This is matched by his receptiveness to new philosophies, seemingly deliberately allegorising the 1960s counter-culture and its explicit challenge to established socio-behavioural norms. The hitherto unimagined coming together of his rhythm and Gloria's song energises the juvenile emperor penguins, creating an insurgence that the traditional orthodoxy is unable to resist. The fear of change that leads to Mumble's initial expulsion from the colony is localised in the figure of the aged Penguin, Noah (Hugo Weaving) – an ironic biblical allusion – and his desperate exhortation for the dancing penguins to 'Stop this unruly nonsense!' and accusing Mumble of bringing 'this disorder, this aberration to the very heart of our community'. The reactionary, xenophobic undertones are brought to the surface when Noah speaks of 'you and your foreign friends [the Amigos] lead[ing] us into your easy ways'. The WASPish fundamentalism, religiosity, rejection of non-conformity and predominantly Yankee accents of the emperor penguins all suggest a satire (or a downright critique) of right-wing US conservatism, which only the freshness and imagination of youth can successfully overcome. And yet, despite all these political inflections, *Happy Feet* can equally be interpreted as an innocent children's film about dancing penguins; it might, for that matter, even be viewed as a 'typically' conservative Hollywood narrative that endorses individualism, family, heterosexual romance, and social unity. It is the ability to encourage and sustain multiple avenues of access that is at the core of these films' success.

While *Happy Feet*, set in the present day, reflects on the need for ecological awareness and the increasing urgency of collective action, Pixar's *WALL-E* shows us what will happen if humanity fails to heed such warnings. The film opens with a curious juxtaposition of shots of outer space overlaid with a performance of Jerry Herman's 'Put on Your Sunday Clothes'. The song continues as the camera roves through images of the post-apocalyptic world drained of life and colour, a dense fog hanging over landscapes marked with crumbling cities and factories, industrial cooling towers and pylons and the occasional wind farm surrounded by vast slag heaps implying a belated, but doomed, ecological drive. The jaunty, all-American popular music serves two distinct functions here. Firstly, it makes melancholia almost inconceivable (Larry David has made a similar observation of the insistently upbeat title music in *Curb Your Enthusiasm* [2000–], his 'comedy of embarrassment'), and so presents an important counterpoint to the potentially depressing visuals. Secondly, and especially for adult audiences, it presents a dialectic of de-familiarisation and familiarisation that ultimately serves an ironic function.

The film then introduces its central character, the benign robot WALL-E (Ben Burtt), who patrols the deserted planet collecting waste. The concept of a lone, automated robot tidying a post-apocalyptic wasteland no longer inhabited by humanity might imply the seeming futility of individual and small-scale ecological drives when the larger problem of industrialisation driven by advanced capitalism continues unabated. A series of tracking shots follow WALL-E as he passes by a huge gas station with the banner 'Buy Large GAS', then a branch of 'BUY N LARGE BANK'. The gas station and the bank represent two key facets of the infrastructure of advanced capitalism: fossil fuels and global finance. The following shots show WALL-E patrolling a huge, empty convenience story, and then a wide shot briefly reveals a metropolis overrun by banners instructing the public to spend and to consume, with invitations to 'BUY LARGE', 'DRINK NOW', 'RUN NOW', and to 'BUY, SHOP' (Figure 3.3). These consumerist exhortations are highly reminiscent of John Carpenter's satirical horror film *They Live* (1988), in which intergalactic capitalists attempt to take over the planet with consumerist messages hidden on public billboards. While this allusion is part of *WALL-E*'s strategy of authorial intertextuality, it carries more subversive meanings. As with *The Lego Movie*, it implies the existence of a huge, ultimately self-immolating capitalist infrastructure that cannot be resisted in any meaningful way (one banner contains a clearly ironic claim to be 'Keeping Power in Our Hands'). Equally disturbingly, these scenes issue a reminder that every one of us partakes, willingly or unwillingly, in a mindless and corrosive cycle of production, consumption and waste.

The film's satire of advanced capitalism is developed further when the action relocates to the Axiom, a huge spaceship carrying the descendants of Earth's evacuated population until they can return to the planet. The actions of the Axiom's literal-minded mainframe, AUTO, which attempts to sabotage humanity's return to the now-fertile but potentially dangerous Earth, reflect a pervasive distrust of mechanisation and reliance on machinery. This unease transcends purely ethical considerations of the treatment of beings with artificial intelligence and gestures towards broader and more abiding anxieties of human extinction. The film's vision of these future humans as obese, cosseted, and disempowered – living in material comfort but lacking the capacity for growth or advancement – requires some discussion. The strong implication

Figure 3.3   The post-apocalyptic city still inundated with consumerist slogans (*WALL-E*, Pixar, 2008). Frame grab.

is that humanity's descent into mindless indolence is a direct result of the fact that technology has already met all material wants and needs. The film captures some of the radical individualism of Herbert Marcuse's critique of advanced capitalist society, particularly his claim that 'the progress of technological rationality is liquidating the oppositional and transcending elements' of what he calls 'higher culture' (moral, intellectual, aesthetic), leading to the condition of the 'one-dimensional man'.[67] The film's solution to this social condition is to reassert a foundational tenet of American ideology: the Protestant ethic. According to Daniel Bell, it was 'puritan restraint', allied to the Protestant ethic, which held 'the unrestrained economic impulse' in check during the early development of capitalism.[68] Equally, the collapse of these principles heralded the age of advanced capitalism, marked by mass production and mass consumption. When all material needs have been met, the psychological and physical need to grow and evolve continues to endure, the film tells us. We must work tirelessly to improve ourselves and society through daily struggle; the alternative is physical and philosophical atrophy.

What is eventually required of the future humans is the recognition that the greed and self-absorption of their forebears is responsible for the planetary extinction. Upon being shown images of the post-apocalyptic Earth, the spaceship's Captain McCrea (Jeff Garlin) remarks: 'Wait, that doesn't look like Earth. Where's the blue sky? Where's the grass?' After McCrea takes possession of the seedling recently discovered on the newly fertile planet, one of its leaves fall off, and the Captain rushes to give it some water, remarking: 'Just needed someone to look after you, that's all . . .' McCrea trails off as he finishes the sentence, gazing at his model globe of the Earth in a meaningful acknowledgement that the past humans (i.e. ourselves) failed to do so. The closing credits roll over a series of traditionally animated graphics that show the humans and the robots working together to repopulate the planet in an idealised, pre-industrial rural agrarianism that evokes the pastoral Golden Age vision of humanity and nature in perfect synchronicity. We see the planting of crops, the building of homes, the digging of water wells, the returning of life to the oceans and humans fishing with nets rather than trawlers, and finally a huge tree grown from the original seedling (now buried in the soil but still rooting from the shoe in which WALL-E had originally placed it). This montage sequence hopefully forecasts a brighter future for these future generations of humanity then their twenty-first-century forebears, avoiding the same pitfalls by applying themselves to cleaner and more sustainable strategies of production and consumption.

However, having visualised the threat of advanced capitalism's overreliance on fossil fuels and the deleterious effects on the world around us in the largely silent opening third, the film ultimately draws back from explicit moralising. Indeed, it chooses to foreground personal concerns rather than political issues, such as the romance between the robot protagonists, WALL-E and EVE (Elissa Knight), and the future humans' self-empowering decision to relinquish the gilded cage of their spaceship and repopulate the Earth. In this sense, the film instead commits itself fully to the wish-fulfilment fantasy in which humanity and its mechanical creations are able to co-exist peacefully and productively. Furthermore, in their benevolence and acquiescence to human authority, these robots are very much the acceptable face of humanity's post-industrial future. Not having the stubbornness of AUTO, or the schizophrenic murderousness of HAL in *2001: A Space Odyssey* (Stanley Kubrick, 1968), these robots represent a somewhat disturbing confluence of childlike wonder and innocence and servility that cannot help evoking, on some level, America's history of slavery.

Certainly, these ambiguities do not suggest a highly developed political agenda on the filmmakers' part. Although the *New York Post* deemed *WALL-E* 'the darkest animated feature ever released by Disney (after "Pinocchio") and certainly the most political',[69] director Andrew Stanton has strongly denied the claim that the film is a deliberate allegory of climate change and ecological awareness:

As [the film] was getting finished, the environment talk started to freak me out. I don't have much of a political bent, and the last thing I want to do is preach. I just went with things that I felt were logical for a possible future and supported the point of my story, which was the premise that irrational love defeats life's programming, and that the most robotic beings I've met are us.[70]

Although Stanton's curiously insistent denial of social comment is hard to credit even on a surface reading, Todd McCarthy's review of *WALL-E* in *Variety* makes a telling point, one that echoes Scott's claim to the film's strategy of deniability: although 'it has plenty to say', it 'does so in a light, insouciant manner that allows you to take the message or leave it on the table'.[71] This multi-voiced, *heteroglossian* style of narrative is further availed by the sublimation of active political commentary to the conventional structures of children's cinema, with endorsements of friendship, kinship and particularly romantic love.

A final representative example of social commentary in Hollywood animation is Disney's *Zootopia*, which remains, at the time of writing, Hollywood's most explicit manifesto for 'diversity' – female empowerment, racial inclusiveness, and acceptance of difference. *Zootopia* has gone on to become one of the highest-grossing films of all time, and only the fourth animated feature to pass $1 billion in global box office takings. The film is set in the fictional city of Zootopia, where anthropomorphised animals live together in a fragile alliance, but ridden by racial and political fractures in close parallel with contemporary Western urban society. The film invites interpretation as an allegory about coming to terms with the darker side of human nature, yet remains palatable (by the normative conventions of family entertainment) because its themes are displaced into the sufficiently unfamiliar milieu of anthropomorphised animal society. *Zootopia*'s protagonist, the seemingly defenceless doe, Judy (Ginnifer Goodwin), overcomes widespread scorn and incredulity to become the first rabbit police officer, but still has to prove herself after initially being assigned menial tasks despite her protests that she is not just a 'token rabbit' (racial and sexual tokenism being a historical reality in modern and contemporary US society). And indeed, the animal society's clearly caste-based system itself allows for comparatively developed, and occasionally subversive, reflections on contemporary racial politics. A seemingly mild-mannered fox and his cub (later revealed to be a con man and his criminal accomplice) are refused custom at an ice cream parlour simply because their species is seen as disreputable, allegorising still-current debates surrounding multiculturalism in Western societies.

The film's second centre, the picaresque fox, Nick (Jason Bateman), is afforded his own origin story that rationalises his later shysterism as a product of his disillusionment after being cruelly muzzled during his induction as a boy scout. Having escaped his tormentors – all of whom are (anthropomorphised child versions of) larger animals not generally known for their cunning or untrustworthiness – Nick is seen privately removing his muzzle and crying. The scene thus establishes his apparent amorality as a defence mechanism against a world of iniquity; Zootopia's supposed utopianism is at best a pious hope and at worst a hypocritical falsity where familiar hierarchies of power operate under a cloak of egalitarianism. As Nick observes, morosely, 'If the world is only going to see a fox as shifty and untrustworthy, there's no point in trying to be anything else.' Judy responds, 'Nick, you are so much more than that.' Both Judy's and Nick's stories are metanarratives of triumph against the odds, embodying the kind of important moral lessons for young people that predominate in children's fiction. But they are also obvious parables for twenty-first-century Western society, where individuals and social groups continue to encounter stigmatisation on a daily basis on account of their gender, sexuality, social class, or ethnic background, and indeed, face more fundamental systematic disadvantages that may be less visible but remain pervasive. If Judy represents the quintessentially empowered career woman (whose struggle for acceptance in a fiercely patriarchal system serves as a reminder of the nature of post-feminist society), then Nick is the socially (certainly racially, perhaps economically) marginalised outsider whose criminality is the predictable product of his status as Other.

In the opening scene, Judy's voice-over reveals: 'Over time, we evolved, and moved beyond our primitive, savage ways. Now, predator and prey live in harmony, and every young mammal has multitudinous opportunities.' Yet the film moves in a more radical direction when she publicly asserts that only predator species have turned savage, and hypothesises that this may be the result of the animals atavistically returning to their supposed biological predispositions towards aggression. As a result of this announcement – which mirrors now-discredited scientific belief that humans from different ethnic groups possess different levels of physical and mental prowess – Nick, as a member of a predator species himself, angrily turns his back on Judy, and the city is overcome by rampant paranoia. There are various moments of political satire: the deputy mayor, a sheep, has engineered the savage predator crisis in order to ascend to power, claiming that 'fear always works' as a means of controlling the populace; a TV news report then shows a clip from the mayor, a lion, admitting falsely imprisoning the affected predators and explaining 'it was a classic "doing the wrong thing for the right reasons" kind of deal', in the kind of blatant self-absolution by a politician that many viewers will find familiar.

Judy's closing monologue might be taken as a shorthand exposition of contemporary Hollywood's politics of liberal humanism. Concepts of social equality – regardless of class, race, gender and sexuality – are brought to the forefront of the narrative:

> When I was a kid I thought Zootopia was this perfect place where everyone got along and anyone could be anything. Turns out real life's a little bit more complicated than a slogan on a bumper sticker. Real life is messy. We all have limitations. We all make mistakes. Which means, hey, glass half-full, we all have a lot in common. And the more we try to understand one another, the more exceptional each of us will be. But we have to try, so no matter what type of animal you are, from the biggest elephant to our first fox – I implore you: try. Try to make the world a better place. Look inside yourself and recognise that change starts with you. It starts with me. It starts with all of us.

Bound up in this piece of dialogue, of course, are conventional ideologies: the valorisation of individualism and community; the homilies of optimism and self-actualisation. But the most telling implication is that the status quo is unacceptable. *Zootopia* presents a vision of society as it all too frequently is, not simply as we would like it to be. The film's representations may be populist and commodified, but they divagate from the overwhelming majority of Hollywood family films that ultimately work to uphold social and behavioural norms by repositioning these causes as something to strive for, much like Jefferson's 'pursuit of happiness', and perhaps with the tacit acceptance that true egalitarianism is something that can never be attained. This closing speech also makes it explicit that Zootopia is not merely an oblique palimpsest of any or all Western nations; it is the United States of America – a nation similarly founded on a claim to perfection (the New Jerusalem; the Land of the Free) whose greatness lies more in the ideals themselves than in their everyday application.

Conclusion

We must end this chapter, as it began, considering the factors that have led to the increasing centrality of allusions to contemporary culture and society within post-1990s Hollywood animation. Although it is important to acknowledge the creativity and ingenuity of filmmakers who explore and sometimes transgress the formal and ideological constraints of a predominantly conservative industry, there is little doubt that commercial imperatives have driven the wider developments discussed here. *The Iron Giant*, *Happy Feet*, *WALL-E* and *Zootopia* share a tendency to satirise society's predilection to externalise and vilify non-conformist groups, ranging from women, gays, blacks, foreigners, and people with disabilities. Their politics are relevant and 'relatable', directly addressing young, liberal Western audiences for whom these issues possess particular resonance. However, the degree of social activism at play here is relatively mild: few people, one presumes, would vehemently oppose messages of peace and tolerance, particularly when they are couched in such metonymic terms. *The Iron Giant*, perhaps the most explicitly political of the four films, presents bigotry and intolerance as undesirable relics of less enlightened times; we are invited to realise that such prejudices are wrongheaded, outdated, and borne through foolish fears that ought to be left in the past. Society has moved on, such films imply, and any viewers that continue to harbour these old intolerances had better get with the programme.

Hollywood remains notoriously conservative in its representations (and non-representations) of race, gender and sexuality. Despite the deniable liberalism of the social comment films discussed here, the politics of the industry tend to be reactive, rather than proactive – necessarily so, since the films must continue to please a highly pluralistic global audience. Indeed, as the following chapter will consider, it may be that these films' satire of illiberalism and endorsement of difference represents a new conformism in Hollywood animation. These metanarratives of inclusion do not simply represent the pious hope of mutual respect and tolerance amongst the disparate creeds, colours and cultural identities of the world, but also reflect – as Lawrence Van Gelder argues in relation to *The Iron Giant* – a comfortable liberalism that, because of the films' mechanisms of plausible deniability, does not have to put its principles on the line.[72] If Hollywood family entertainment has an overarching ideology, it is the politics of consensus: the shared cultural referents of its strategies of intertextuality, and the fashionable but deniable liberal satires of modern society. Both forms exemplify the 'hip, edgy' approach that Jeffrey Katzenberg brought to the Disney, Pixar and DreamWorks features of the mid-to-late 1990s. The currency of being 'modern', 'current', and 'relatable' has never been higher.

4. WAYS OF BEING: IDENTITY AND HOLLYWOOD ANIMATION

This chapter examines how contemporary animated films have negotiated changes in attitudes towards individual and group identity, particularly (though not exclusively) in relation to gender, sexuality, race and ethnicity. As we have already seen, one of the central projects of post-1990s Hollywood animation is that of accommodating difference; this is reflected in numerous mission statements in which the major studios – while emphasising the border-crossing universalism of their products – proclaim their commitment to values of diversity, inclusiveness and multiculturalism. Such statements are solidly underpinned by commercial pragmatism: films must address a pluralistic, global audience to remain profitable, and therefore must be able to reconcile a multitude of different interests, backgrounds and perspectives. However, affirmations of this kind also respond to current debates regarding the social desirability, and the political capital, of diversity in its many forms. I am concerned in this chapter not only with how different kinds of identity are represented in contemporary animation, but also how valorisations of difference are reconciled with the utopianism traditionally embodied by the Hollywood family film.

DISNEY IN TRANSITION: SEXUAL POLITICS IN THE EARLY FILMS OF THE 'DISNEY RENAISSANCE'

To modern-day eyes, the sexual and racial politics of classical-era Hollywood feature animation (i.e. films produced between the 1930s and 1960s, almost exclusively by Disney) are liable to appear highly regressive. The films reflect a strongly patriarchal worldview: white, male, heterosexual, and ideologically conservative. This is not to argue that they are intentionally political, much less deliberately offensive; rather, they are broadly reflective of contemporary attitudes in society-at-large at a time when 'diversity' in film as it is now widely understood – that is, as pertaining to the on-screen and off-screen representation of repressed minority groups – had not yet emerged as a prominent discourse. It is useful to turn to Jack Zipes's delineation of the narrative formulae of the classical Disney fairy tale:

> Each film is framed by a prince on a quest for the proper mate, essentially a young virginal woman, a trophy princess, who will serve his vested interests, and the quest ends with a marriage in a splendid castle, in which the prince and princess will be attended by admiring if not obsequious servants. The manner in which the prince attains his goal depends on the collaboration of the underlings, the dwarfs and enchanted objects, and the ingenuity and valour of this sympathetic prince. Songs are strewn along the plot as flowers to enliven and brighten the action, just as comic gags are used to divert us from the serious nature of the business at hand – ruthless competition for power. But everyone knows his or her role, and their roles are all geared to guaranteeing the happiness of the heroes, seemingly born to lead, take power, and to be admired, as fetishist objects. They will eventually reside in a palace, a utopian realm, that few people are privileged to inhabit, unless you are one of the chosen servants. The goal is not only a reconciliation of conflict and the defeat of evil, but also acclamation of those who deserve to rule by those who deserve to serve.[1]

While Zipes admits that his schemata may appear 'overly crude', he maintains its validity – with minor variances – when applied to the entire canon of Disney fairy tale films from *Snow White and the Seven Dwarfs* (David Hand et al., 1937) into the new century.[2] The Global Disney Audiences Project (GDAP), an international survey of audiences' reception to Disney films conducted around the turn of the millennium, found a high level of agreement in respondents' perception of 'the classic Disney formula':

> Overall, expectations about Disney films were quite consistent – beautiful heroines seeking romance, brave heroes, evil villains, and happy endings with good triumphing over evil and the chaste couple united. Our respondents are strongly disposed to read Disney texts in these terms, regardless of an individual's particular feelings about the company.[3]

Although Zipes's definition is much more concerned with ideologies of class and power, there is a high degree of agreement as to the prototypical narrative structure of the Disney feature film. It is also significant that this consensus appears to be shared equally by people who approve and who disapprove of Disney, which suggests that claims to the films' narrative conservatism are not confined to those with an ideological axe to grind.

On closer inspection, both schemata are somewhat reductive, applying primarily to animated fairy tale films. In actuality, as Amy M. Davis observes, a relatively small proportion of Disney animated films are adapted from established fairy tale pre-texts.[4] Furthermore, just as animated films comprise only a relatively small proportion of Disney's theatrical releases (James R. Mason puts the figure at 27 per cent between 1937 and 2015), few of its live-action films could be categorised as fairy tales.[5] Yet Disney animation's close association with the fairy tale mode is more significant than it might appear. As we saw in the previous chapter with DreamWorks' *Shrek* (Andrew Adamson and Vicky Jenson, 2001), by the early 2000s fairy tales were beginning to be viewed as clichéd and old-fashioned, not simply on account of the familiarity of their generic codes, but also the perception that they advance regressive models of race, gender and other forms of identity.[6]

More generally, though, both male and female characters in pre-1990s Hollywood animation operate at the level of archetypes, with little pretence that they are fully formed, three-dimensional individuals. This is not to denigrate the films in question, merely to point out that they were made under a different set of conventions. In previous chapters, I have discussed the high premium now placed on 'relatable' characters in nearly all forms of modern fiction. Aside from a contemporary linguistic idiom, the protagonists of Hollywood animated films must exhibit special and supposedly 'unique' characteristics in terms of style, cultural background, fantasies, desires, beliefs, quirks and neuroses – in a word, their *identity*. In contrast, classical Disney films are populated, in the main, by character 'types' – figures that represent broad ethical and behavioural traits, such as goodness and wickedness, innocence and knowingness, physical (and thus moral) beauty and ugliness, and which are largely interchangeable with their equivalents in other films of the period. Just as classical-era Disney protagonists might now appear flat and under-developed, the characters that inhabit contemporary Hollywood animated features would probably be incomprehensible in all sorts of ways to movie-goers of the 1930s and 1940s.

Although it is difficult to apply precise periodisation, the current premium placed upon conceptions of individual and group identity can be traced to the so-called 'Disney Renaissance' films of 1989–99, a phase that began with *The Little Mermaid* (Ron Clements and John Musker, 1989) and ended with *Tarzan* (Kevin Lima and Chris Buck, 1999). As we have seen in previous chapters, this period coincided with growing awareness of changing family dynamics (particularly in terms of gender roles) and a broad embedding of contemporaneousness in a medium traditionally associated – rightly or wrongly – with non-realist, escapist fantasy. Changing definitions of identity in the United States underpin many of the most significant developments in post-1990s animation: the men and women who struggle to reconcile their social responsibilities (particularly to their families) with individualist desires to free themselves from traditional models of gender stratification and pursue their own interests; the representatives of minority groups (e.g. non-white, LGBT or disabled audiences) who wish to see characters that represent their own interests on screen; the broader recognition that many viewers desire 'relatable' characters that look, act and sound similar to themselves. One corollary of this is Disney largely abandoning animal-centred stories during the 1990s in favour of narratives focusing on human protagonists.[7] This is to say that 'identity' in post-1990s Hollywood goes beyond representations of 'inclusiveness' and 'diversity' (though these are significant elements) and reflects a broader preoccupation with conveying the multicultural plurality of contemporary society – a plurality that implicitly rejects the middlebrow homogeneity of the United States during the mid twentieth century, and thus carries important political resonances.

Disney, of course, was the dominant force in Hollywood feature animation until the mid 1990s. By the time Pixar and DreamWorks emerged as significant players, Disney was already trying to establish its credentials as a studio that takes gender and racial equality seriously. During the tenure of Michael Eisner as Disney's CEO (1989–2005), the composition of Disney's executive body shifted from one of almost complete 'male-dominance to, if not full equality, at least a greater presence of women in leadership roles'.[8] This behind-the-scenes development parallels more liberal discourses in 'Disney Renaissance' films such as *The Little Mermaid*, *Beauty and the Beast* (Gary Trousdale and Kirk Wise, 1991), *Aladdin* (Ron Clements and John Musker, 1992), *Pocahontas* (Mike Gabriel and Eric Goldberg, 1995) and *Mulan* (Barry Cook and Tony Bancroft, 1998). Do Rozario argues that most female protagonists of the 'Disney Renaissance' are active, self-motivated figures. Whereas 'Walt's princesses scrubbed and waited with boundless cheerful energy [. . . and] twirled like ballerinas and sang of princes who would come and dreams that would be fulfilled', their latter-day counterparts 'undertake no chores, neglect their obligations, and run wild'.[9] This perception appears to be shared by many consumers. Whilst we should be wary of the pitfalls of interpreting popular acclaim as an index of ideological approval, director Ron Clements's claim that *The Little Mermaid* was taken up by teenagers as a 'date movie' gestures to its ability to speak to the sensibilities – if not *necessarily* the politics – of contemporary youth.[10]

Nevertheless, every one of these 'Disney Renaissance' features has been seen as politically problematic in one way or another. In investigating these issues, we must first uncouple the films' contemporary semantics (e.g. location, idiom, aesthetic) from their more traditional syntactic (e.g. narrative, ritual, ideological) patterns. Although *The Little Mermaid* and *Beauty and the Beast* position themselves as 'modern', 'updated' iterations of classical-era fairy tales, upon closer inspection many of the prototypical elements of the Disney film as identified by Zipes and respondents in the GDAP remain evident: the beautiful (white) female protagonist in search of idealised heterosexual romance; the struggle and eventual victory of good over evil; the happy ending signalled by the romantic union of the beautiful princess and the handsome, virtuous prince, with its tacit implication of marriage and children that upholds the sanctity of the family and establishes inter-generational continuity. Indeed, for all its stylistic innovation, Roberta Trites sees Disney's adaptation of 'The Little Mermaid' (1837) as even more ideologically conservative than Hans Christian Andersen's nineteenth-century fable, introducing changes 'in characters, images, and conflicts that rob women of integrity'.[11] Much of Trites's criticism of Disney's version centres on its reimagining of the mermaid, Ariel (Jodi Benson), as singularly obsessed with marriage, whereas Andersen's Ariel construes love as a means to an end in her pursuit of an immortal soul. She also takes issue with the film's implication that 'the only beings worth marrying are those who are perfect and that perfection is not only somehow attainable but is actually necessary for a man to be loveable', a puritanical position that – as we shall see later in the chapter – Disney eventually revisited and disavowed in *Frozen* (Chris Buck and Jennifer Lee, 2013).[12]

Davis is kinder in her appraisal of the sexual politics of the 'Disney Renaissance' films. While acknowledging that 'the heroines of 1990s Disney films, although more in keeping with feminist attitudes, are not by any stretch of the imagination heroines to feminists' and that their lives and adventures are 'at least sanctioned, if not rewarded' by patriarchal society, she nonetheless perceives them as transitional texts that strongly reflect liberal 'political correctness', which itself represents 'arguably the most pervasive discursive influence of the 1990s'.[13] In contrast to classical-era Disney princesses such as Snow White, Cinderella and Sleeping Beauty, *The Little Mermaid*'s Ariel 'actively seeks adventure and works hard to achieve goals she has set for herself'; Davis also praises the character's 'willingness to gamble, her determination to make her own choices, and her tenacity in working toward what she wants out of life'.[14] Similarly, she regards *Aladdin*'s Jasmine (Linda Larkin) as 'strong, intelligent, well-balanced [. . . and] fiercely independent'.[15] At a push, then, we might say that *Aladdin* possesses feminist cadences because it emphasises the agency and self-determination of the princess – her right to choose her destiny. However, it still upholds 'traditional' values of heteronormativity, marriage and patriarchal power structures. Furthermore, as Davis argues, *Beauty and the Beast* hearkens back to classical-era Disney constructions of femininity, with the film's portrayal of Belle (Paige O'Hara) suggesting that 'the woman who is selfless, giving, and uses her wisdom only to support others is the good woman deserving a reward', and that 'an unselfish act by a man improves nothing, but an unselfish act by a woman can transform the world'.[16]

DIVERSITY AND CONTEMPORARY DISNEY FILMS

Disney does appear to take criticisms of its cultural politics seriously, particularly when they threaten to expose the disjuncture between the company's brand identity as a purveyor of universal, utopian 'family' entertainment and its more troubling on-screen representations of marginalised groups. Since the mid 2000s, it has been on a highly visible inclusivity drive. In 2008, Gary Marsh, then president of Disney Channels Worldwide, claimed, 'We talk about [diversity] daily.'[17] Since 2011, the company has employed a 'chief diversity officer'; both incumbents in the role to date – Paul Richardson and Latondra Newton – are African American. In 2014, Richardson explained:

> Diversity is a pillar of our growth strategy. Our content, products, attractions and other entertainment offerings include a multitude of ideas and experiences that strive to meet the needs of the diverse global consumers, guests, fans and viewers we serve every day. Disney is committed to appealing to a broad array of audiences and reflecting the diversity of our consumers.[18]

Senior Disney executives have expressed similar sentiments in the media. Disney CEO Robert Iger explains that 'diversity is not only important; it is a core strategy for the company'; Sean Bailey, president of production at Walt Disney Studios, claims that 'inclusivity is not only a priority but an imperative for us, and it's top of mind on every single project'; and Disney chairman Alan Horn emphases that the company's mission is to 'tell inclusive stories – both in front of and also behind the camera [. . .] It's one of the most important issues facing our industry, and we continue to seek out and work with filmmakers and creatives [sic] who understand and share our commitment to making films that reflect the world around us'.[19] These sentiments are underlined by Disney's 'Diversity and Inclusion Commitment' statement, which has appeared on its website since April 2018:

> From our media networks to our movie studios, from our theme parks to our products, very few companies touch the hearts and minds of generations of people around the world the way Disney does. With this rich opportunity comes a deep sense of responsibility for creating the most authentic stories and experiences. Today, audiences are rapidly diversifying, new generations are shaping the nature of work, and changes in society increasingly impact employees everywhere.

> Our focus and intent encourages people from every nation, race/ ethnicity, belief, gender, sexual identity, disability and culture to feel respected and valued for their unique contributions to our businesses. It informs our guiding principles and defines our relationship with guests and consumers, who trust and believe in the Disney brand in ways that are meaningful to them. Simply put, diversity and inclusion reminds us all – from Disney fans to employees – that we belong.[20]

The sentiments espoused in these mission statements are not simply altruistic (although many Disney executives do appear to be socially liberal), nor can they be reduced to simple PR for the benefit of Western audiences. Rather, they respond to the demands of the market. Disney's diversity mission is under-pinned by its aim to be the world's leading multimedia organisation for decades to come. This goal requires not just sensitivity to the needs and beliefs of differ-ent demographic groups in the United States and the Western world, but also the cultivation of stories and modes of representation that are capable of tran-scending borders such as culture, language, and ethnic background. In its 1999 annual report, Disney described itself as having 'underpenetrated overseas', and the company has since emphasised the necessity to 'move with agility' in foreign markets by 'exploiting international opportunities'.[21] One of the great confidence tricks of corporate marketing is the ability to make the consumer believe that the product belongs to them, intimately and uniquely. Hollywood studios foster this perception through strategies of localism and individualisa-tion. To a degree, this has always been the case; since its beginnings, Disney has taken its stories from international traditions of folk tale and fairy tale. Subtitling, dubbing and local marketing and release strategies are all familiar ways of retailoring North American media to local markets. However, these strategies have intensified. Since the 1990s, for instance, the dubbing of songs as well as dialogue has become more widespread, allowing Disney – as one executive put it – to 'take our movies around the world and make them sound like local movies'.[22]

However, although 28 per cent of respondents in the GDAP did indeed view the company's films as 'universal', a significantly higher number – in the region of 50 per cent – thought Disney to be 'uniquely American', citing its perceived expression of prototypically US ideologies.[23] A less favourable manifestation of this is the belief that Disney's aggressive international manoeuvring amounts to 'cultural imperialism'. However, Disney's relationship with its global audiences is a two-way process. Just as the company benefits commercially from access to international markets, so it must also weigh its own values as a brand against the complex, sometimes turbulent and inherently heterogeneous nature of global politics. One especially thorny and pertinent example is Disney's treat-ment of LGBT issues and characters. James R. Mason's recent survey of adults' engagement with Disney films found that, although approximately 90 per cent of respondents claimed to enjoy Disney films as adults, the most common reason (66 per cent) for *disliking* them was the company's treatment of gender, sexuality, race and disability.[24] As Mason observes, Disney has a long tradition of under-representing LGBT concerns, yet 'how far Disney films might go in terms of LGBT+ representation in the future may depend on international censorship',[25] taking into consideration the continued hostility towards queer identities in many countries across the world.[26]

This preoccupation with identity is a relatively recent phenomenon. Marie Moran argues that the 'widespread refraction' of individuality and subjectivity through the 'popular idiom' of identity only really took hold after the 1950s. Before then, she claims,

> there was quite simply no discussion of sexual identity, ethnic identity, political identity, national identity, consumer identity, corporate identity, brand identity, identity crisis, or 'losing' or 'finding' one's identity – indeed, no discussion at all of 'identity' in any of the ways that are so familiar to us today, and which, in our ordinary and political discussions, we would now find it hard to do without.[27]

By no means is this heightened interest in identity unique to the United States. The results of several World Values Surveys have revealed that 'post-materialist' values such as 'trust, tolerance, subjective well-being, political activism, and self-expression' are invariably privileged in post-industrial societies that enjoy 'high levels of security'; indeed, 'beyond a certain point, diversity is not only tolerated, it may be positively valued because it is interesting and stimulating'.[28] In contrast, in less economically developed countries, so-called 'survival values' predominate to a much higher degree, and people 'tend to emphasise economic and physical security above all other goals, and feel threatened by foreigners, by ethnic diversity and by cultural change'.[29] Results show 'an almost linear' trend in the rise of 'self-expression values' in the US since 1981 (the date of the first survey), a finding that accords with Moran's claim that, by the 1980s, what has become known as 'identity politics' was 'completely embedded' in popular and academic discourses.[30]

However, it is important to note the relation between current conceptions of identity and foundational national mythologies of individualism in the United States. As Wayne E. Baker observes, 'self-expression is an especially American orientation; it appears to have blossomed in recent years, but it has always been an American preoccupation'.[31] We can see this in valorisations of the rugged, self-reliant pioneering spirit of the European settlers of the North American continent. The American frontiersman Davy Crockett (1786–1836) – the subject of the jingoistic live-action Disney film, *Davy Crockett, King of the Wild*

Frontier (Norman Foster, 1955) – embodies this particular view of US history as built on the legendary feats of individual heroes as much as the collective will of the people. The particular centrality of individualism in the nation's folk history helps to rationalise the current view of identity, because 'everyday uses of the term to articulate relations of social similarity and difference were likely to be expressed in a distinctively personal form'.[32] By the same token, Moran sees the turn to identity politics as a means of *retaining* individuality in a society marked by post-industrial standardisation; personal identity, in this context, becomes 'a means of obscuring the basic sameness engendered by the relentless logic of the commodity behind a vision of "individual" [. . .] distinction'.[33] Running parallel with this notion of 'individual' identity (which, as Moran observes, could take an almost limitless number of permutations) is the 'social' interpretation of it, which began in earnest with the race- and gender-based civil rights movements of the 1960s and emphasises 'group oneness, cohesion and solidarity over individual distinction'.[34]

In this sense of conceptualising a shared history, heritage and way of life, identity 'had explanatory power but also political potential, as it encouraged a strengthening of in-group solidarity and the expression of group-based pride' – in short, what has become known as 'identity politics'.[35] A follower of Raymond Williams' cultural-materialist approach, Moran also views identity politics not merely as an escape from the massification and standardisation engendered by advanced capitalism, but as actively consolidating its interests. It is worth noting the easy slippage between 'identity politics' as an act of organised political resistance and as a discourse ripe for commodification, in the sense of offering up yet more 'exploitable' consumer markets ('the grey dollar', 'the pink pound', and so on). What began as a means of articulating the shared interests and history of marginalised social groups has metamorphosed into a more 'libertarian' form 'where identity operates primarily to facilitate consumption on a global scale'.[36] This final point relates to Benjamin Barber's claim that the neo-liberal capitalist structure 'infantilises' adults into compulsive, lifelong consumption by promoting an ideology of privatism that 'associates liberty with personal choice of the kind possessed by consumers'.[37] The inextricable link between modern conceptions of identity and aspects of Western modernity is especially pertinent in context of contemporary cinema's obsession with individuality.

Disney's success in its efforts to cater to multiple identities (i.e. 'diversity') within its potential consumer base is harder to gauge – partially, no doubt, because the company's recent films form part of a long-term project with no specific end-date. From a commercial standpoint, Disney has continued to consolidate its international dominance in the family entertainment arena. Since the 1990s, with the loosening of trade barriers, it has expanded its theatrical presence in developing markets such as India, Russia and, most spectacularly,

China (which now constitutes the second most lucrative domestic territory in the world, behind North America, and where it opened Shanghai Disneyland Park in June 2016). While classical-era Disney adaptations of international fairy tales tend to retain the non-American setting, but otherwise palimpsest character types and political positions recognisable and explicable to US audiences, Disney's post-1990s excursions into foreign territory strongly emphasise cultural heritage. Examples of Disney's pursuit of authenticity in its representations of international cultural traditions include mobilising an 'advisory team' comprising 'anthropologists, cultural practitioners, historians, linguists, and choreographers from islands including Samoa, Tahiti, Mo'orea, and Fiji' when producing *Moana* (Ron Clements and John Musker, 2016), the collaboration of 'cultural consultants' on the Sámi people of Northern Scandinavia in *Frozen II* (Chris Buck and Jennifer Lee, 2019), and the hiring of local creative personnel in films such as *Coco* (Lee Unkrich, 2017).[38]

Just as extended passages in *Moana* and *Pocahontas* are given over to exploring the tribes' close affiliation with the landscape, and their cyclical patterns and structures of life, the conventional quest narrative in *Coco* is told against a backdrop suffused with recognisably 'local' cultural elements, including the Mexican tradition of the *Día de los Muertos* and the ritualistic significance of the family *ofrenda*. Perhaps to pre-empt charges of 'cultural appropriation', the release of *Coco* was accompanied by statements asserting its boundary-breaking universalism, with director Lee Unkrich claiming that 'the movie is about family, and I think that you don't need to be a member of a culture to appreciate a family that's about someone else's culture.'[39] The *New York Times'* A. O. Scott concurred, arguing that 'the cultural vibe of "Coco" is inclusive rather than exoticizing', and that the representation of family 'is both specific and universal'.[40] Despite this, Disney continues to be accused of 'diversity deficiency'.[41] A report on diversity in North American film and television published by the USC Annenberg School for Communication and Journalism in 2016 found that Disney performed poorly in its metrics for on-screen representation of minorities, as well as for the proportion of minority groups employed behind the scenes.[42] Sampling the full range of theatrically released Disney films in 2014, the report noted that female characters comprised only 25 per cent, characters from 'under-represented' groups 22 per cent, and LGBT characters less than 1 per cent, of the total.[43] Furthermore, there were no female directors, and female writers made up only 10 per cent. It should be noted that Disney's performance in these areas was neither substantially better nor worse than that of the other major Hollywood studios; indeed, the report concluded that the film industry 'still functions as a straight, White, boy's [sic] club'.[44]

The intersection of gender and race in post-1990s Disney films requires particular consideration. In particular, *Pocahontas* and *Mulan*, Disney's first animated features featuring non-white female protagonists,[45] bear interesting comparison with representations of race and ethnicity in later films such as *The Princess and the Frog* (Ron Clements and John Musker, 2009) and *Moana*. As we will see, the level of expectation surrounding Disney's treatment of these issues has risen considerably since the 1990s. At that time, the mere presence of non-white, non-American figures in the central role was widely seen as a significant end in itself. Today, 'authenticity' of representation – a word that gestures vaguely but powerfully to the perceived sincerity and accuracy of the portrayal of the indigenous culture – is a necessary prerequisite, not just to assuage North American critics of media 'diversity', but also in recognition of the consumer power of global markets.

Pocahontas marked something of a turning point in the so-called 'Disney Renaissance'; it grossed little more than a third of that of *The Lion King* (Rob Minkoff and Roger Allers, 1994), and its original storyline – ostensibly an exploration of the conceit that 'if we don't learn to live with one another, we will destroy ourselves' – was widely seen as hackneyed and historically inaccurate in its depiction of the historical Pocahontas and the Powhatan people.[46] The most obvious reconfiguration is that the real-life Pocahontas (real name: Matoaka), an 11-year-old when she saved the life of English colonialist John Smith from execution at the hands of her tribe in Jamestown, Virginia in 1607, is reimagined as a 1990s Disney princess: statuesque, feisty, impressionable, idealistic and strong-willed. If she is not quite 'American' at the outset of the film, she is certainly open to ideological repositioning at the hands of the Western coloniser. Nevertheless, *Pocahontas* is explicit in its portrayal of the British settlers as plunderers of the Native American tribes. The opening musical number, 'The Virginia Company' – sung by a chorus of British privateers – contains the lyrics:

> We'll kill ourselves an Injun, or maybe two or three
> We're stalwart men and bold of the Virginia Company!

In contrast, the Powhatan tribe's establishing number, 'Steady as the Beating Drum' (which bears a close resemblance to 'Circle of Life' in *The Lion King*) establishes their largely peaceable affiliation with the environment, their naturalness and the cyclical nature of their existence:

> O Great Spirit, hear our song
> Help us keep the ancient ways
> Keep the sacred fire strong
> Walk in balance all our days.

While Disney has a long history of representing British people as villainous – with nefarious English colonialists in films such as *Rob Roy, the Highland Rogue* (Harold French, 1953), *Kidnapped* (Robert Stevenson, 1960) and *The*

Fighting Prince of Donegal (Michael O'Herlihy, 1966) – on this occasion it is the pre-history of US society that is called into question. The villainous Governor Ratcliffe (David Ogden Stiers), who refers to the Native Americans as 'bloodthirsty savages', is clearly figured as the undesirable face of British imperialism, but John Smith (Mel Gibson) embodies the heroic virtues of pioneers of repute such as Davy Crockett. Despite actually being English, the character's American accent and appearance (blond, tall, slim, blue-eyed) differentiate him from the physically and morally unattractive sailors who accompany him on the voyage. The fundamental difference between the American-coded Smith and his British-coded shipmates is underlined when a young sailor falls overboard, and Smith ignores their demands to leave the boy behind by jumping in to rescue him.

The romantic union between the noble white man and the free-spirited Native American woman is hardly devoid of cliché – not least in the *deus ex machina* that allows Pocahontas (Irene Bedard) to understand English and communicate with the settlers. Yet it does serve to reaffirm the pious hope of American multiculturalism, upholding a broad liberal principle of expanding to accommodate (or absorb) different cultural traditions within the overarching laws and structures of the union. The ending of the film sees the parting of Pocahontas and John Smith; she remains with her people, and he returns to England. In this sense, although the film is unable to repudiate colonialism, it does at least refrain from depicting it as an ennobling or civilising apparatus. Furthermore, in not allowing Pocahontas to fall into the domestication that, hitherto, was the ultimate trajectory for almost every Disney heroine, the film's sexual politics appear to make a concession to contemporary feminist discourses. However, the fact that her 'destiny' is ultimately bound up with that of a white colonialist still proved controversial. Janet Maslin's *New York Times* review lamented the film's advancing of the adolescent real-life Pocahontas to a 'flirty, full-grown vixen [. . .] concerned with finding Mr. Right'.[47] Furthermore, it was noted that *Pocahontas* fails to disavow the charge of cultural hegemony that has long been levelled at the company. Sarah Vradenburg, writing in the *San Jose Mercury News*, accused the film of treating 'a piece of real history like a fairy tale' and concluded that 'after seeing "Pocahontas", I realized nothing was safe from Disney-fication'.[48]

Mulan, as with *Pocahontas*, can be viewed in context of Disney's quest for alternative narrative modes to the Westernised fairy tale film; it also continues the process of 'modernising' Disney females. At the outset of the film, it is made explicit that Mulan (Ming-Na Wen), a teenage girl living in Ancient China, is unable adequately to fulfil the duties of wife and mother and thus bring honour to her family the 'traditional' way. The metanarrative of the young protagonist coming to terms with their own identity is again pre-eminent here; after an elaborate musical sequence in which Mulan is beautified in the traditions of contemporary

Figure 4.1   The noble white man and the free-spirited Native American woman (*Pocahontas*, Disney, 1995). Frame grab.

Chinese civilisation (made to look a 'porcelain doll', she observes) in preparation of being matched with an appropriate husband, her clumsiness ruins an important meeting with the local match-maker, who angrily prophesises that she will never bring honour to her family. The following sequence sees a distraught Mulan, having removed the make-up from her face while looking into a mirror, singing, 'When will my reflection show who I really am?'

Early sequences establish Mulan's more 'masculine' credentials as a heroic, resourceful figure, particularly when she chooses to 'pass' as a man by conscripting in the Chinese army to fight the invading Huns. In the musical number 'A Girl Worth Fighting For', a deliberately anachronistic portrait of femininity is presented as prize to be won through masculine prowess:

> I want her paler than the moon with eyes that shine like stars
> My girl will marvel at my strength, adore my battle scars
> I couldn't care less what she'll wear or what she looks like
> It all depends on what she cooks like.

Mulan's attempt to redirect the song in a more enlightened direction ('how about a girl who's got a brain, who always speaks her mind?') is instantly dismissed by her brothers-in-arms. Ultimately, however, the structurally inevitable romantic union between Mulan and the head of the Emperor's army, Captain Li Shang (B. D. Wong), is built on more egalitarian foundations than the clearly patriarchal match-making hinted in the early scenes. Indeed, her divagation from the demure women this society prizes is signalled at the end of the film, when – having saved the Emperor from assassination – she continues to disobey orders from her superiors, refuses a position of authority in the Emperor's court so that she can return home to her parents, and impulsively hugs the Emperor in a violation of protocol. Again, though, the film teases the probability of heterosexual romantic union: in the final scene, Li Shang, having initially been hostile to Mulan after her disguise is blown, follows her to the family home in an unspoken admission that his rejecting her was misguided, and is invited to dinner.

In presenting a female protagonist who thinks and acts in a similar fashion to relatively emancipated 1990s American teenagers, but placing her in an anachronistic feudal society, *Mulan* is able to acknowledge and negotiate changing gender norms. However, in its attempt to assert the fundamental universalism of its core values, the film is far less concerned with cultural, ethnic and racial specificities. To this extent, both *Mulan* and *The Princess and the Frog* share a similar agenda: the reconciliation of 'difference' within the overarching, liberal-humanistic politics of consensus. They also reflect the conviction, which might equally be interpreted as utopian or colonialist, that differences in cultural background are relatively insignificant, and that transcending (without necessarily effacing) such borders is a desirable goal. But increasingly, animated Hollywood family films must balance the genre's inherent utopianism with the need to preserve group identities, particularly at the level of race and ethnicity; the alternative risks the perception that the films are merely commodifying difference (once again, 'cultural appropriation') and perpetrating a neo-colonialist flattening of multiculturalism that serves only to reinscribe the dominant ideology.[49]

Loosely adapted from E. D. Baker's 2002 novel, *The Frog Princess* – itself a retelling of the Brothers Grimm's 'The Frog Prince' (1812) – *The Princess and the Frog* updates the source text's fairy tale mythology to 1920s Louisiana. Set in an impoverished, largely African American community in a historical period in which racial discrimination was a quotidian reality, it attempts to engage with still-relevant issues of caste-based social inequality. *The Princess and the Frog* marked Disney's much-trumpeted return to cel animation, a style last utilised in the poorly received *Home on the Range* (Will Finn and John Sanford, 2004). It is a throwback in two other regards: it was Disney's first self-proclaimed fairy tale film since *Beauty and the Beast*, and its directors, Clements and Musker, were studio veterans who had directed the earliest of the so-called 'Disney Renaissance' releases, *The Little Mermaid*. These 'traditional' markers are significant, as *The Princess and the Frog* is Disney's first film featuring an African American 'princess', yet was regarded as only partially successful in reflecting the historical realities of African American life in the Deep South of the 1920s; indeed, some contemporary critics were explicitly hostile, deeming it a pernicious example of Hollywood 'whitewashing'.

The film presents a historically dubious but seductive view of 1920s New Orleans as an oasis of cultural cosmopolitanism and ethnic accord. It is a fantastical palimpsest – celebrated by the Randy Newman musical number 'Down in Orleans', which evokes a place where 'the women are very pretty', where 'they got music [that's] always playing', where 'there's some sweetness going around' and where 'dreams do come true' – that puts one in mind of the nostalgic, sentimental turn-of-the-century Midwest of *Meet Me in St. Louis* (Vincente Minnelli, 1944). The initial scenes focus on the friendship between Tiana (Anika Noni Rose), the daughter of an African American seamstress, and Charlotte (Jennifer Cody), the pampered daughter of a wealthy Southern industrialist. Whereas Charlotte lives in an opulent mansion, Tiana's family live on a row of small huts as part of a tight-knit, multiracial community. This image of social cohesion among working-class communities is a common trope of fiction that deals centrally with marginalised groups in US society (cf. Steinbeck's *The Grapes of Wrath* [1939]), but *The Princess and the Frog* offers a more specific representation of racial egalitarianism through its allegorical treatment of its central characters. In an early scene that epitomises the film's humanistic spirit, the young Tiana makes gumbo that her father proclaims the best that he has ever tasted, and Tiana then invites all of their neighbours to share it. As people of various skin colours eat together on the front porch, Tiana's father – who dreams of becoming a chef – remarks, 'You know the thing about good food? It brings folk together from all walks of life.'

Aside from her skin colour, in every regard Tiana is a classical Disney heroine: industrious, gentle, kind, loyal, empathetic, dreamy, romantic, heterosexual, and – by the end of the film – ready to take her place as wife and mother. An early exchange between Tiana and her elderly mother, Eudora (Oprah Winfrey), concerns Tiana's obsession with opening a restaurant to the exclusion of all else, realising her now-deceased father's wish for her to become a professional chef but thereby overriding Eudora's desire to see her daughter married and having children:

> EUDORA: Babycakes, I'm sure this place is going to be just wonderful, but it's a shame you are working so hard.
>
> TIANA: But how can I let up now when I'm so close? I got to make sure all daddy's hard work means something.
>
> EUDORA: Tiana, your daddy may not have gotten the place he always wanted, but he had something better. He had love. And that's all I want for you, sweetheart: to meet your prince charming and dance off into your happily ever after.

What is at stake here is the reconciliation of Tiana's individualist fantasies with socially prescribed gender roles that she is unable to resist. Yet, as with all Disney films that end with heterosexual coupling, the union is entered into voluntarily, in deference to the transformative powers of romantic love.

The difference here is that the marriage between Tiana and Naveen (Bruno Campos), the playboy prince of a fictional Arabian kingdom, is explicitly presented as being mutually beneficial: in the film's final scene, they open their own restaurant in New Orleans. Tiana and Naveen each possess skills and frailties lacking in the other; as an interracial couple, their coupling also highlights the film's central theme of reconciling difference. Their character traits are clearly defined from the outset: she is highly driven and hard-working but is unable to countenance the possibility of indulging herself (deferred gratification); he is spoiled, arrogant and concerned only with living in the moment (immediate gratification). These characteristics only change due to the other's intervention. He teases her as a 'stick in the mud' incapable of having fun; she, in return, diagnoses him as 'a no'count, philandering, lazy bump on a log'. But just as Tiana teaches Naveen to cook (representing her pragmatism), he teaches her to dance (a metaphor for non-productive play, specifically sexuality) and loosen up. Naveen abandons his apparently innate self-absorption and attempts to sacrifice his happiness by brokering a deal with Charlotte in which he marries her in return for funds for Tiana's restaurant. But Tiana prevents him from doing so with the remark: 'My dream wouldn't be complete without you in it.'

It is, perhaps, in keeping with its charmingly ersatz visual aesthetic that *The Princess and the Frog* – a cel animation in an age of computer animation – hearkens back to more traditional, didactic modes of Hollywood family entertainment. On some levels, it might be seen as a homily on the need to balance hard work with play, and in its vision of a young black woman overcoming poverty and racial discrimination to establish her own business, it does not wear its progressive credentials lightly. Endorsements of principles of equality of opportunity (the 'American Dream') are commonplace in contemporary family films, and tend to be dealt with much more overtly than the largely naturalised ideological affirmations of family and community that typically underpin the form. Yet for all its much-vaunted liberalism, the film explicitly views Tiana's life as incomplete without Naveen; she is repeatedly prevailed upon not to work so hard by her friends and mother, as if her single-minded pursuit of career is axiomatically 'bad' (we may recall Sally Field's enervated careerist single mother in *Mrs Doubtfire* [Chris Columbus, 1993]). Only when she reconciles these ambitions with a classically Disneyesque form of aristocratic domesticity (she becomes a princess by marrying Naveen) is she seen to be complete. The film stops short of asserting, as the classical Disney fairy tale did, that marriage and domesticity are the truest and most profound markers of fulfilment for a young woman. However, it is still incumbent upon the female protagonist to balance her individualistic fantasies with the responsibilities of wife and mother.

The clear implication is that ethnicity is irrelevant; the virtues possessed by Disney princesses from Snow White to Tiana (and beyond) are presented as timeless and universal. At the time of the film's release, Disney executive Kathy Franklin told *The Hollywood Reporter*: 'Our hope is that she will fit in as all the other princesses have fit in. We hope that she is very inspirational for little girls and that little girls will want to play out her story.'[50] The contrary argument is that while skin colour may largely be irrelevant (or purely cosmetic, as some critics claimed of Tiana), cultural heritage is not. Numerous critics and lobbies found fault with the film's representation of race, arguing, variously, that Tiana spends too much time under a spell transformed into a frog; that Naveen is not really 'black', and thus the narrative disallows the possibility of a black prince (a troubling claim, since it appears to preclude identification as such to anyone not of African descent); that the New Orleans setting leads to cultural stereotyping (bayous, gumbo, jazz, voodoo) or, worse, that it is inappropriate and insensitive in the wake of the city's recent humanitarian tragedy of Hurricane Katrina in August 2005.[51] To some degree, these criticisms might be seen as a form of 'blowback' of the kind Disney has experienced at various points over its history; when contentious issues are dealt with by any large public organisation, a backlash is virtually inevitable.[52] Yet Disney's chequered history in its cultural (mis)representations of 'Otherness' has engendered a prevailing culture of suspicion, if not outright cynicism, amongst minority groups and liberal commentators.

Centring on the daughter of the chief of a Polynesian tribe and her desire to leave her island community for a life of adventure, *Moana* was described on release as Disney's 'most culturally sensitive film ever' by the *Washington Post*.[53] As in *Pocahontas*, there is a strong emphasis on cultural heritage: the myths and legends of the tribe, the close affiliation with the landscape, and the cyclical patterns and structures of life are all foregrounded. In an early scene, Moana (Louise Bush as an infant; Auli'i Cravalho as a 16-year-old) is told by her mother (Nicole Scherzinger) that she will do great things, but her father, Tui (Temuera Morrison) immediately adds: 'But first you must learn where you're meant to be.' The song 'Where You Are' then plays over a montage sequence showing images of Moana progressing to young adulthood, and emphasises her growing sense of stultification in the self-contained island from which, as she observes, 'no one leaves'. The song is performed mostly as a call-and-response number between Moana and her over-protective father who tells her:

> Moana, it's time you knew
> The village of Motunui is all you need
> The dancers are practising; they dance to an ancient song

> Who needs a new song? This one's all we need
> This tradition is our mission [. . .]
> You must find happiness where you are.

Like most of Disney/Pixar's post-1990s releases, this lyric emphasises a familiar tension between the desires of the individual and the needs of the community. Moana (like her recalcitrant father before her) desperately wishes to leave her island and venture out into the ocean in search of adventure and fulfilment. The island may 'give us all we need', but it remains a place of confinement; Moana's yearning for escape ('there's more beyond the reef') represents the young adult's desire to break from the restraints of childhood. Yet the daring young female protagonist is not wholly isolated from the traditions of her ancestors; as in *Pocahontas*, there is a wise, rebellious grandmother (Rachel House) that encourages the girl to lead her people into a new, more enlightened, future. The sexual politics of these films seems to acknowledge, tacitly or otherwise, a long history of patriarchal repression that is localised in apparently subservient but actually free-thinking grandmothers who, nonetheless, have failed to break out of their confinement.

These grandmothers serve an important narrative function. In both films, the young female heroine overcomes the recalcitrance of their father and effects a dramatic change in his worldview. This is doubly significant, because the father is the head of the tribe, and thus also represents the patriarchal Law in the Lacanian sense. These 'modern' heroines succeed where their spirited but disempowered female ancestors failed. The film's dramatic climax is also given an explicitly feminine coding. The monstrous fire demon, Te Kā, is revealed as the spirit of the benevolent goddess Te Fiti, who became corrupted after losing her heart. It is Moana, and not the legendary demigod Maui (Dwayne Johnson) – an exaggeratedly masculine, would-be hero who fails in his attempt to defeat Te Kā in physical combat – that recognises Te Kā's true nature and is able to return her heart, restoring the island to fecundity. According to directors Ron Clements and John Musker, it is Moana's empathy – widely perceived as a 'feminine' characteristic – that 'got her started on this whole journey' and allows the eventual peaceable reconciliation between the two sides.[54] We might compare these climactic sequences to those of *The Little Mermaid*, in which the heroic Prince Eric (Christopher Daniel Barnes) impales the sea witch, Ursula (Pat Carroll), through the heart with a ship's bow. Although *Moana*'s vision of heroism remains undeniably gendered, it is the title character's virtues of gentleness and rationalism that not only save her people, but do so in a way that averts the traditional (male-coded) trope of Hollywood heroism: that of resolving conflict through violence.[55]

The projection of authenticity is clearly central to the film. Its complex mythology is avowedly rooted in Polynesian cultural history; many of the

Figure 4.2   The restored Te Fiti as an image of nurturing feminine fecundity (*Moana*, Disney, 2016). Frame grab.

actors (e.g. Auli'i Cravalho, Dwayne Johnson, Temuera Morrison) are of Polynesian background; the Hollywood-based Maori filmmaker Taika Waititi was attached to the project as an advisor early in the production; and, notably, Disney assembled a so-called 'Oceanic Story Trust' composed of anthropologists, historians, linguists and choreographers from across several Pacific islands to advise on Polynesian culture. However, Disney remains susceptible to the charge of reinscribing the very 'coloniality' such films appear to disavow, appropriating local cultures for commercial purposes while disingenuously claiming to uphold 'diversity'. *Moana* has been accused not merely of appropriating Polynesian heritage for the purposes of corporate profiteering, but also of producing a banal assemblage of mythic elements from across several different cultures. For instance, a New Zealand Member of Parliament and a Samoan rugby player alleged that the film – in rendering Maui as extremely large – upheld offensive stereotypes that Polynesians are obese.[56]

Part of the issue, as Michelle Anya Anjirbag argues, is that conceptions of 'diversity' continue to be rooted in what we might call the 'situatedness' of Western social and political discourse, which 'relies on binaries as a mode of communication', particularly in terms of 'white' and 'non-white'.[57] Ventures such as Disney's Oceanic Story Trust are problematic, in Anjirbag's estimation, because they presuppose that 'all members of a group will hold the same opinion'.[58] Obviously, this cannot be so; New Zealand educator Tina Ngata publicly criticised Waititi for ratifying Disney's reinterpretation of Polynesian culture, claiming that 'the story of our voyaging tipuna is not just yours to place into the hands of Disney [. . .] The placing of this narrative in the hands of Disney is, at best, cavalier – and at worst a complete sellout.'[59] Furthermore, 'diversity' has become such a prominent and potent political discourse that, according to Anjirbag (via Sara Ahmed), there is considerable 'aesthetic and cultural value conferred through something being labelled as diverse'.[60] Consequently, 'it is the *designation of diversity itself* that holds value or political economy' (my emphasis); the form that diversity takes in the text itself, and even the impact on the people whose culture is being invoked, assume lesser importance.[61] From a socio-political standpoint, then, what emerges through films such as *Pocahontas, Mulan, The Princess and the Frog* and *Moana* are ambivalent examples of a multinational conglomerate purporting to be 'inclusive' and acting with sensitivity and authenticity, yet – as often as not – imbricating itself within the very colonialist practices it claims to repudiate. From a commercial perspective, of course, the picture is much clearer: many of Disney's 'glocal' films have been colossal money-makers, continuing to consolidate the company's international dominance of the family entertainment market. For this reason, the tensions inherent in Disney's treatment of diversity and multiculturalism are unlikely to be resolved in the near future.

WOMEN AND THE CONTEMPORARY PRINCESS FILM

As seen earlier in the chapter, Disney's representation of women and femininity in the 1990s was typified by ambivalent sexual politics, caught between 'traditional' models of domesticity and subservience to male authority and more 'modern' principles of independence and autonomy. *Tangled* (Nathan Greno and Byron Howard, 2010), as with *The Princess and the Frog*, is something of a transitional text in the neo-Disney canon in that it continues to focus on heterosexual coupling while attempting to emphasise gender equality. However, since the early 2010s, there has been a further shift in representations of female identity in Disney/Pixar releases, which often de-emphasise or dispense altogether with the courtship–marriage plot and its attendant inflections of patriarchal inequality. Instead, other relationships come to the fore: *Brave* (Mark Andrews and Brenda Chapman, 2012) explores the bond between a mother and daughter, *Frozen* between two sisters, and *Inside Out* (Pete Docter, 2015) between an adolescent girl and her own, personified, 'emotions'. In their treatment of these different relationship types, however, the films are careful not to suggest that individual (or collective) identity ought to be sacrificed to whatever duties or responsibilities that bond might traditionally have entailed.

One of the most important shifts in what we might still loosely term Disney 'princess films' since the release of *Tangled* has been the attempt to broaden the appeal beyond the presumed core audience of pre-teen girls. Loosely adapted from the German fairy tale 'Rapunzel' (1812), *Tangled* was originally produced with the working titles of 'Rapunzel' and 'Rapunzel Unbraided', but these were eventually vetoed under the belief that a gender-specific title would alienate large sections of the market. Pixar's Ed Catmull recalled that Disney's marketing department had warned against using the word 'princess' in the title of *The Princess and the Frog*, but that the filmmakers had stood firm, arguing that 'the quality of the film would trump that association and lure viewers of all ages, male and female'. This belief proved to be unfounded, and scheduling the film's release against James Cameron's *Avatar* (2009), in Catmull's reckoning, 'only encouraged moviegoers to take one look at a film with the word princess in the title and think: That's for little girls only'.[62] In the event, although the gambit of retitling the film was roundly ridiculed, it paid off at the box office: *Tangled* grossed approximately $600 million worldwide.

It is also the relative earnestness of films such as *The Princess and the Frog*, *Tangled* and *Frozen* that distinguish them from the deconstructive lampooning of the early DreamWorks releases. In *Tangled*, for instance, while the film's narrator assumes a knowingly self-conscious address to the audience, and several of the characters converse in a modern, demotic style, the narrative is largely free from interrogative irony. Humour is largely confined to character moments and the odd sight gag (such as a horse vengefully chewing up a wanted poster at impossible speed) or comical verbal exchange rather than, as in films such as *Shrek*, from the perceived absurdity of generic conventions. Furthermore, although it purports to represent its characters in an emotionally realistic fashion, the film ultimately contains at its heart an idealistic fantasy of heterosexual romance between Princess Rapunzel (Mandy Moore) and the reformed thief, Eugene (Zachary Levi). The closing narration – delivered to the audience by Rapunzel and Eugene – is notably strait-laced:

> EUGENE: Well, you can imagine what happened next. The kingdom rejoiced, for the lost princess had returned. The party lasted an entire week, and honestly, I don't remember most of it. Dreams came true all over the place [. . .] At last, Rapunzel was home, and she finally had a real family. She was a princess worth waiting for. Beloved by all, she led her kingdom with all the grace and wisdom that her parents did before her. And, as for me, I started going by 'Eugene' again, stopped thieving, and basically turned it all around. But I know what the big question is: did Rapunzel and I ever get married? Well, I'm pleased to tell you that after years and years of asking . . . I finally said yes.
> RAPUNZEL: Eugene!
> EUGENE: Ok, I asked *her*. And we're living happily ever after.
> RAPUNZEL: Yes, we are.

This dual narration can be seen as a strategy intended to pre-empt the accusation that this is not a relationship between equals, even down to Rapunzel's final confirmation of Eugene's claim that they are living 'happily ever after'.

Nevertheless, in other regards Rapunzel is yet another 'classical' Disney princess: white, conventionally beautiful, kindly, sheltered, innocent, attuned with nature, perfectly at home in the domestic environment, and yet possessed with enough feistiness that the portrayal does not seem intolerably anachronistic. Eugene, a double-dealing, petty thief, hardly appears a promising match for Rapunzel, but the moment he privately admits his true name/identity (having previously gone by the name 'Flynn') represents a turning point. Eugene is no 'fixer upper' in the vein of Kristoff from *Frozen* (whose imperfections are actively celebrated), but rather undergoes a metamorphosis into a simulacrum of ideal manhood. This fantasy of transformation through romantic love is a familiar trope of the Hollywood romance, being central to wish-fulfilment romantic films such as *Dirty Dancing* (Emile Ardolino, 1987) where the rough edges of the rugged, working-class male object of desire are smoothed out by the gentler, refined, idealistic girl on the cusp of adulthood. The desire to move away from such representations may have as much to do with studios' desire to appeal to male audiences as with the perception that they peddle old-fashioned sexual politics.

Brave – Pixar's first feature with a female protagonist – takes a very different approach to the princess narrative. Co-director Brenda Chapman has spoken of her desire for a 'real girl' in the leading role, one that did not have 'tiny, skinny arms, waist and legs' and who could 'give girls something to look at and not feel inadequate'.[63] Claudia Puig, reviewing the film in *USA Today*, wrote that *Brave* 'introduces audiences to a new breed of Disney princess – one brimming with self-confidence, strong opinions, athletic skills, determination, loyalty and a head full of unruly curls [. . .] Indefatigable and fierce, she's a role model for girls in the 21st century.'[64] However, it is not just the passivity of Disney princesses that is being disavowed, but also the 'girliness' of earlier fairy tale films. Dave Hollis, the company's executive president of worldwide distribution, argued: 'You have to draw men and boys as well to see this number [. . .] the themes in the movie – bravery, fighting for your fate – transcend gender.'[65] This strategy appears to have paid off: according to ComScore's PostTrak exit polling service, 43 per cent of audiences during the film's opening weekend were male, the exact same proportion as for *Frozen*, released the following year.[66]

While *Brave* trades on the idea of the 'relatable' protagonist, the generic conventions of the fairy tale film are subject to modification. Chapman herself recognised that 'fairy tales have gotten kind of a bad reputation, especially among women'.[67] Consequently, the film entirely eschews the romantic plot. Although the focalisation usually remains with the individualistic teenage princess, Merida (Kelly Macdonald), the 16-year-old daughter of the king of a medieval Scottish clan, the film is primarily concerned with her relationship with her traditionalist mother, Elinor (Emma Thompson). The opening scene emphasises their close bond, as Elinor and the infant Merida play hide-and-seek to the delight of the child. It is when Merida grows into a young adult that fractures develop in their relationship, with Merida resisting her mother's attempts to mould her into a 'perfect' princess. Her self-reliance and eschewal of traditional gender roles is signalled in the opening scene, when her father, King Fergus (Billy Connolly), gives her a bow as a birthday present. Elinor objects, 'She's a lady!' but Fergus laughs, as if recognising the absurdity of the claim. Merida later rails against the incessant rote-teaching she receives in preparation for being a princess who 'strives for perfection', and the apparent inevitability that she will eventually 'become. . . *my mother*'.

The primary site of dramatic conflict surrounds Merida's refusal to consent to her betrothal to the son of one of her father's allies. As with *The Princess and the Frog*, *Tangled* and *Frozen*, the film presents an image of female empowerment more befitting the prevailing mood of twenty-first-century Western society, recognising that the princess need not be bound by patriarchal, patrilineal traditions which demand that the young woman willingly negate her own ambitions. Although all of the Disney fairy tale films from *The Princess and the Frog* onwards allegorise changing gender norms, *Brave* examines this as a potential site of disharmony between the daughter, who initially rejects self-abnegation in any form, and the mother, who understands the magnitude of the self-sacrifice but ultimately remains committed to convention for the stability and consensus it brings. The fact that the film refuses wholly to endorse or to repudiate either point of view perhaps reflects its intended cross-demographic appeal to mothers and daughters. In one sequence, after a heated argument between the two women, both are seen separately rehearsing a speech intended to placate the other with detailed explanations of their respective positions; the camera intercuts between these speeches, as if to assert the essential similarities between the characters and the validity of their perspectives.

The film's *deus ex machina* magical transformation of Elinor into a bear (and back again) initiates a reversal of roles that allows both characters not only to reach a mutual understanding, but to prove willing to sacrifice their own beliefs for the sake of the other. The key sequence occurs when Merida announces to the assembled court: 'I've been selfish. I tore a great rift in our kingdom. There's no one to blame but me. And I know now that I need to amend my mistake and mend our bond.' She begins to announce her betrothal, but notices Elinor – still in bear form – in the background frantically urging her not to. Duly emboldened, she confirms her intention to break with tradition and speaks of the importance that people 'write their own stories, follow their hearts, and find love in their own time'. At the end of the film, when Elinor has returned to human form, Merida exclaims 'You changed!' and Elinor responds, 'We both have.'

It is worth comparing *Brave* with two Disney films released shortly afterwards: the CG animated feature, *Frozen*, and the primarily live-action feature, *Maleficent* (Robert Stromberg, 2014). Just as *Frozen* is loosely adapted from Hans Christian Andersen's 'The Snow Queen' (1844), *Maleficent* is loosely adapted from another classic fairy tale, Charles Perrault's 'Sleeping Beauty' (1697). Besides their considerable international popularity on theatrical release (*Frozen* grossed almost $1.3 billion; *Maleficent* more than $750 million), what links these films is their radical reinterpretation of the source texts. In both cases, the film's co-protagonist is a sympathetic and 'relatable' revision of the original story's villainous female: the Snow Queen is recast as Elsa (Idina Menzel), whose powers engender fear in herself as much as in her subjects; and Maleficent (Angelina Jolie), though she remains an antihero, is far from the repulsive, evil fairy she appears in Disney's 1950s adaptation of *Sleeping Beauty* (Clyde Geronimi et al., 1959). In both films, the primary villain is a duplicitous male figure not present in the source text. This revisionism may have a pragmatic commercial basis: for all their purported gender neutrality, these productions, in contrast to the majority of male-oriented family-adventure movies, are intended for girls (and their parents) more than boys. But it is also explicitly, and self-avowedly, political: a determined movement away from the dyadic representations of 'good' and 'bad' femininity that has long bedevilled children's fiction. In *Frozen* and *Maleficent*, the female protagonists are freed from a reliance on romantic love in order to achieve personal (or social) fulfilment. A conventional, heterosexual romantic coupling is teased, but ultimately disavowed when the character set up to be the male hero betrays the central female character.

While the consequences of these betrayals are still devastating for their victims, the key relationship in both films is between two women: sisters (*Frozen*) and mother and daughter (*Maleficent*). In both films, an act of pure, selfless love from the putatively villainous female restores the stereotypically 'good' princess to health. Unusually, for Hollywood fairy tale films, this family bond is seen to be at least equal, if not superior, to the intimacy and transformative power of romantic union. The implication of these acts of revision (both to the source text and to the Disney fairy tale film) is twofold. Firstly, women are seen to be sufficiently empowered and self-sufficient not to require a man in their life. Secondly, while heterosexual romance and marriage are still fulfilling choices for many, they need not be 'happily ever after'. This deconstructive impulse allegorises current social trends (the normalcy of divorce and/or alternative family structures) and self-reflexively debunks conventions – of courtship, romance and marriage – that have become too clichéd or outmoded to be presented in the earnest, uncynical and politically regressive manner of previous Disney fairy tale films.

As noted above, one important aspect that differentiates *Frozen* (and many other Disney films) from the narrative-cartoonalism popularised by Dream-Works is the de-emphasising of authorial intertextuality. But whilst the film is not a *bricolage* of modernity in the vein of *Toy Story* (John Lasseter, 1995) or

Shrek, this is not to deny its deep reflexivity. It reveals Disney to be in the midst of an ongoing process of rewriting its own seemingly inviolable conventions. Because these rewritings tend not to be overtly comedic or explicitly decon-structive in the vein of *Shrek*, they may not register as parodic at all. However, the revisionism that characterises Disney fairy tale films of the 2010s can be seen, essentially, as reparative: they deliberately rewrite the established conven-tions of the form in order to 'resuscitate' it (to use Dan Harries's term).[68]

Parody, in this sense, is a creative act that serves to 'weed out' clichéd or outmoded conventions.[69] In several regards, *Shrek* resembles the last of Thomas Schatz's four stages of generic development (experimental, classic, refinement, baroque).[70] However, rather than signalling the end of the fairy tale genre, it supports Harries's supposition that parody of this kind can 'end up reinvigorat-ing and extending the genre'.[71] In many ways, though – and to borrow Rick Altman's semantic/syntactic approach to genre – films such as *Brave*, *Frozen* and *Maleficent* are even more substantive parodies than *Shrek*.[72] *Shrek* might seem like a radical take on the fairy tale film, but the parody is largely at the *semantic* level: the conventions of the form are roundly ridiculed, but they are still broadly upheld. The more recent female-centred Disney/Pixar films – in moving away from heterosexual romance as the traditional narrative goal of the protagonist – are engaging in a more fundamental revisionism at the *syntactic* level.

The de-emphasising of the romantic mode has coincided with a growing interest in films that invest their protagonists with 'emotional realism'. *Frozen*, in particular, repeatedly diffuses the idea of the physically and psychologically 'perfect' princess, not just because it represents a largely male-oriented image of ideal femininity, but also because the doll-like princesses of classical-era Disney films are not considered especially 'relatable' to contemporary audiences. The film must reconcile the archaisms of its fairy tale realm with everyday reali-ties comprehensible to twenty-first-century audiences. Thus Elsa's sister, Anna (Kristen Bell), may look rather like a classic Disney princess – she is white, beautiful, romantic, kind-hearted, and uncynical – but we also see her waking up drooling with strands of hair in her mouth, wondering if the feeling in her stomach on the day of her sister's coronation is because she is 'elated or gassy', and singing of her desire to 'stuff some chocolate in my face'. The film also appropriates something of the kooky, rapid-fire exchanges of contemporary female-oriented comedies such as *The Gilmore Girls* (2000–7), as when Anna bumbles comically at Elsa's coronation:

ELSA: Hi.
ANNA: Hi . . . oh, 'hi' me? Hi.
ELSA: You look beautiful.
ANNA: Thank you. You look beautifuller. I mean, not 'fuller'. You don't
    look fuller. But, but more beautiful.

Later, a group of trolls sing Anna a song that lays out a new manifesto for Disney's portrayal of romantic love. The song, 'Fixer Upper', concerns her prospective relationship with the stoic but somewhat hapless iceman, Kristoff (Jonathan Groff), and contains the lyrics:

> We're not saying you can change him, 'cause people don't really change
> We're only saying that love's a force that's powerful and strange
> People make bad choices if they're mad or scared or stressed
> But throw a little love their way and you'll bring out their best
> True love brings out the best
> Everyone's a bit of a fixer-upper, that's what it's all about
> Father! Sister! Brother!
> We need each other to raise us up and round us out.

The song is a homily on the 'true' nature of love, suggesting that no romantic coupling is 'perfect', that 'love at first sight' is an idealistic or even dangerous fallacy, that compromise is at the heart of any relationship, and that love is ever-changing. The assumption that it exists as a latent state in characters whose sole destiny is to discover their one, immutable 'true love' is disavowed here. This constitutes a marked departure from previous Disney films (and from most children's fiction), instead expressing a pragmatic, less misty-eyed conception of romance more characteristic of YA literature.

Anna perhaps represents Disney's quintessential representation of the 'typical' twenty-first-century American teenager: self-conscious, goofy, eager to please but increasingly secure in her own abilities and desires. In contrast, her older sister, Elsa, embodies more complex and problematic feelings of estrangement from mainstream society – a milder version of the self-consciously non-conformist protagonists discussed in the following chapter. *Frozen*'s (gender-neutral) title, of course, refers to the Snow Queen's frozen heart, and it is her inability (or her *feared inability*) to control her own power indiscriminately to freeze people that is film's primary problematic, and the vehicle through which sisterly love can be explored. The opening song, 'Frozen Heart', prefigures the main storyline in its assertion (by a group of rugged ice harvesters) of the strength, hardness, beauty and danger of ice, and its repeated references to breaking through 'the frozen heart'. Throughout the film, ice is construed not merely as a tangible physical phenomenon but as a metaphor for loneliness, alienation, self-denial and the emotional barriers that people build to protect themselves from others.

The theme of Elsa having to control her powers, reining in her magical abilities for the good of herself and those around her – particularly Anna, whom she almost freezes to death – can be seen as another metonymy for the child's need to acquire self-discipline and come to terms with the responsibilities of the adult world. In an early scene, the Troll King (Ciarán Hinds) tells Elsa, 'Your power will only grow. There is beauty in it, but also great danger. You must learn to control it.' On the other hand, her parents' subsequent decision to keep Elsa isolated from the outside world, and from Anna, is seen as equally harmful: an enforced repression of individuality that corrodes the family from the inside out. As her powers continue to grow, Elsa's father (Maurice LaMarche) gives her cotton gloves, advising her to 'conceal it', 'don't feel it', and 'don't let it show'. Not comprehending the reasons for Elsa's withdrawal, Anna sings (in the number 'Do You Want to Build a Snowman'):

> Come on, let's go and play.
> I never see you any more, come out the door
> It's like you've gone away.
> We used to be best buddies, and now we're not
> I wish you would tell me why.

Subsequently, after the death of their parents, Anna plaintively reprises the song, appealing to Elsa (from behind a closed door) to

> Let me in
> We only have each other; it's just you and me
> What are we going to do?

The traditional ideal of the 'perfect' princess weighs heavily on both sisters; it is the disjuncture between this socially constructed idea of desirable femininity and their 'real' identities (flawed, human) from which the film derives much of its dramatic impetus. At times, this is used as a comedic mechanism: as if to underline the fact that Anna is an altogether more modern Disney heroine, she rebukes the seemingly virtuous, actually villainous Hans (Santino Fontana) for his 'frozen heart' before delivering a crushing sock to the jaw that sends him hurtling off a bridge into the fjord below. Humour is derived from the comic incongruity of a Disney princess knocking out a man twice her size, but this moment is also cathartic for the characters – and, by extension, the audience – since it underlines one of the film's central messages: that women are just as strong, capable and self-sufficient as men.

One of the central threads of the film is Elsa's reconciliation of her perceived need to repress her powers and her parallel desire fully to express her own individuality. In the number 'For the First Time in Forever', on the day on the coronation, Elsa sings:

> Don't let them in, don't let them see
> Be the good girl you always have to be.

(At this point there is a point-of-view shot as Elsa gazes at a large portrait of her imposing, now-deceased father.)

> Conceal, don't feel, put on a show
> Make one wrong move and everyone will know.

However, this strategy proves ineffective; she accidentally reveals her powers to her court, leading one nobleman to denounce her as a 'monster', and leaves the kingdom to build her ice palace. In the iconic musical number 'Let it Go' (a top-five hit in the US charts), she finally accepts her own identity:

> It looks like I'm the queen
> The wind is howling like this swirling storm inside
> Couldn't keep it in, heaven knows I've tried
> Don't let them in, don't let them see
> Be the good girl you always have to be
> Conceal, don't feel, don't let them know
> Well, now they know
> Let it go, let it go, can't hold it back any more.

It should be emphasised that the tone, tempo, melody and orchestration of 'Let it Go' in no way imply that Elsa's condition is monstrous, or even undesirable. It is a sweeping, orchestral, mid-tempo romantic ballad that expresses the cathartic bursting forth of innate desires that she can no longer suppress. Having finally let loose her 'true' self, Elsa goes on to sing:

> I don't care what they're going to say
> Let the storm rage on
> The cold never bothered me anyway
> [. . .]
> That perfect girl is gone.

This symbolic 'coming out' has been interpreted by many fans and critics as a parable of self-acceptance of queer identity. However, the debate that surrounds Elsa's sexuality is yet another manifestation of the strategy of 'deniability' that suffuses post-1990s Hollywood animation; while there is sufficient evidence to sustain the possibility that Elsa is gay, there is certainly not enough that viewers who prefer to believe otherwise are forced to accept it as fact.[73] Elsa's inability to control her magical powers might be taken to represent an entirely *non-sexual* loss of rational self-control; equally, it may suggest coping with a mental illness, or any number of alternative interpretations.

In either event, *Frozen* presents a double-voiced discourse of maturation, cautioning the need to control base impulse but emphasising the necessity of retaining self-expression and individualism. If the first position is a hallmark of Grecian philosophies and Freudian theorising on the necessity of maintaining order in civilised society through self-repression (in a sense, self-abnegation for the common good), the second is more redolent of current attitudes towards the pursuit of self-actualisation. If there is a broad (if largely unconscious) metanarrative that links almost all contemporary Hollywood animation it is this: the holding of seemingly contrary pulls of self and community in delicate balance. Usually, this dialectic is manifested in a classically American form of individualism, where a measure of difference among individual people (in appearance, philosophy, and behaviour) is held as desirable and necessary, but only insofar as it serves the larger needs of civilisation. Elsa's apparent mastery of her powers at the end of the film – when she turns the central square of her kingdom into an ice rink and her subjects merrily engage in the festivities – demonstrate her newfound ability to harness her abilities in a way that preserves her independence and individuality but that also benefits the entire community.

Models of Masculinity

Changes in representations of male figures in Hollywood animation since the 1990s are perhaps less visible, and considerably less documented. Nonetheless, they remain significant in what they reveal about contemporary constructions of masculinity in the United States. As noted earlier in this chapter, the Disney non-animal male hero largely conforms to basic character tropes, such as strength, bravery, loyalty, nobility and moral 'goodness'; his narrative function is to defeat evildoers and, in the case of grown-up figures such as The Prince (Harry Stockwell) in *Snow White and the Seven Dwarfs*, Prince Charming (William Phipps) in *Cinderella* (Clyde Geronimi et al., 1950) and Prince Phillip (Bill Shirley) in *Sleeping Beauty*, successfully courts his female counterpart, thus partaking in a broader reaffirmation of heterosexual love, family, tradition and continuity. This quintessential model of masculinity recurs in the majority of human male Disney heroes until the 1990s, when values of 'relatability' and 'emotional realism' began to impose modifications in representations of male and female protagonists, framed against broader shifts in sexual politics. As we have seen, the core elements of the classical Disney male hero remain evident in post-1990s figures such as John Smith in *Pocahontas*, and – in the popular imagination – continue to register as a kind of ghostly presence, to the extent that the 'typical' Disney hero is still widely seen as embodying the prototypical characteristics listed above, while films that deviate from this pattern are held to be participating in a slightly unexpected, and laudable, act of textual revisionism.

As we saw in Chapter 2, success for adult male protagonists such as Mr Incredible, Carl Fredericksen from *Up* and Héctor from *Coco* typically depends on negotiating a path between fulfilling paternal responsibilities and their pursuit of individualist fantasies of self-actualisation. However, other recent films recast the traditional heroic archetype in the form of individuals whose appearance and conduct may appear, on the surface, to be decidedly non-heroic, but who nonetheless ultimately embody classical virtues such as bravery, perseverance and loyalty – a select list might include Mumble (Elijah Wood) from *Happy Feet* (George Miller, 2006); Remy (Patton Oswalt) from *Ratatouille* (Brad Bird, 2007); Flint (Bill Hader) from *Cloudy with a Chance of Meatballs* (Phil Lord and Christopher Miller, 2009); Hiccup (Jay Baruchel) from *How to Train Your Dragon* (Chris Sanders and Dean DeBlois, 2010); Ralph (John C. Reilly) from *Wreck-It Ralph* (Rich Moore, 2012) and Forky (Tony Hale) from *Toy Story 4* (Josh Cooley, 2019). This practice can be viewed as an example of what John G. Cawelti calls 'stereotype vitalisation', a technique used in multiple genres of fiction to invest 'significant touches of human complexity or frailty to a stereotypical figure'.[74] Protagonists of this kind can also be understood in light of what Ken Gillam and Shannon R. Wooden identify as the 'New Man' archetype in post-millennial Hollywood animation. Having characterised pre-1990s male Disney protagonists as 'two-dimensional', they argue that new models of masculinity were required in order to respond to 'post-princess' femininity.[75] Indeed, they suggest that figures such as Woody and Buzz in *Toy Story* undergo genuine character development over the course of the narrative, and ultimately arrive at a 'New Man' model, which they characterise in the following terms:

> they all strive for an alpha-male identity; they face emasculating failures; they find themselves, in large part, through what Eve Sedgwick refers to as 'homosocial desire' and a triangulation of this desire with a feminized object (and/or a set of 'feminine' values); and, finally, they achieve (and teach) a kinder, gentler understanding of what it means to be a man.[76]

These films thus reject, and even ridicule, the so-called 'alpha-male' identities initially inhabited by characters such as Buzz Lightyear, Mr Incredible, Maui, Gru (Steve Carell) from the *Despicable Me* series and Dracula (Adam Sandler) from the *Hotel Transylvania* series; figures whose exaggerated masculinity eventually proves to be 'fraudulent, precarious, lonely, and devoid of emotional depth'.[77]

What is most notable in *How to Train Your Dragon* is the way conflict is framed as an ideological battle between two opposing models of masculinity. The first is the 'alpha male' figure, which is represented by the Viking settlement in which the film is set; the second is the 'New Man', embodied by the film's young protagonist, Hiccup, the son of the Viking chieftain. Hiccup's difference is signalled by his name and by his small frame and twenty-first-century mannerisms in a community of hyper-masculine Vikings. Early in the film, his non-conformism is highlighted by his dismayed father, Stoick (Gerard Butler):

> From the time he could crawl he's been . . . different. . . When I was a boy, my father told me to bang my head against a rock and I did it. I thought it was crazy, but I didn't question him. And you know what happened? That rock split in two. It taught me what a Viking could do [. . .] He could crush mountains, level mountains, tame seas. Even as a boy, I knew what I was, what I had to become. Hiccup is not that boy.

Hiccup's more 'modern' appearance (nerdy, clean-shaven, almost hipsterish) and Canadian accent mark him out as someone with whom we are encouraged to identify; in essence, audiences are asked to invest any aspect of themselves that they regard as non-conformist in Hiccup. In contrast, the burly, Scottish-accented Vikings represent patriarchal orthodoxy, rejecting anyone and anything that they regard as 'Other', and thus a threat to their way of life. If Hiccup represents modernity in its most attractive forms (warm, tolerant, forward-thinking), Stoick – whose name, suggestively, is pronounced the same as 'stoic' – initially stands for extreme authoritarianism, evident in his intolerant paternalism and inability to engage with his son. These attributes are wedded to a doctrinaire social conservatism that works to marginalise difference and disallow the possibility of different ethical or behavioural schemas.

Part of the film's psychological conception of the 'New Man' protagonist lies in Hiccup's refusal to relinquish supposedly 'childlike' virtues such as innocence and empathy. Unlike the rest of his tribe, he does not fear the fire-breathing dragons that share this world with the Vikings, nor reject them for being different, but instead reaches out and attempts to forge a connection of trust. Hiccup's simpatico relationship with the dragon he names 'Toothless' leads to his discovering that 'everything we know about you guys is wrong'; he later admits that he was unwilling to kill the defenceless dragon because 'he looked as frightened as I was. I looked at him and I saw myself.' As in films such as *Old Yeller* (Robert Stevenson, 1957), the animal is a psychological mirror for the human child: innocent, inarticulate, instinctual, and lacking civilised affectation. But here the dragons, in their diversity of appearance and colour, perhaps serve as a metaphor for other nationalities or ethnicities in human society. It behoves the non-bigoted Hiccup to re-educate his fellow Vikings on the possibility of inter-species accord, borne through peaceful and respectful action. On every occasion that Hiccup disarms himself and gently talks to a dragon, it responds in kind, abandoning its threatening behaviour; as in *Moana*, the clear moral is that violence begets violence.

During an elaborate initiation ceremony in which Hiccup is single-handedly expected to slay a fearsome dragon, he lays down his weapon and his Viking helmet and, addressing the creature, announces: 'I'm not one of them.' The other Vikings react with alarm to Hiccup's actions, and fearfully capture Toothless when he comes to defend Hiccup. It is Hiccup's young friend, Astrid (America Ferrera), who makes the required logical jump: Hiccup is the first Viking not to kill a dragon, and also the first to make friends with one. He represents the possibility of peaceful co-existence that is realised in the film's final scenes, in which Vikings ride dragons as a matter of course. The eventual transformation in Stoick's character is perhaps too easy to be credible, although it is serves the narrative function of reaffirming family unity (especially important here, since Hiccup and Stoick are the only surviving members of their family). In this reconciliation, Hiccup is able to negotiate a necessary change in his community without renouncing his heritage as a Viking, and Stoick retains his authority, in part, through his admission that his actions have been misguided. Indeed, Stoick's admission of fallibility invests him with strength: another 'New Man' virtue, the film reminds us, is having to courage to admit failure and learn from it.

In contrast, *Wreck-It Ralph* presents a comically exaggerated personification of 'bad' masculinity in the figure of the title character (John C. Reilly), a villain in a 1980s arcade game whose relentless objective is to smash and destroy, with his enormous fists, anything in his path. The comic disjuncture at the heart of the film is that Ralph is a soft-hearted individual who is thoroughly disenchanted with being a 'bad guy' and – to the scorn and amusement of his acquaintances – desires to be the kind of 'New Man' represented by the repairman hero of his game, Fix-It Felix (Jack McBrayer). *Wreck-It Ralph* thus represents yet another exploration of contemporary masculinity in the

Figure 4.3   The peaceful accord between Hiccup and Toothless (*How to Train Your Dragon*, DreamWorks, 2010). Frame grab.

Pixar tradition of everyday, 'relatable' characters and situations.[78] Rejecting the moral binaries of the classical-era films, it also suggests that the desire and the capacity for emotional-behavioural development is an important facet of contemporary 'maleness'; the protagonists' desire to be something greater than that which they are – while eschewing the need for traditional heroic deeds beyond the more outwardly modest capacities of the 'New Man' – undergirds the narrative trajectories of Hiccup and Ralph. Heroism, we are told, may take many forms and abide in the least expected places.

Equally, these films emphasise the plurality of contemporary masculinity, reaffirming one of the central tenets of the Hollywood family film: individualism. The scene in *Wreck-It Ralph* in which a group of video game antagonists meet in a parody of an intervention group to discuss their various levels of existential crises over their intractable villainous identities culminates with the so-called 'bad guy affirmation', which is chanted simultaneously by each member of the group: 'I'm bad, and that's good. I will never be good, and that's not bad. There's no one I'd rather be than me' (Figure 4.4). However, Ralph's visible reluctance gestures to the dangers of 'groupthink'. The film persistently warns against the mindless and repetitive tyranny of the homogenised collective, which is embodied in several undesirable guises: the minor characters in the Fix-It Felix game, all of whom are explicitly hostile towards Ralph and attempt to exclude him from their after-work socialising; the Barbie-like inhabitants of the Sugar Rush game who condemn the game's second protagonist, the eccentric young princess Vanellope von Schweetz (Sarah Silverman), as a 'glitch'; even the viral 'Cy-Bugs' which unthinkingly destroy everything in their path in the arcade. Ralph and Vanellope are heroes – albeit unconventional ones – precisely because they assert their own difference and uniqueness, breaking their own programming and pursuing their own fantasies.

Figure 4.4   Personifications of 'bad masculinity' attempt to come to terms with their destructive inclinations (*Wreck-It Ralph*, Disney, 2012). Frame grab.

Wreck-It Ralph might easily be interpreted as a quintessential exposition on the need forcibly to repress the destructive egoism of childhood and assume the responsibilities – and self-repression – of adulthood, thereby enacting what Freud calls 'the reality principle'. But the eventual acceptance of Ralph's chaotic predispositions (which never cross over into malicious destructiveness), by his friends as well as himself, suggests a different set of moral lessons. If we take Ralph's instinctual capacity for destructiveness not as a metaphor for violent adults, but for children yet to master their own innate desires, we are probably closer to the mark. Children are not always calm and demure, but have the capacity to be fractious, opportunistic and selfish. Furthermore, Ralph is a social outsider, as with so many recent Disney protagonists, but his behaviour invites interpretation through other lenses. In particular, it calls to mind other physiological conditions dimly understood until recent years, and still rarely invoked in children's films, such as autism, bipolar disorder and ADHD.

Ralph's heroism lies precisely in his ability to overcome his disability (i.e. his computer-programming) while retaining his individualism. In such a context, Vanellope's insult to Ralph – 'stinkbrain' – becomes not only a term of affection but a marker of the authenticity of their relationship in a universe literally composed of computer code. Vanellope is a more conventional 'outsider' in her sassiness, keen sense of irony and frequent indulgence in toilet humour (anticipating characters such as Anna in *Frozen*). When she is transformed back into a simulacrum of a fairy tale princess at the end of the film, she immediately casts off that identity: 'The code may say I'm a princess, but I know who I really am.' Ralph's own ultimate validation comes in the final lines of the film, when he explains, 'Turns out I don't need a medal to say I'm a good guy. Because if that kid likes me, how bad can I be?' A similar metonymy for disability is presented in *Toy Story 4* in the character of Forky, the plastic spork crudely fashioned into a 'toy' by the human child, Bonnie (Madeleine McGraw). Initially convinced that he is 'trash' – a belief that manifests itself in his constant desire to hurl himself into the nearest bin – he is nonetheless welcomed by Bonnie's more outwardly 'perfect' toys, and ultimately comes to accept his status as a toy (an object of desire) and his individualism in the final scene, when he announces: 'we are all special, unique'.

CONCLUSION

Many of the characters discussed in this chapter speak to the broader valorisation of different kinds of individualism in recent Hollywood cinema, where peaceable diversity in background, appearance and philosophy is held as the hallmark of a civilised, integrated global society. The Hollywood family film has a strong tendency to utopianism. However, 'utopia' is always a social construct. The recent changes in Disney's politics can be seen as a broad attempt to refute the substance of Jack Zipes's telling observation that the company seeks to 'establish ownership of utopia'.[79] However, Disney's vision of it (reified in its films, media, theme parks and other paratexts) continues to circumscribe difference and diversity in all kinds of ways. Equally, it is important to recognise that the popular appeal of such films, to invoke Richard Dyer's observation on mass entertainment, often rests on their projection of 'what utopia would feel like rather than how it would be organised'.[80] Even if we recognise the accord such films project as a logical impossibility (or worse, a pernicious falsehood), we may still wish to partake in the humanistic fantasy – or, at least, the pious hope – that individual differences may be accommodated and celebrated because more unites than divides us as a species.

Of course, this appearance of consensus can only be sustained because the films' *heteroglossian* strategies of 'deniability' allow controversial positions (e.g. Elsa's sexual orientation) to be couched in ambiguity. In other words, they deliberately occlude social and political fractures that, if given full expression, would annihilate the utopian illusion. As Baker points out, the United States is a unique case amongst post-industrial countries in that its values are simultaneously 'post-materialist', with a strong emphasis on self-expression (i.e. identity, diversity and inclusivity), and highly traditional, 'with levels of religiosity and national pride comparable to those found in developing societies'.[81] These values would appear to be in direct conflict with one another. The textual ambiguities that undergird many mainstream animated films conceal such fractures, not because Hollywood studios are genuinely motivated by utopian philosophies, but because they are guided by a commercial logic that demands the transcendence of social and political disunity.

Nonetheless, as the final chapter of this book will argue, in recent years a counter-tendency has emerged in which benign 'otherness' is *not* always reconciled with accepted conventions of social normalcy. Finding its fullest expression in the work of filmmakers such as Tim Burton and Wes Anderson and studios such as Laika, this tendency lacks the broadly universalistic inflections of Disney, Pixar and DreamWorks. Although such films share a similar preoccupation with 'identity', they nonetheless foreground non-conformist representations of unregenerate weirdness that deliberately tap into sub-cultural identities. As such, they do not aspire to 'relatable' majority tastes, and are rarely utopian in character.

5. ON THE BORDERS: CHILDREN'S HORROR AND INDIEWOOD ANIMATION

This chapter will focus on a recent tradition of Hollywood animated films which mine the intersection between the 'mainstream' and 'cult' firmaments. While there is a long history of experimental or leftfield animation in the United States (e.g. the films of Ralph Bakshi), the films discussed here are characterised by a duality specific to post-1990s Hollywood cinema: they target a mass market while simultaneously addressing audiences that may, ordinarily, reject mainstream animation in its more conventional iterations.[1]

What has become known as the 'children's horror film' is one of the most visible sites of stylistic innovation in post-1990s Hollywood animation. Tim Burton is perhaps the key influence on the development of the 'children's horror' style. A future legend of leftfield commercial cinema, Burton was one of several young Disney animators that expressed frustration at the studio's perceived artistic decline in the late 1970s and early 1980s. His early Disney shorts, *Vincent* (1982) and *Frankenweenie* (1984), evinced a macabre sensibility that deviated markedly from the wholesomeness of the classical Disney film. Viewed with suspicion by Disney executives, Burton left the company in 1984, but his trademark appropriation of gothic horror iconography for mainstream consumption in live-action films such as *Beetlejuice* (1988) and *Edward Scissorhands* (1990) significantly widened the generic parameters of the post-1990s Hollywood family film. Animated children's horror films such as Burton's *The Nightmare Before Christmas* (Henry Selick, 1993), *Corpse Bride* (2005) and the feature-length remake of *Frankenweenie* (2012), and Laika's *Coraline*

(Selick, 2009) and *ParaNorman* (Sam Fell and Chris Butler, 2012), all utilise similar textual strategies: they present grotesque imagery with sufficient wit to appeal to leftfield sensibilities, while still delivering the pleasing emotive content associated with mainstream family entertainment.

This is also true of another recent cycle of animated features that I refer to here as 'indiewood animation'. Films such as *Fantastic Mr. Fox* (Wes Anderson, 2009), *Rango* (Gore Verbinski, 2011) and *Isle of Dogs* (Wes Anderson, 2018) are also ambivalently positioned between the mainstream and cult firmaments, but their textual strategies are somewhat different from those of children's horror films. They exhibit a comparatively cerebral patented kookiness and trippy, offbeat humour, congruent with their stars' (George Clooney, Johnny Depp, Scarlett Johansson, Bill Murray) personae as heroes of independent Hollywood, and aim to mobilise a more culturally literate audience that may disparage mainstream animation for its perceived sentiment and juvenility. Collectively, I will argue, the 'children's horror' and 'indiewood' animated films represent a compromise between the perceived requirements of mass audiences and the promise of additional credibility and cachet associated with cult cinema.

CHILDREN'S HORROR AND CONTEMPORARY HOLLYWOOD

As scholars such as Sarah Smith have discovered, children have enjoyed horror films since the early days of commercial cinema.[2] However, what is now understood as the 'children's horror film' – a production that draws on horror tropes but is intended primarily for the consumption of child audiences – is a more recent invention. Catherine Lester traces its origins in the United States to 1968, the point at which the modern-day Hollywood ratings system came into effect, thereby establishing 'adult horror' as a legitimate generic entity.[3] Liberated from the strictures of the industry's system of self-censorship, the Production Code (which was intended to maintain movie-going as a family entertainment activity in which children could partake), films were free to engage with more mature themes and explicit content. As Lester observes, adult horrors such as *The Exorcist* (William Friedkin, 1973) and *The Texas Chainsaw Massacre* (Tobe Hooper, 1974), by their very existence, opened 'a space for child-oriented horror films with unrestrictive ratings'.[4] Hollywood's introduction of the 'PG-13' rating in 1984 was also a major watershed; for the first time, films such as *Ghostbusters* (Ivan Reitman, 1984) and *Gremlins* (Joe Dante, 1984), which explicitly contained horrific elements unsuitable for young children (and which, by extension, would appeal to teenagers), could be marketed towards family audiences.[5]

The initial wave of children's horror films were primarily live-action and, as Filipa Antunes argues, represented a genuine fusion of horror tropes with the conventions of children's film.[6] However, Hollywood's post-1990s cycle of animated children's horror films is much more comedic in tone, with horror iconographies usually parodied rather than upheld. The foundational figures in this tradition are Tim Burton and his erstwhile collaborator, Henry Selick (another former Disney animator). *The Nightmare Before Christmas* – developed and produced by Burton and directed by Selick – was a modest success upon initial release, but has since emerged as one of the most influential post-1990s animated features. Like several other films discussed in this chapter, it asserts its difference through the medium of stop-motion animation. Historically, stop-motion is more associated with European traditions; as such, it is ideally suited to the non-conformist milieux of the films, bespeaking artisanal craft (in an age of mechanical or digital reproduction) and putting one in mind of earlier mavericks such as Willis O'Brien and Ray Harryhausen.

In this sense, *The Nightmare Before Christmas* embodies a specific dialectic between creative experimentation and mainstream commercial considerations, one that has come to characterise Hollywood children's horror in its wider iterations. The film's incubation began during Burton's tenure at Disney in the early 1980s, when he developed a story based around the character of Jack Skellington, a spidery, skeletal figure who rules the land of Halloween Town. In these initial stages, Burton did not manage to produce much more than concept art; Disney apparently viewed the project as 'too weird' and he left the studio to carve out an increasingly successful career as a director of self-consciously quirky live-action films such as *Pee-wee's Big Adventure* (1985), *Beetlejuice*, *Batman* (1989) and *Edward Scissorhands*. Disney's revived interest in Burton's concept reflected, in large part, the director's burgeoning reputation as a visionary auteur capable of producing high-concept films with proven box office appeal.

The film relates Jack Skellington's discovery of Christmas Land and his subsequent, well-intentioned attempts to co-opt the holiday by impersonating Santa Claus and delivering presents to children, but succeeding only in outraging bourgeois society with his inappropriately ghoulish offerings. Although suffused with the same kinds of comic grotesquery Burton supplied in *Beetlejuice*, the film ultimately reverts to a predictably upbeat final act, in which order is restored and Jack embraces his identity as the leader of Halloween Town. Yet it is instructive that *The Nightmare Before Christmas* was released under the Touchstone Pictures label, which was reserved for more adult-oriented fare that did not fit the wholesome Disney brand. As James M. Curtis has shown, its subsequent critical and commercial success was considerable, but it was not until 2006 that the film – 'once the proverbial black sheep of the Disney family' – was rebranded as a Walt Disney Pictures release, a move that underlines the legitimisation of children's horror within the Hollywood family entertainment mainstream.[7]

The popularity of *The Nightmare Before Christmas* has generated a sub-industry of Hollywood family films (both live-action and animated) that deal with macabre surface pleasures and which are locatable within the generic conventions both of children's cinema and horror film. The impulse behind such films is largely creative, but there is also an element of pragmatic product differentiation. Indeed, the children's horror cycle is inherently reflexive, appearing to reject the unbridled sentiment and the narrative certainties associated with more mainstream iterations of Hollywood animation. In a fiercely competitive marketplace, filmmakers like Burton, Henry Selick, Shane Acker and Travis Knight offer narrative and aesthetic attractions that Disney, Pixar and DreamWorks do not. Yet in industrial terms, children's horror films are very much a part of the Hollywood system, being funded and distributed by companies such as Disney and Warner Bros. The Portland-based animation studio, Laika, the best-known purveyor of US animated children's horror films, is typically referred to as 'independent', yet most of its films have been distributed by Focus Features, a subsidiary of Comcast (owner of Universal), and it is owned by the billionaire business magnate Phil Knight, the co-founder of Nike.

Formally, films such as *The Nightmare Before Christmas*, *Corpse Bride*, *Coraline*, *ParaNorman*, *Frankenweenie* and *The Boxtrolls* (Graham Annable and Anthony Stacchi, 2014) all reside 'on the borders', as it were; they test the limits of (perceived) suitability and appropriateness for children in terms of standards of taste and decency. Common tropes in these films include the idea of a magical, often dangerous 'Other World' running parallel with our own, accessible only to certain people (i.e. the films' protagonists, and, by extension, ourselves as viewers); an emphasis on hauntings and the supernatural; a cosmetically appealing or respectable facade obscuring a darker shadow reality; the foregrounding of death, monstrosity and the grotesque, often presented through a form of comic abjection that revels in the kinds of morbid, scatological detail traditionally anathema to mainstream children's film; and the use of nightmarish fairy tale settings, aesthetically influenced by German Expressionist cinema (particularly in the films of Tim Burton) and European animation (e.g. the work of Lotte Reiniger, Jan Švankmajer and Soviet fairy tales). They also bring to mind Judith Halberstam's claim that

> animated films nowadays succeed [. . .] to the extent that they are able to address the disorderly child, the child who sees his or her family and parents as the problem, the child who knows there is a bigger world out there beyond the family, if only he or she could reach it.[8]

These films certainly address individuals who view themselves as outsiders in some way, and such is the current premium on values of diversity and self-expression that many more young people of the current generation may identify as such. However, their radicalism should not be overstated; their moral ambiguities and depictions of death, decay, and so on are made palatable by a combination of humour and fantasy that serve to inoculate against unmediated feelings of horror or revulsion. Moreover, they are recognisable as family films, and any sense of alterity they might project is regulated by the conventions of the genre.

Like most of the films discussed in this book, leftfield Hollywood animation is closer to 'mimesis' than 'abstraction' in Maureen Furniss's continuum,[9] but it does eschew the narrative-cartoonalism that Sam Summers identifies as central to millennial-era CGI features.[10] Hollywood children's horror films – particularly those of Laika and Tim Burton – capture an alternative vision of America where oddness and danger lie just below surface conformity. Laika's attempt to differentiate *Coraline*, its first feature film, from the Disney/Pixar norm is evident from director Henry Selick's professed desire to 'revive' the more gothic, fairy tale sensibilities of Disney's early features, notably the 'Night on Bald Mountain' and 'The Sorcerer's Apprentice' sections of *Fantasia* (Ben Sharpsteen et al., 1940).[11] While the film does soften some of the more disturbing aspects of Neil Gaiman's graphic novel (a medium in which greater experimentalism is permissible), Selick claims to have resisted instructions from the film's distributor, Universal, to 'lighten the story'. Instead, the art direction borrows from the low-key lighting and gothic expressionism of Tim Burton's films and of Selick's own *The Nightmare Before Christmas*, largely eschewing the pastels and neutral tones of Dave McKean's artwork from Gaiman's graphic novel. The oppressively drab colour palette in *Coraline*'s 'real-world' scenes – replete with dull, craggy landscapes, rough-hewn deciduous trees, and ominously dark clouds – register an immediate and radical departure from the bright tones and graphic richness which are the hallmarks of the Pixar style.

Figure 5.1   The unconventional child and her grey, barren everyday world (*Coraline*, Laika, 2009). Frame grab.

Furthermore, Selick's recruiting of a Japanese artist, Tadahiro Uesugi, to produce concept art for the film represents an attempt to internationalise the film's aesthetic, broadening the expressive range of Hollywood animation beyond Disney-style hyper-realism. Uesugi consciously made the film's fantasy landscape more colourful and vibrant than the 'real world' (thus building on films like *The Wizard of Oz* [Victor Fleming, 1939], where the shift from monochrome to colour is literal). In this sense, at least, the Laika films perhaps come closest among mainstream Hollywood animated features to realising Paul Wells's conviction that 'animation as a film language and film art is a more sophisticated and flexible medium than live-action film, and thus offers a greater opportunity for film-makers to be more imaginative and less conservative'.[12] *New York Times* critic A. O. Scott identified stylistic influences in *Coraline* from more avant-garde stylists such as David Lynch, director of *Eraserhead* (1977) and *Mulholland Drive* (2001), and Guillermo Del Toro, director of *Pan's Labyrinth* (2006). But he also found resemblance at the level of narrative as well: 'Mr. Selick is interested in childhood not as a condition of sentimentalized, passive innocence but rather as an active, seething state of receptivity in which consciousness itself is a site of wondrous, at times unbearable drama'.[13]

In other regards, however, the narrative ideology of the Hollywood children's horror film is largely conventional. Although the films may appear to give free rein to the Freudian Uncanny, disturbing or horrific elements are tightly regulated: these are still family films, adhering largely to the structural norms of the wider genre. *The Nightmare Before Christmas* and *Coraline*, for instance, remain clear examples of the 'circular journey' narrative structure, which, according to Maria Nikolajeva, 'can be traced in practically any children's text'.[14] In this story pattern the central child (or childlike) figure leaves home and embarks on a journey to another place (which is often fantastical), encounters difficulties and hardships, but ultimately returns home with newfound skills and psychological maturity.[15] Lewis Carroll's *Alice's Adventures in Wonderland* (1865), L. Frank Baum's *The Wonderful Wizard of Oz* (1900) and J. M. Barrie's *Peter Pan* (1911) are notable examples of this narrative pattern, as are most of the Disney features. Several of these films also exemplify Bruno Bettelheim's belief in fairy tale as a therapeutic mechanism through which real-world anxieties can be managed psychologically and overcome. Bettelheim's proposition that 'the form and structure of fairy tales suggest images to the child by which he [sic] can structure his daydreams and with them give better direction to his life' is borne out in the narrative trajectory of *Coraline* and *ParaNorman*, which underscore their young protagonists' ultimate psychological shift from unhappiness and boredom to vibrancy and autonomy.[16]

As with Laika's later films, *Coraline* positions its child protagonist, Coraline Jones (Dakota Fanning), as a mild non-conformist. Her name – easily confused with that of Caroline, the kind of 'ordinary' name she despises – registers an unusual quality, as does her appearance (blue-haired, wearing a bright yellow raincoat), her brandishing of a dowsing rod in the early scenes, and calling her friends in Michigan her 'best trolls'. In contrast, her family name (Jones) and parents' occupations (editors of a gardening catalogue) are resolutely prosaic. Moody and discontented, Coraline's main source of unhappiness seems to be the division of parental roles between her parents. Her mother (Teri Hatcher) is brusque and inaccessible, consumed with her work. Her father (John Hodgman) is more accommodating but defers to the authority of her mother. When Mr Jones dishes out some unappetising food at the dinner table, Coraline asks, 'Why don't *you* ever cook, mom?' Mrs Jones replies, impatiently, 'Coraline, we've been through this before. Your dad cooks, I clean, and you stay out of the way.' Mrs Jones thus appears, to her daughter, to be abnegating her maternal duties.

This paves the way for Coraline's adventures in the Other World, which contain apparently kindlier, more attentive versions of her parents – outwardly perfect except for the disturbing detail that their eyes have been replaced by buttons sown into their heads. As in children's fantasy novels such as Catherine Storr's *Marianne Dreams* (1958), the adolescent girl's adventures in the Other World are manifestations of unconscious fantasies that must be worked through. (The fact that Coraline's 'Other Father' rides a giant mechanical praying mantis is pertinent in light of the fact that a mantis prop is earlier seen on Coraline's bedside table.) On some levels, this Other World is mere wish-fulfilment: the simulacra of Coraline's parents initially appear much more appealing than the genuine articles, with her 'Other Father' telling her that 'Everything's right in this world, kiddo'. Moreover, the fantasy gives free rein to her own narcissism, with the Jones's bare, wintery garden transformed into a wondrous parade of tropical flowers and birds that, when viewed from a distance, resembles Coraline's own face.

Inevitably, Coraline discovers that this fantasy world is too good to be true. Having been alarmed by the Other Mother's desire to sew buttons into her eyes, Coraline then discovers the ghosts of other children locked in a hidden room in the Other World. In chorus, they explain that the 'Beldam' – the Other Mother – 'spied on our lives through the little doll's eyes and saw that we weren't happy. So she lured us away with treasures and treats and games to play. Gave all that we asked, yet we still wanted more.' The fact that the Other Mother literally loves these neglected children to death invokes the didacticism of the old aphorism, 'be careful what you wish for'. It also avails the classical children's fictional trope of the circular journey as a narrative mechanism through which the child can reconcile themselves to the necessities, if not exactly the pleasures, of their everyday world ('there's no place like home'). It is only after Coraline loses her parents (when the Other Mother kidnaps them) that she learns to appreciate them. For the first time in her life, we presume, she puts their welfare above her own, returning to the Other World in an attempt to save them, and dismissing her realisation that she is walking into a trap by reiterating, simply, 'They are my parents.'

The Other Mother's desire to sew buttons into Coraline's eyes may well represent an attempt to infantilise the adolescent, or else forcibly to repress maturation and suspend her in permanent childhood. The Other Mother informs Coraline that she can remain forever in the Other World, and Other Father tells her that 'We'll sing and play games, and Mother will cook your favourite meals'. The substitution of buttons for eyes surely represents a macabre metaphor for childhood, representing the sublimation of individuality to doll-like conformism and impassivity; an image of perfection with all the edges smoothed over ('Our little doll', as the Other Mother calls Coraline while handing over the buttons). If the Other Mother's seeming kindly solicitude represents Coraline's fantasy of ideal parenthood where the mother, not the father, cooks and cleans, the Coraline-doll ('Other Me', as Coraline calls it) might imply a parallel, if presumably suppressed desire on the part of her real mother for a more demure, obedient, 'ordinary' daughter, an impossible, Shirley Temple-type image of ideal girlhood rather than the awkward contrarianism and sexual awakenings embodied by the adolescent Coraline.

Coraline's eventual psychological maturation is confirmed by an exchange with her mother at the end of the film that revisits a previous point of contention between them. In an earlier sequence, Coraline selects a blue colour scheme (the same colour as her hair) for her school uniform rather than the typical grey. When her mother refuses to accede, Coraline protests: 'The whole school's gonna wear boring, grey clothes. No one will have these.' Mrs Jones is unmoved, but tells Coraline that if the book pitch is successful she will 'make it up'; an apathetic Coraline replies, 'That's what you always say.' At the end of the film, Coraline's mother gives her a gift of the gloves that she had earlier been refused, as if to suggest that the two characters – although different in many regards – are willing to compromise for the sake of their relationship. But as with many fantasy films, the narrative allows the child protagonist to retains elements of the Other World despite their return to 'our' world. In the final sequence, the barren, wintery landscape is replaced by spring-like fecundity, mother and father are seen planting flowers, and all of the family's eccentric neighbours are gathered round for a garden party. The Freudian pleasure principle, then, is not absolutely supplanted by the reality principle. Equally, Coraline's friendship with the similarly awkward adolescent, Wyborne (Robert Bailey Jr), is back on track, and she even remarks, 'I'm glad you decided to stalk me.' Laika's films are replete with moments in which perversity is reaffirmed within clearly defined limits. While the primacy of the nuclear family has been reasserted, there is space in this offbeat, topsy-turvy universe for the unconventional and the absurd.

Laika's next film, *ParaNorman* – sold by the filmmakers as 'John-Carpenter-meets-John-Hughes' – occupies much of the same terrain.[17] As with Coraline Jones, Norman (Kodi Smit-McPhee) is a youthful non-conformist on the cusp of adolescence. The opening scene of the film sees him watching a gory zombie movie, and fruitlessly attempting to explain the conventions of the genre to his elderly grandmother (Elaine Stritch). When his mother (Leslie Mann) asks him what he has been watching, he responds, impishly, 'sex and violence'. Although Manohla Dargis, in her *New York Times* review of the film, describes Norman as 'an unreconstructed little weirdo', he is an agreeable child, immediately acceding to his father's (Jeff Garlin) request that he takes out the garbage.[18] These children are not rebels in the James Dean mould, they are 'normal' people with diverse interests who reject the wholesome, ingratiating model of childhood typically advanced in classic children's fiction. Norman himself alludes to the less-desirable alternative of youth delinquency when he responds to his father's remark, 'Can't you be like other kids your age and pitch a tent in the yard or have a healthy interest in carpentry?' with the pithy retort, 'I thought you said kids my age were too busy shoplifting and joyriding?' The message here is not only for children who feel excluded, but also for parents who vainly desire 'normality' in their offspring. As with *Coraline* and *Frankenweenie*, on one level the film can be seen as a celebration of difference. *ParaNorman* does not hold back in portraying the social impact of this non-conformity: Norman is shunned by most children at school (everyone in the playground turns to stare at him in unison when he arrives, and the word 'freak' is scrawled on his locker) and is the subject of ridicule and dismay in equal measure amongst his immediate family.

While *Coraline*'s aesthetic is heavily indebted to gothic expressionism and draws on recognisable traditions of fairy tale animated film, *ParaNorman* is less self-consciously 'dark', and also appropriates several conventions of live-action cinematography. In one sequence, a dolly zoom (popularly known as a 'vertigo shot') is employed when a character opens a door and unexpectedly finds a zombie on the other side. The shot serves two functions. On one level, it utilises a stylistic device widely associated with horror and suspense cinema to evoke shock and unease. As Lester notes, *Coraline* uses similar techniques, employing voyeuristic point-of-view shots that suggest the 'assaultive gaze' of a killer.[19] However, for cine-literate audiences these intertextual cinematographic appropriations fulfil a contrary function, diffusing tension through the use of parody: there are almost identical shots in films such as *Vertigo* (Alfred Hitchcock, 1958) and, particularly, *Jaws* (Steven Spielberg, 1975), when the police chief realises that the shark is attacking children playing in the water. Like live-action family films such as *E.T.* (Spielberg, 1982), *ParaNorman* also employs numerous point-of-view shots and camera set-ups at the height of the child protagonist's face to facilitate the viewer's identification with the character. In one early scene, Norman is stuck between his bickering mother and father, and the camera lingers on his face tracing his response as he is framed by their flabby midriffs. The camera then follows a disconsolate Norman as he walks away, and the point of audition remains with him as he overhears his over-zealous father expounding on his perceived oddness:

> FATHER: I'm nothing if I'm not liberal, but that limp-wristed hippie gar
> bage needs to be nipped in the bud. This behaviour might be ok with
> your side of the family, but I'm not putting up with it any more. Not
> me! This isn't the west coast, Sandra. People talk, they do.
> MOTHER: He's just sensitive, Perry.
> FATHER: Oh, please! Sensitive is writing poetry and being lousy at team
> sports.

Point-of-view editing is also used during the film's most notorious instance of comic abjection, when Norman goes to the house of his deceased Uncle Prenderghast (John Goodman) to retrieve a book held in the dead man's hands. Rigor mortis having set in, Norman struggles to release the book from Prenderghast's hands; eventually he hauls the man to his feet and pulls the book clear, but the cadaver then falls on top of Norman, pinning him to the ground. Moments later, Prenderghast's tongue lolls out on to Norman's horrified face (Figure 5.2). The entire scene might easily be pitched as dark comedy but for the lightness of the music that underpins it, which creates an ironic counterpoint to the action.

Figure 5.2　The abjection of Prenderghast's tongue lolling on to Norman's horrified
face (*ParaNorman*, Laika, 2012). Frame grab.

Thematically, the film is a parable of tolerance (if not outright acceptance) of difference, and a repudiation of violence, bigotry, populism and mob sentiment. Eventually, Norman discovers that the demonic entity that periodically haunts the town is the vengeful spirit of Agatha Prenderghast (Jodelle Ferland), an 11-year-old girl who was burned for suspected witchcraft in the eighteenth century. Norman successfully reasons with Agatha by accusing her of the same crimes as her oppressors: bullying, bigotry and violence. Yet the film is at pains to emphasise that the zealotry that drove the eighteenth-century townspeople to kill Agatha still abides in the twenty-first century, with shots of torch-wielding maniacs threatening to kill Norman because he appears to be in collusion with supernatural entities. A gesture towards overcoming prejudice is made by Norman's cheerleader older sister, Courtney (Anna Kendrick), who seems to represent the 'typical' American teenager in her preoccupation with boys and fashion. She addresses the crowd with an appeal to listen to Norman (for the first time in his life); Norman's friends Neil (Tucker Albrizzi), Mitch (Casey Affleck) and Alvin (Christopher Mintz-Plasse) then join her in her appeal, Mitch pointing out, 'All you wanna do is burn and murder stuff, burn and murder stuff; just burning and murdering.' Norman underlines the point (made repeatedly in George A. Romero's films) that the zombies are 'just like you'. Neil, who ascribes his victimhood to the fact that 'I'm fat. And my allergies make my eyes leak. And I sweat when I walk too fast. And I have a lunch box with a kitten on it. Ooh! And I have irritable bowel syndrome,' makes the telling observation, 'You can't stop bullying; it's part of human nature. If you were bigger and more stupid, you'd probably be a bully too.' In the film's final scene, with Agatha appeased and the zombies no longer haunting the town, Neil asks whether everything will return to normal; Norman replies, 'Well, as normal as it could be.'

Alongside *Zootopia* (Byron Howard and Rich Moore, 2016), *Coraline* and *ParaNorman* remain the most overt reaffirmations of cultural diversity in mainstream Hollywood animation. Liberal discourses and child psychology have both asserted the inherent plurality of childhood and the need to understand and encourage degrees of difference. Whereas post-1990s Disney releases have tended to interpret difference largely in terms of race and gender, the children's horror films acknowledge a rather different form of deviation, subverting representational norms of childhood innocence. The innocent child archetype has long constrained representations of children and childhood in popular fiction, disallowing engagement with seemingly unwholesome realities (e.g. death, a primary focus of both *ParaNorman* and *Frankenweenie*) or supposedly adult preoccupations such as violence or sex. Unusually, *ParaNorman* makes an explicit allusion to sexual maturation when the gauche adolescent, Neil, is seen eating popcorn while watching a freeze-framed image of a lycra-clad woman's buttocks on his mother's aerobics video. (The joke, admittedly, is facilitated by the fact that Neil is figured as a comically grotesque character in his own right, being morbidly obese and disgusting in his personal habits – 'gross' in every sense of the word.) But the point is that childhood is not a homogenous category, and each child must learn to come to terms with their own identities and their place in the world. Both Coraline and Norman are eventually accepted by their families, friends and neighbours, having initially been marginalised and assaulted for their failure to ascribe to broader social conventions of child behaviour.

Arguably, the process of learning amongst these films' adult characters is at least as important: they must begin to listen to the children, not simply cosset them with outdated or otherwise misguided preconceptions of 'ideal' childhood. In the process, the eccentric or sometimes bizarre proclivities of these characters become normalised. Moreover, the socialisation process is seen as dialogic – adults learn lessons about tolerance and forgiveness from children whose minds are comparatively open and unprejudiced. To some degree, this dynamic hearkens back to the Romantic conceptions of the child as untainted by worldly corruption and thus embodying a morality that is pure and natural. But it also reflects a more historically specific pious hope in the potential of children – the next generation – to transform society for the better.

These films thus tend to represent the prevailing tenets of US liberalism: freedom and individualism bound up with sexual and racial egalitarianism; acceptance of diversity in its many forms (within specific moral constraints); resistance to cultural as to social homogeneity; and a belief in a better future that must, nonetheless, be pursued and worked for. All of the film's children – the strange but gentle and perspicacious Norman, the obese, kindly and gregarious Neil, the quintessential all-American cheerleader Courtney, the stereotypical jock Mitch (who is finally revealed as gay in a comically unexpected reversal in the penultimate scene), and the imbecilic, rap-loving school bully Alvin – learn to accept each other's non-conformities. Conversely, the brief scene at the end of the film where various townspeople attempt to absolve themselves of responsibility for their murderous rampage seems to echo the murderous actions of their eighteenth-century counterparts who were responsible for Agatha's death. This suggests that human nature is slow to change, if it ever changes at all, and gestures towards a broader struggle for a future of tolerance and freedom from bigotry that perhaps can never be attained. The scene in which a policewoman, remonstrating with a member of the public shooting at zombies, exclaims, 'What do you think you're doing firing at civilians? That is for the police to do!' may be an amusing joke, but the satire is difficult to stomach given the everyday realities of marginalised and vulnerable groups being targeted by police in the United States. It is an unusual moment of mild political subversion in a Hollywood family film, where the arms of the state have tended to be unimpeachable.

Frankenweenie is similarly ambivalent in its attitudes towards adult authority and the institutions of society as forces for good. The film is a remake of Burton's 1984 Disney live-action short of the same name, which had not been considered suitable for child audiences and led to Burton's dismissal from the studio (or his forced resignation, depending on the source). As the title implies, it is a semi-comic retelling of Mary Shelley's *Frankenstein* (1818), except that the adult scientist is reimagined as a boy genius, Victor (Charlie Tahan), who is obsessed with reanimating Sparky, his beloved dog, after it is killed in a road accident. As in *Coraline* and *ParaNorman*, the central child figure is a socially withdrawn adolescent whose interests are viewed by the parents as unhealthy. Having watched Victor's homemade monster movie pastiche, his father (Martin Short) observes, 'A boy his age needs to be outside with his friends', to which his mother (Catherine O'Hara) replies: 'I don't know that Victor has friends, dear. Other than Sparky.' Father responds, 'I don't want him to turn out, you know . . . weird.' As in *Coraline* and *ParaNorman*, accepted images of childhood normalcy – a state characterised by Romantic conceptions of innocence and pre-sexual adventure – are invoked as a model against which the 'unconventional child' is positioned. Both films delight in comic abjection. In *Frankenweenie*, children's beloved pets are transformed into monstrous destructive forces, subverting the children's fictional convention that animals are benign and share a natural affinity with children. And both films culminate in scenes of enraged townsfolk descending into mob violence having erroneously identified the central character as the source of the supernatural happenings.

Despite their similarities, there is an important difference between the two films. *ParaNorman* is an allegory of accepting difference in a society that upholds conformity (or at least the appearance of it); the central child is alienated from society by supernatural abilities that represent 'Otherness'. In *Frankenweenie*, by contrast, Otherness represents virtually the totality of society, despite the conventional suburban setting that the film shares with Burton's own *Edward Scissorhands*, another quintessential narrative of suburban dysfunction. Whereas *ParaNorman* juxtaposes its extraordinary events with a familiar, recognisable suburban milieu, the logic at the heart of *Frankenweenie* is topsy-turvy, with the central child residing in a gothic shadow world in which almost every member of the local suburban community is a grotesque, from the gaunt, East European science teacher, Mr Rzykruski (Martin Landau), to the sinister, foreign-accented humpbacked schoolboy, Edgar (Atticus Shaffer).

Again, though, it is the outwardly 'normal' inhabitants of the community that are the most dangerous. The film channels the local community's distrust for Victor's invention into a comment on the dangers of anti-intellectualism. The outwardly sinister but nonetheless inspirational Mr Rzykruski is harangued at a community meeting for imparting strange and supposedly dangerous ideas to children in his class. One of the local parents laments that her daughter has been 'asking all sorts of strange questions about things I've never even heard of'. The teacher then addresses the audience:

> Ladies, gentlemen, I think the confusion here is that you are all very igno-
> rant. Is that right word, 'ignorant'? I mean 'stupid', 'primitive', 'unen-
> lightened'. You do not understand science, so you are afraid of it like a
> dog is afraid of thunder or balloons. To you science is magic and witch-
> craft because you have such small minds. I cannot make your heads bigger
> but your children's heads – I can take them and crack them open. This is
> what I try to do: to get at their brains!

Subsequently, Rzykruski is sacked from his position and replaced by a clearly incompetent gymnastics teacher who brazenly admits 'Sometimes knowing too much is the problem'. A later exchange between Rzykruski and Victor charac-terises the problem as a cultural one:

> RZYKRUSKI: Back home everyone is a scientist. Even my plumber wins
> Nobel Prize. Your country does not make enough scientist. Always
> needs more. You should be a scientist, Victor.
> VICTOR: Nobody likes scientists.
> RZYKRUSKI: They like what science gives them, but not the questions,
> no. Not the questions that science asks.

Just as the film clearly equates science with reasoned thought and rational-ism, the problems in society are attributed to ideological populism. The nor-mative institutions of socialisation are stripped of moral agency: government is represented by the appallingly authoritarian and anti-intellectual mayor, Mr Burgemeister (Martin Short), the local school is ruled by fear of scientific advancement, and, most tellingly, the film implicitly disavows religion – one of the ideological pillars of socialisation – through its secular refusal to condemn Victor's resurrecting his deceased pet. (Rather, the somewhat vague suggestion is that humanity must use science responsibly.) Victor's father's admission that 'Sometimes adults don't know what they're talking about' might be seen as a shorthand concession that the hierarchies of authority between children and adults are more tenuous than they used to be, or, alternatively, that they *ought* to be more tenuous than they actually are. It also underlines the fact that the film's moral centre does not abide with adults, and sometimes not even with parents. Victor, like Norman, possesses insight that grown-ups do not. The scene in which the town's adults assist Victor in resuscitating Sparky under-lines this broader point. If all of these films are narratives of individuation, self-expression and tolerance, they also allegorise (or anticipate) the emanci-pation of bright, resourceful and independent children from social structures that work to nullify difference. To a large degree, then, these 'children's horror' films are parables of individualism – the qualities possessed by these children are seen as important to a functioning, multicultural democratic system.

The obvious similarities between *ParaNorman* and *Frankenweenie* – which were released in close proximity to one another – might go some way to explaining their relative underperformance at the box office: *ParaNorman* was a modest hit; *Frankenweenie* a slight loss-maker after costs. Alternatively, it may be that macabre, stylistically quirky films that extol the virtues of non-conformist pursuits simply do not appeal strongly to mainstream audiences. Laika's third children's horror feature, *The Boxtrolls*, also underperformed at the box office. Furthermore, the film's release was widely viewed by the critics as the point at which Laika tipped over into self-parody with its insistent foregrounding of the grotesque and the macabre. The strategy of product differentiation underpinning the Laika business model was picked up by numerous critics, one of whom remarked that the film 'seems to have been masterminded by people thinking, "Everyone loves Pixar. So let's do everything the opposite!"'.[20] Adapted from English children's author Alan Snow's best-selling 2005 novel, *Here Be Monsters!*, *The Boxtrolls* bears close comparison with the feature films of the British animation studio, Aardman, which similarly trades on a marketable vision of an eccentric Britishness – marked by a curious juxtaposition of quaintness and grotesquery – that is temporally and culturally removed from the milieu of contemporary America. Where the film clearly divagates from the earlier children's horror films discussed in this section is that it is almost impossible to place it within the context of twenty-first-century America. Set in the fictional country of 'Norvenia', *The Boxtrolls* develops a pseudo-gothic steampunk aesthetic that corresponds to Laika's differentiation from Disney/Pixar hyperrealism. However, the deliberate, cultivated oddness of the world it evokes serves to dislocate the film from its socio-cultural contexts.

The human protagonist of *The Boxtrolls*, a boy called Eggs (Isaac Hempstead Wright) – so named because he wears a large egg box in lieu of standard human clothing – is yet another iteration of Laika's 'unconventional child'. Abandoned as an infant and raised by the eponymous Boxtrolls, benign subterranean troll-like creatures that are hated and feared by the city-dwelling humans, Eggs subverts and reaffirms the Victorian child archetype in equal measure. He is dirty, occasionally destructive, and assuredly 'gross' in his personal habits; simultaneously, however, he is artless, unaffected and unequivocally morally good. In an early scene, he is given a teddy bear as a present by his surrogate father, the Boxtroll Fish (Dee Bradley Baker), but after holding it tight to his face momentarily, Eggs tears off its head and pulls out a clockwork music box from inside; he greedily partakes in a banquet of live creepy-crawlies with the other Boxtrolls, and later scratches at his genitals in public, drawing a harsh rebuke from the prim-and-proper city-dwelling Winnie (Elle Fanning), who exclaims

'You don't scratch there in public! That's why they're called "privates"!'. He elicits shock and disgust at an aristocratic soirée when his lack of socialisation manifests itself in a number of graceless faux pas, including repeatedly kissing, then innocently licking, a lady's hand, and stuffing his face with cheese before he realises that a number of guests are looking at him with disapproval, where-upon he regurgitates the food back on to a plate. Much of the film's comedy is generated by behavioural transgressions of this type, a form of humour that is largely regressive, appealing both to the child's enjoyment in violating strict adult codes and to the willing adult's desire to withdraw, temporarily, from social codes of propriety. As with Laika's earlier releases, the film's strategies of double address rest more on comic abjection than on intertextual allusive-ness in the manner of DreamWorks and Aardman, although there is an isolated comic intertextual allusion: in one sequence Eggs tumbles out of his box, and the other Boxtrolls immediately turn and point at him while emitting a piercing shriek, in parody of the aliens' attack siren in the 1970s remake of the horror classic, *Invasion of the Body Snatchers* (Philip Kaufman, 1978).

The film's story concerns the efforts of Boxtroll exterminator and aspiring social climber, Snatcher (Ben Kingsley), to wipe out the creatures and establish himself as a member of the elite White Hats society, which is led by the town's leader, Lord Portley-Rind (Jared Harris) and concerns itself only in the cease-less pursuit and consumption of exotic forms of cheese. The rulers' fixation with cheese is clearly a metonymy for power and privilege, and their subjuga-tion of the Boxtrolls is equally interpretable – deliberately so, I would suggest – as an assault on marginalised peoples in contemporary society. But the cheese fetishism is mostly sourced for comic grotesquery: Snatcher, despite his obses-sion with cheese, is also violently allergic to it, but periodically eats it anyway (to the despair of his lackeys) as part of his wish-fulfilment fantasy of rising up the social ladder. His face horribly reddened and swollen, Snatcher insists, 'I belong up there in the tasting room, chomping on the choicest cheeses, every-one in town bowing down to me, not a gentleman, a lord!' At the film's climax, Snatcher's inability to resist eating a rare cheese, despite having already swol-len to enormous proportions, leads to him literally exploding. Yet this horrific moment is prefaced by a serious homily, in which Eggs advises Snatcher: 'Don't do it. It won't change who you are. Cheese, hats, boxes – they don't make you. *You* make you.'

Despite its unconventional surface pleasures, the valorisation of ideal par-enthood developed by the film remains ideologically conventional, articulating the potential strengths of non-nuclear and otherwise unconventional fam-ily structures in the manner of other Laika releases (and post-1990s anima-tion more broadly). At one point, Winnie lists desirable attributes in a father: 'Someone who'll do anything to help you. They always listen and never get angry. They guide you when you don't know what to do. They're there when it's dark, when you're scared or lonely. And they are never, ever too busy to talk to you.' Eggs then replies, 'Like Fish?' and a point-of-view shot shows Eggs looking directly at the Boxtroll who had raised Eggs as an adopted son despite their biological and cultural differences and who returns his glance. Conversely, the distant, self-regarding Lord Portley-Rind is clearly figured as a bad father. It is only at the end of the film, after Winnie has turned Snatcher's gruesome demise into a macabre song-and-dance performance for the whole town, that Portley-Rind resumes his paternal duties. Her taking delight in the grotesque detail ('Trapped in his sweaty armpit until he swelled like a balloon and pop! An ocean of guts exploded over us like a hurricane of yuck!') appears to liberate Portley-Rind from the burden of presiding over a conventional family; delighted, he greets her as 'My little angel! My weird little angel!'

The end of the film also posits a rapprochement between the humans and the Boxtrolls, with both groups happily co-habiting. The initially 'othered' creatures are apparently accepted, but not fully assimilated into society; the final shot of a Boxtroll disappearing into the sewers suggests that they retain their own culture and rituals. The social allegory is intended for any viewers who wish to claim it, and it is sufficiently broad as to be applicable to any number of real-world situations. The film's other two major social allegories – those of class and family relations – are dealt with less ambivalently. The eventual return of Eggs's father, long presumed deceased, restores a sense of ideological conservatism to the earlier vision of an orphaned child raised by a sympathetic but monstrous-looking personification of 'Otherness'. The film does not wholly negate Fish's symbolic fatherhood, with the final scene showing Eggs, his father and Fish all riding out of town listening to the Italian opera LP that the Boxtrolls had listened to while working underground. Rather, it delineates a tripartite family arrangement that acknowledges the prevalence of non-nuclear structures but remains avowedly unorthodox. As with all the Laika films, the ultimate model for contemporary society appears, broadly speaking, to be one of 'sameness with difference': family and friendship continue to be upheld as pillars of society, but their definitions have expanded to encompass all forms of benevolent non-conformity.

The children's horror cycle responds to a number of socio-cultural trends in contemporary America. One of these is the rise of so-called 'identity politics', a phenomenon explored in the previous chapter. Another has been the legitimisation of 'monster' narratives in children's and youth fiction that allegorise the dialectics of marginalisation and integration of social groups that are labelled, or label themselves, as different from mainstream norms. We might trace the rise of sympathetic monster narratives to 1960s family sitcoms such as *The Addams Family* (1964–6) and *The Munsters* (1964–6), or the children's books of Roald Dahl. But these early examples of sympathetic monstrosity work largely by comic inversion of acceptability; they extract humour from the juxtaposition of perversion with the appearance of normalcy. There is no implication that these families' behaviours would be tolerable in the 'real world'. In contrast, many of these later films present the 'monsters' themselves as ordinary, or as ordinary as can be expected in a society that is rotten to the core. They reflect a more contemporary attitude towards society as fractured, dysfunctional, conflicted and amoral, embodying Jiddu Krishnamurti's famous observation that 'it is no measure of health to be well-adjusted to a profoundly sick society'. A parallel body of recent fiction – e.g. Stephanie Meyer's *Twilight* novels (2005–8) and the TV series *Being Human* (UK 2008–13; US 2011–14) – also establishes humans and 'monsters' as essentially conterminous. The latter position is also implied by children's horror films in which humans and monsters engage successfully in romantic union, such as the *Hotel Transylvania* films (2012–); as Dracula (Adam Sandler) nonchalantly remarks in *Hotel Transylvania 3: Summer Vacation* (Genndy Tartakovsky, 2018), 'Humans, monsters, what's the difference?'

'INDIEWOOD' ANIMATION

The films under discussion in this section can be located within the post-1990s 'indiewood' tradition in US popular cinema. As the term implies, 'indiewood' describes the broad convergence of the low-budget, prestige 'indie' film tradition of the 1980s and the mainstream Hollywood studio apparatus. In industrial terms, this process of convergence was a gradual one; Hollywood studios had provided funds towards the Sundance Festival, the largest 'independent' film festival in the United States, from its inception, and most studios financed and distributed nominally independent films throughout the 1980s. But the major industry watershed was Disney's acquisition of Miramax in 1993. Quentin Tarantino's *Pulp Fiction* (1994), funded and distributed by Disney via Miramax, was the film that announced 'indiewood' as a dominant aesthetic style and industrial reality, blurring 'the boundary between mainstream Hollywood product and the independent fringe'.[21] As Geoff King explains, indiewood films contain 'features associated with dominant, mainstream conventions and markers of "distinction" designed to appeal to more particular, niche audience constituencies'.[22] According to Yannis Tzioumakis, common characteristics of indiewood production include the presence of established stars, the use of a strongly recognisable generic framework, an appeal to well-defined niche audiences, and an emphasis on authorship (e.g. a directorial 'brand' or signature).[23] These elements are all apparent in the films under discussion in this section – particularly those of Wes Anderson. (The other dominant textual feature of indiewood, in Tzioumakis's estimation – the pronounced presence of sex and violence – is generally absent even in Anderson's more 'adult' releases.)

Ultimately, each of the indiewood animated features define themselves through their alterity; the impression that they represent something that is distinct from the mainstream orthodoxy. Whereas the children's horror films appear to be aimed at disaffected or marginalised youth, the indie films avowedly target groups which reject unsophisticated, lowest-common-denominator entertainment (hipsters, ironists, literati, cineastes, and so on). But if the children's horror films are centrally concerned with the politics of identity, then the indiewood films are built on implicit hierarchies of taste and distinction. There is broad overlap between James MacDowell's identification of the 'quirky' impulse of many post-millennial indiewood films and Michael Z. Newman's category of 'movies for hipsters'. In a sense, both scholars approach similar territory from different perspectives: MacDowell is concerned largely with identifying shared generic features,[24] while Newman analyses the textual strategies the films employ to mobilise the so-called 'hipster' audience.[25] MacDowell suggests that the 'quirky' indie cycle shares several recurrent aspects, including

> (1) a combination of varied comic styles such as deadpan, comedy-of-embarrassment and slapstick; (2) a type of 'self-consciousness' in visual style which hints at a sense of surreal artificiality and/or fastidious neatness; (3) a thematic preoccupation with childhood and innocence; and, perhaps most importantly, (4) a tone that is often concerned to create tensions between 'ironic' distance from and 'sincere' engagement with protagonists.[26]

Although MacDowell refers primarily to live-action films, these traits (and the fourth one in particular) are highly prominent in the animated features under discussion here. Newman argues that there is a natural affinity between 'indie' and 'hipster', since 'to be indie is to aspire to hipness, and to be a hipster is to invest one's identity in the aesthetic legitimacy of indie'.[27] Such films are seen as artefacts of late modernity, as Newman points out:

> Millennials come of age in a time of allegedly 'post everything': post-Fordist, post-industrial, post-consensus society, but also postfeminist, postracial, and post-modern culture. Theirs is a hypersaturated consumer capitalism and also a world of fluid identities and hyperconsciousness of cultural difference, meritocracy, and egalitarianism, particularly within the privileged communities of white, elite cosmopolitanism culture wherein educational institutions promote such ideals as received wisdom.[28]

The corollary of this is a social condition in which individual and group identities are thrown into question, and the socio-cultural boundaries between childhood and adulthood are blurred. Many of the textual features of the 'hipster' cycle Newman identifies – particularly 'the prolongation of childhood into adulthood' and, by extension, the perpetuation of 'consumer identities of youth into adulthood' – have been applied to Western consumer culture more broadly by critics such as Benjamin Barber, and in my own work on family entertainment and 'kidult' culture.[29]

Seen in this light, there is a natural affinity between Hollywood indie hipsterism and contemporary Hollywood animation. Indeed, with its frequently ironic, postmodern 'hip' sensibility, orientation towards youth and simultaneous affiliation with 'kidult' culture, post-1990s Hollywood animation may be the natural home for this mode of contemporary cinema. Newman sees Wes Anderson as 'embody[ing] hipness and hipsterism', but we might view Anderson's animated films not as isolated forays into another medium, but as the truest expressions of his creative drive.[30] Peter C. Kunze has identified numerous intertexts of children's literature and culture even in ostensibly adult-oriented Anderson films, such as *The Royal Tenenbaums* (2001) and *The Life Aquatic with Steve Zissou* (2004),[31] while Newman notes the 'frequent idealisation' of childhood in his oeuvre.[32] No doubt these intertextual borrowings are deliberate, to a point, but we must also view Anderson's films in context of a contemporary culture that, in Barber's words, develops 'an ethos of induced childishness: an infantilisation that is closely tied to the demands of consumer capitalism in a global market economy'.[33] As the population of the developed world ages, Barber observes, 'the definition of youth simply moves up'.[34] Yet the indie films' blatant fascination with (and nostalgia for) childhood does not manifest itself merely in simple-minded 'childishness'. Indeed, *Fantastic Mr. Fox* and *Isle of Dogs*, as with *Rango*, are relatively sophisticated narratives replete with textual strategies that appeal, semi-ironically, to adults, and thereby run the risk of alienating child audiences.

There is a strong curational aspect to the indie animated films. The *mise-en-scène* are highly determined (all the films having been several years in the making) yet avowedly artisanal; Anderson's stop-motion films, in particular, are rough-hewn, full of textures and detail that implicitly disavow plasticity. The films also contain many cultural signifiers that align them with hipster culture and bespeak 'quirky' as a sensibility. The voice casts are studded with icons of indie Hollywood, such as George Clooney, Jason Schwartzman, Bill Murray, Scarlett Johansson and Johnny Depp. As with Anderson's live-action features, *Fantastic Mr. Fox* features an achingly hip, but nostalgic, soundtrack featuring 'retro' artists such as The Beach Boys, The Rolling Stones and Art Tatum. Newman points out that this kind of curational work asks the spectator to appreciate the assemblage of 'perfectly ironic or beautiful or nostalgically charming images and sounds', inviting us 'to share a taste culture' with the filmmakers or the film's characters, or at least 'aspire to do so'.[35] Pierre Bourdieu theorised that one of the ways individuals may accumulate 'cultural capital' is through investment in 'higher' cultural forms that reflect positively on 'the quality of the person, which is affirmed in the capacity to appropriate an object of quality', such as theatre-going, or partaking in art-house films.[36] Art films do this, in part, by providing pleasures that cannot easily be decoded. In other words, they can only be understood – *fully understood*, at least – by consumers who possess 'higher' levels of aesthetic taste, intelligence and learning.

As we saw in Chapter 3, a version of this practice can be seen in contemporary Hollywood animated films that employ intertextual strategies that can only be comprehended by audiences able to 'decode' their allusions. The indiewood films operate in a slightly different way: they are hardly highbrow, but much of their appeal is in the slightly snobbish rejection of the more 'obvious' pleasures of Disney and Pixar. *Variety* speculated that *Fantastic Mr. Fox* may attract people 'who would rather drive a 1953 Jaguar XK 120 than a new one'.[37] Indeed, the discourses that have surrounded these films have tended to emphasise their quirkiness and experimentalism, attributes that are bound up with the perception of the films as 'quality' cinema. As with the children's horror cycle, this high esteem is partly related to the films' supposed rejection of the sentimentalism and commercialism of mainstream Hollywood. For example, *Variety* described *Fantastic Mr. Fox* as 'the season's defiantly anti-CGI toon'.[38] Equally, the *New York Times* viewed it as Anderson's 'most fully realized and satisfying film', rationalising its incongruity with the mainstream aesthetic by observing that 'the point of everything Mr. Anderson has ever done is that truth and beauty reside in the odd, the mismatched, the idiosyncratic'.[39] The film scored two other notable registers of critical approval on its initial release, opening both the BFI London Film Festival and the AFI Festival in Hollywood.

Such accolades are rare for Hollywood animated features. Given traditional critical distaste for mass culture, it is significant that the indiewood films are not usually massively profitable, at least by the standards of Disney, Pixar and DreamWorks (*Fantastic Mr. Fox* recouped less than $50 million in worldwide theatrical grosses, against the initial outlay of $40 million). The relative box office failure of Anderson's films might also be attributed to their more adult-oriented pleasures. *Variety* suggested that it was the 'retro charms' of *Fantastic Mr. Fox* that would 'likely appeal more strongly to grown-ups than to moppets', whereas the *New York Post* noted that it was 'unusually dark for a family film'.[40] As these responses indicate, numerous critics have placed *Fantastic Mr. Fox* and *Isle of Dogs* within the auteurist context of Anderson's cinema, de-emphasising their credentials as family entertainment. Certainly, the generic identity of these films is slightly unclear. *Fantastic Mr. Fox*'s artisanal stop-motion aesthetic drew critical comparisons to *The Nightmare Before Christmas* (indeed, Anderson and Henry Selick originally planned to collaborate on the film), but the comparison is largely impressionistic, based on the fact that any major Hollywood features that break from the models of Disney/Pixar hyper-realism or DreamWorks 'narrative cartoonalism' tend to get bundled together. Other critics noted that *Fantastic Mr. Fox* exhibits 'stop-and-start rhythms' and 'scruffy looks' and is 'both precious and rough-hewn'.[41]

In focusing on the films' aesthetic attractions, however, their narrative and ideological conservatism has remained largely unacknowledged. Given Anderson's auteurist credentials, it may be surprising to find that *Fantastic Mr. Fox* is far less politically progressive than any of the children's horror films discussed above. While the stop-motion aesthetic is charmingly artisanal, its allusive style of humour is highly derivative of strategies employed in Pixar's and, especially, DreamWorks' films, and in Anderson's own live-action features. As with productions such as *Shrek*, it not only alludes to other popular texts in wide currency, but also draws heavily on self-reflexive metatextuality, signalling its own artifice with a series of fourth-wall-breaking jokes. For example, when Mr. Fox and his friends succeed in outwitting a group of human farmers, digging horizontally until they reach the chicken farm, British pop star Jarvis Cocker (or rather a stop-motion figurine of him) inexplicably appears, performing a song that narrates the action up to this point; at the end of the number, the villainous farmer, Mr Bean, berates Cocker for poor song-writing. At such points, the film treads a path between the quirky, self-referential mode of Anderson's live-action films and the intertextual comedy of post-1990s Hollywood animation. The film's politics, too, are identifiable within a more mainstream stratum of Hollywood family entertainment. Ultimately, it valorises what Ann Oakley has called 'the conventional family' with its emphasis on stable parenthood (eschewing individualistic desires when not explicitly in the service of the family) and a child that adheres to traditional registers of normalcy – in this case, the adolescent boy who is loyal, brave, impressive in his physicality and appears, in essence, as a younger and less evolved version of his father, demonstrating inter-generational continuity.[42]

Quirkiness aside, *Fantastic Mr. Fox* bears more comparison with Pixar's *The Incredibles* (Brad Bird, 2004) than the children's horror oeuvre. In both movies, an exaggeratedly masculine middle-aged protagonist is unwilling to relinquish a former life of adrenaline-pumping daredevil action and reconcile himself to an unfulfilling life of domesticity. In the film's opening scene, Mr Fox stands, laconically, against a tree on top of a hill, listening to 'The Ballad of Davy Crockett', a quintessential celebration of American individualism originally featured in Disney's 1950s miniseries, *Davy Crockett* (1954–5). Mr Fox views himself in a similar vein to the outlaw hero: as a cunning, powerful and indomitable 'man alone' who lives by his wits and whose innate skills can outmatch any opposition. The incompatibility between his individualistic desires and his patriarchal responsibilities is at the core of the narrative. At the insistence of his pregnant wife, Mr Fox gives up his career as a bird poacher (an occupation that puts him in constant danger of being shot by farmers) and begins writing a dull newspaper column that he is certain no one reads, embodying a classic middle-aged male malaise regarding the seeming futility of everyday life and the perceived, inexorable loss of potency.

Against the explicit advice of his wife and his lawyer, Mr Fox moves his family out of their underground burrow into a tree house adjacent to three villainous farmers, a move that is explicable only as an attempt to reinject some excitement into his life (he rationalises it by remarking that he is now aged seven, almost the age his father was when he died). He then begins secretly stealing from each of the farmers, to the point that they group together and attempt to kill the entire family. In the following scene, Mrs Fox berates her husband for his lack of responsibility as a husband and father. She rejects his justification that he is 'a wild animal', and – in an archly self-aware piece of dialogue – remarks that 'this story is too predictable [. . .] in the end we all die, unless you change'. Later, when it seems that he must hand himself over to the farmers to prevent them from eradicating their entire community, Mr Fox tries to explain himself to his wife: 'I think I have this thing where I need everyone to think I'm the greatest, the – quote unquote – "fantastic Mr Fox" – and if they aren't completely knocked out and dazzled and kind of intimidated by me then I don't feel good about myself.' Like prototypical Anderson male figures, such as Bill Murray's Bloom from *Rushmore* and Gene Hackman's Royal from *The Royal Tenenbaums*, Mr Fox is a representation of flawed, rugged American masculinity. But whereas those middle-aged men are motivated entirely by their own fantasies, Mr Fox – more typically for a mainstream Hollywood production – ends up sacrificing his own freedom for the sake of the family unit.

In the children's horror film, there is a definite thematic relation between style and ideology: the aesthetics reflect the subjectivity of characters who define themselves by an Otherness that is ultimately, and emphatically, unregenerate. Where *Fantastic Mr. Fox* differs is that its leftfield credentials scarcely go beyond its quirky veneer. In amalgamating the four children of Dahl's novel into one – an adolescent boy struggling to live up to the legacy of his father – the film reverts to a recurrent thematic in the Hollywood cinema, the relationship between father and maturing son. Whereas Mr. Fox is a legendary figure in his community, known for his athletic prowess, cunning and determination, Ash is small and clumsy. His vain struggle to match (let alone surpass) the accomplishments of his mercurial father form a background theme in the film, and his resentment is intensified by the arrival of his physically impressive cousin, Kristofferson, which triggers an inferiority complex. There is a telling scene in which Mrs Fox attempts to impress on Ash the need for him to accept himself and not worry about fitting in with the crowd.

> MRS FOX: Ash, I know what it's like to feel different.
> ASH: But I'm not different . . . am I?
> MRS FOX: We all are. Especially him [points at Mr Fox]. But there's
>   something kind of fantastic about that, isn't there?

[She leaves.]

ASH: Hmm. Not to me. I'd prefer to be an athlete.

Ash's final line in this exchange subverts the usual pat moral homilies about self-acceptance and embracing difference. Ash, who is neglected by his father and ignored by female foxes his own age, retains his desire to assimilate. The irony here, which is not lost on Ash, is that Mrs Fox appears to represent the socially desired qualities (beauty, intelligence, strength, compassion) that he lacks, and as such she cannot possibly understand his feelings. Part of Mr Fox's subsequent redemption is sitting Ash down and telling him that he's happy that Ash is his son, but it is not until the cub has been taught karate by Kristoffer-son, and has played his part in foiling the farmers, that Mr Fox accedes that he is 'an athlete' and gives him a bandit hat – a symbol of masculine self-reliance. In other words, the classic children's fictional trope of the child's coming-of-age (and following in his father's footsteps) is evident here, yet in a way that rejects the ingratiating triteness of Mrs Fox's earlier speech and simultaneously reaf-firms Ash's primary identity as a wild animal. The joke here – one that is made several times over the course of the film – is that these animated characters mostly act like analogues of human beings, yet occasionally behave in a way that re-emphasises their animalism.

Despite his undoubted prowess as a filmmaker, Anderson seems unwilling, or perhaps fundamentally unable, to move beyond the conventional narrative ideology of mainstream Hollywood animation. While his contributions to the medium are not outwardly didactic, their ironic pleasures nonetheless give way to familiar reaffirmations of the primacy of friendship, family and commu-nity, and the importance of moral codes of kindness, decency, and maintaining law and order. *Isle of Dogs*, Anderson's second animated feature (and ninth in total), embodies many of these tensions. The film is set in the fictional Japanese metropolis of Megasaki City after an epidemic has spread through the city's canine population, leading the mayor, Kobayashi (Kunichi Nomura), to exile all dogs to Trash Island, a remote, festering wasteland close to the mainland. The narrative is told largely from the perspective of the English-speaking dogs; the film's most prominent joke is that the Japanese human characters' dialogue is not dubbed or subtitled, making their speech as unintelligible to most West-ern viewers as it is to the dogs. Eventually, it transpires that the dog-hating mayor and his military adjutant, the vampiric Major Domo (Akira Takayama), engineered the dog illness as an excuse to purge the city of the animals, and ultimately to wipe them out.

The two human teenage protagonists in *Isle of Dogs*, the Japanese boy Atari (Koyu Rankin) and the American foreign exchange student and political cru-sader Tracy (Greta Gerwig), are not dissimilar to the young heroes and heroines of the Tim Burton and Laika features. On the one hand, they look or sound vaguely unusual: Atari's Japanese dialogue is unintelligible to most of the film's viewers, while the teenage reporter Tracy – who sports a colossal blonde afro – imagines herself as a fearless moral crusader. On the other hand, their bravery and perspicacity differentiate them from the remote, corrupt or wholly villainous adults that surround them. While Tracy is determined to expose Mayor Kobayashi's criminal misdemeanours, Atari is motivated solely by his obsessive desire to be reunited with his loyal canine bodyguard, Spots (Liev Schreiber), and to reverse Kobayashi's exile of the city's dogs. Spots only regretfully turns his back on Atari because he now has a family – a female dog and a litter of newborn puppies to support (his shift in loyalties ascribes to a broader social expectation that immediate family supersedes even close friendship). Spots' brother, Chief (Bryan Cranston), initially an aggressive social outcast, reforms after Atari befriends him and he begins a relationship with the former show dog, Nutmeg (Scarlett Johansson), while simultaneously becoming Atari's official bodyguard. Even Kobayashi – who plans to wipe out the dogs using a toxic chemical – is made to see the error of his ways, and donates one of his kidneys to the injured Atari to save the boy's life.

The film's conclusion may not entirely be utopian, but it falls squarely into the category of the 'happy ending', with the victory of unambiguously virtuous characters, the reform of morally ambivalent ones (such as Chief and, to a lesser degree, Kobayashi), and the defeat and punishment of contemptible ones (Major Domo). As we have seen, both *Fantastic Mr. Fox* and *Isle of Dogs* consciously resist generic categorisation and invite comparisons with the director's live-action films. Anderson apparently feels a need to distance himself from the perhaps too-clichéd syntax of the family film. Yet in most other regards, the narrative and ideological conventions of the genre are upheld to the extent that any disavowal remains, at best, ambiguous. Rather than reflecting his spirit of independent artistry (as is usually suggested), one wonders the extent to which films like *Fantastic Mr. Fox* and *Isle of Dogs* actually represent Anderson's assimilation into the mainstream.

To an even greater degree than the Anderson features, *Rango* was marketed as an antidote to the narrative ideology of the Disney/Pixar films. Distributed by Paramount, its budget of $135 million places it squarely within the blockbuster firmament (even though its worldwide box office of around $245 million constituted a significant underperformance). The development of an appropriately 'indie' tone and aesthetic was a conscious strategy on the part of the filmmakers. According to Paramount vice chair Rob Moore, 'We wanted to get out in front of other animated movies – *Mars Needs Moms*, *Hop*, *Rio* – and it worked [. . .] *Rango* is ambitious creatively, and that's the thing we expect to keep the movie going.'[43] The pedigree of its director, Gore Verbinski (*Pirates of the Caribbean*), and screenwriter, John Logan (*Gladiator*, *The Aviator*), should also temper grandiose claims of the film's indie credentials. However, the fact that it garnered the Academy Award (2011) and BAFTA (2011) for Best Animated Film points to the considerable critical acclaim that it met upon release. The *New York Times*' A. O. Scott, having observed that 'feature animation currently finds itself in a golden age of mediocrity, with sensationally inventive technical means tethered, more often than not, to drab and cynical imaginative ends', admiringly used adjectives such as 'odd', 'anarchic', 'rambling', and 'eccentric' to describe *Rango*.[44] The *Washington Post* also compared the film positively to other Hollywood animated features of the period, pointing out that:

> If a spew of old-movie allusions guaranteed greatness – if mere pastiche equalled masterpiece – then every Quentin Tarantino flick would be genius, and an animated film need only hire the manically talented Robin Williams to toss off film quotes like some Imdb.com algorithm on hyperdrive.[45]

However, as with several films discussed in this chapter, critics were unsure as to its intended audience, with *Variety* calling it 'astonishingly adult-skewing' yet suggesting that it possesses 'kid appeal aplenty'.[46] *USA Today* concurred, acknowledging 'wide-ranging cultural and cinematic references, from journalist Hunter S. Thompson, artist Salvador Dali, author Carlos Castaneda, "spaghetti Western" filmmaker Sergio Leone and the 1974 movie *Chinatown*' and 'verbose, polysyllabic dialogue', but noting that the film's 'level of humour – much of it distinctly of the bathroom variety – is aimed squarely at the under-13 set', resulting in 'cacophonous mishmash'.[47] It was reported in the US trade press that only 46 per cent of attendees during the film's opening weekend were under the age of 25, an unusually low number for a nominally family-oriented animated feature.[48]

It is likely that *Rango* was simply too esoteric for the notoriously fickle family market. Unlike the children's horror films produced by the likes of Tim Burton and Laika, *Rango* generally resists the unambiguous didacticism that characterises Hollywood feature animation. In its non sequiturs, puns, and deliberately obscure allusions, it is more reminiscent of the playful, adult-oriented classical-era Hollywood shorts of Tex Avery and Chuck Jones. As in those productions, there are few concessions to child audiences beyond the aesthetic level (anthropomorphised animals, comedic visual incongruities), but the film's extended length allows for many more longueurs, and the storyline of political intrigue and corruption in a frontier desert town freely engages with tropes of the western genre.

The existentialist crisis suffered by the central character, the chameleon Rango (Johnny Depp), might be viewed as a self-conscious allusion to the disorientation engendered by the film's own generic hybridisation. The film begins with the writerly, self-aware conceit of Rango attempting to define himself as a hero, and realising that in order to be a hero he requires conflict. The fact that Rango is a chameleon is suggestive, implying the absence of a core identity; he seeks to inhabit a series of archetypal roles in search of himself. When he arrives in the old-west town of Dirt, he is told that strangers don't last long, so determines to 'blend in' with the town's inhabitants, and immediately begins imitating the idiosyncratic gaits of first a cockroach, then a vulture, and finally a porcupine. Moments later, Rango is asked the direct question, 'Who are you?' Turning towards a mirror to stare at his own reflection, he muses, 'Who am I? I could be anyone.' At this point, he assumes the identity of a tough gunslinger and announces to the crowd, portentously, that his name is 'Rango' – a word that has dual connotations of 'range' (prairies, freedom) and the Latin languages (gesturing to the spaghetti western). Later in the film he is exposed as a fraud, and leaves town in disgrace when he is forced to admit, 'I am nobody.' In the film's most quixotic passage, Rango has a vision in which he meets Clint Eastwood's Man with No Name from Sergio Leone's 'Dollars Trilogy' (Figure 5.3):

> RANGO: I don't even know what I'm looking for any more. I don't even know who I am. They used to call *you* the Man with No Name.
> MAN: These days they got a name for just about everything. Doesn't matter what they call you. It's the deeds make the man.
> RANGO: Yeah, but my deeds just made things worse. I'm a fraud. I'm a phony! My friends believed in me, but they need some kind of hero!
> MAN: Then be a hero.
> RANGO: No, no, no, you don't understand. I'm not even supposed to be here.

Figure 5.3   Rango engages in existentialist dialogue with The Man with No Name
(*Rango*, Paramount, 2011). Frame grab.

MAN: That's right. You came a long way to find something that isn't out here. Don't you see? It's not about you. It's about them.

Rango's initial negation of self leads, paradoxically, to his discovery of his true self, a reification of his heroic ideal. On one level, the portrayal of the central character can be viewed as a satire of the individualistic, goal-oriented, and phallically omnipotent male protagonist of classical Hollywood cinema, just as the film – with its John Huston-like villainous tortoise – pastiches *Chinatown* (Roman Polanski, 1974). Yet the character of Rango can be read differently, as a maturing child still developing his own identity separate from that of the parent. If the film, boiled down to its essence, has a 'message' it may be the conventional reaffirmations of individual identity bound up with duty and obligation to one's friends and family. Once again, the veneer of oddball quirkiness only partially obscures a narrative that is both reassuringly familiar and predictably conservative.

The dialectic between sincerity and irony is integral to the indie animation cycle. Indeed, MacDowell argues that this tonal balance is 'perhaps the most immediately tangible aspect' of the 'quirky' film sensibility in its wider iterations.[49] In these films, hip inflections are mediated by the narrative demands of family animation, which emphasises humanistic values and bears powerful moralistic overtones within a narrative structure that ultimately rehabilitates ironic distantiation and allows apparently sincere Manichean values to triumph. Strategies of emotive uplift are also evident, with audiences (particularly adult males) invited to take pleasure in the seemingly impossible reconciliation between ironic individualism and devoted family member. The victory of the hipsterish protagonists coincides with their moral and behavioural reform; these directionless, mildly picaresque individuals embrace friendship, family, duty, and moral obligation wholesale. Yet the tone of these films remains faintly inscrutable. One is never entirely satisfied that the conventions of family entertainment are being uncritically upheld as much as semi-ironically lampooned; there is enough ambiguity – especially for those familiar with the work of the filmmakers involved – to believe that the apparently sincere speeches given to George Clooney's Mr Fox and Johnny Depp's Rango are spoken with a forked tongue. The 'plausible deniability' that Ellen Scott identifies as central to Pixar's adult address may be repurposed here: the indie films invite – and are able to sustain – both an 'ironic' and a 'sincere' interpretation.[50]

HYBRIDISATION

As we have seen, several of the children's horror and 'indiewood' films evidence greater degrees of aesthetic experimentation than is permissible within the Disney/Pixar hyper-realist approach. In this section, I will discuss two films – the dystopian fantasy *9* (Shane Acker, 2009) and the Japanese folklore-influenced

Kubo and the Two Strings (Travis Knight, 2016) – that can be located within the industrial logic of 'indiewood' cinema (having been distributed by the Universal-owned Focus Features), but which also evidence the increasing influence on mainstream Hollywood of global animation, with its more diverse set of stylistic codes. Hollywood has always assimilated aesthetic styles from other national cinematic traditions, yet this trend has accelerated since the turn of the millennium. Films such as *9*, *Kubo and the Two Strings* and *Isle of Dogs* employ hybrid styles that largely eschew narrative cartoonalism or hyper-realism, and reflect the popularity of world traditions such as Japanese anime among Western filmmakers and audiences alike. Furthermore, in recent years a higher proportion of animated features have employed non-American creative personnel in pivotal roles. For instance, *9* was a co-production between Tim Burton and Timur Bekmambetov, a Russian-Kazakh writer-director known mostly for Russian-language fantasy films, and *Coraline* drew on the concept art of Tadahiro Uesugi.

9 is unusual within contemporary traditions of North American animation in two key regards. Firstly, it deals with fantasies (and realities) that are materially unpleasant, even to the extent that its suitability for family audiences is questionable. Secondly, it pointedly avoids the prevalent strategy of using humour to diffuse discomforting themes or imagery. We might compare it with the largely upbeat vision of post-apocalyptic life in *WALL-E* (Andrew Stanton, 2008), which immediately announces its playful detachment with Jerry Hernan's 'Put on Your Sunday Clothes' (itself, perhaps unconsciously, recalling the semi-ironic use of Vera Lynn's 'We'll Meet Again' as dozens of atomic explosions ravage the surface of the planet at the end of *Dr. Strangelove* [Stanley Kubrick, 1964]). Where *WALL-E* and *9* are in accordance is in attributing the apocalypse to human action or inaction: in *WALL-E* it is man-made pollution and climate change, and in *9* it is the abuse of technology that leads to the planet's destruction. Similarly, both films envision a possible post-apocalyptic future for humanity's descendants, the success of which ultimately rests on the ability of the survivors to avoid the mistakes of the past (or, for audiences who grasp the allegory, the present and the near future); the final line of dialogue in *9* is, 'This world is ours now. It's what we make of it.' Both films, therefore, have a didactic underpinning.

While Laika's *Coraline*, *ParaNorman* and *The Boxtrolls* consciously invoke tropes of the grotesque, horror and comedy are tightly interwoven so that suspense is diffused, whereas *9* is so serious and strait-laced that its disturbing details suffuse the narrative. *Variety*'s Todd McCarthy is correct in noting the film's placement 'on the edge between commercial considerations and genuinely eccentric creativity'.[51] In one sense, this works to the film's advantage: not burdened by the need to retain suitability for young children (it received a 'PG-13' rating in the US), it positions itself 'beyond the confines of cautious family fare', as the *New York Times* put it, and thus escapes the narrative predictability of many Hollywood family films.[52] Whereas the darker aspects of family-oriented features such as *WALL-E* are ultimately redeemed by endings that are both unambiguous and emotionally uplifting, *9* ends more ambivalently, with the future of the leading characters – and the world – still in the balance. Many of the film's attractions, though, are aesthetic in nature. While there are gothic, expressionist cadences in the *mise-en-scène* and cinematography that evoke producer Tim Burton's own films, Acker's influences are avowedly international: the animators Jan Švankmajer, Christoph and Wolfgang Lauenstein, and the Brothers Quay's uncanny stop-motion short, *Street of Crocodiles* (1986). This is a radical artistic decision in the context of Hollywood animation (which places emphasis on story, transparent narrative, character, and emotional realism) and probably explains the relatively lowly box office grosses of just under $50 million worldwide, despite Focus Features' high-end marketing and distribution strategies.

Similarly, *Kubo and the Two Strings*, while still containing the mildly scary moments that have characterised Laika's output, is much more experimental than its earlier films. A fantasy quest narrative far removed from the suburban 'relatability' of much post-Pixar animation, it is more akin to the folklore-derived oriental fantasy of Studio Ghibli (with which it shares a similar graphic richness and artisanal aesthetic), with its *mise-en-scène* of samurai warriors, kung fu action sequences, and Bon festivals. The opening voice-over narration immediately emphasises the importance of the viewer registering the detail and intricacy of the narrative:

> If you must blink, do it now. Pay careful attention to everything you see and hear, no matter how unusual it may seem. And please be warned. If you fidget, if you look away, if you forget any part of what I tell you, even for an instant, then our hero will surely perish.

The script, in its somewhat playful, self-referential way, asserts that this is no passive spectatorial experience, but rather a complex, multifaceted film that requires sustained engagement. This fact will no doubt resonate with audiences already familiar with Laika's output, for it is central to the company's brand identity that it continues to position itself as distinct from the more aesthetically and narratively conventional terrain that most Hollywood feature animation treads.

The film's characters and situations are deliberately quixotic, from the Japanese boy hero, Kubo, who has the capacity to animate origami with his guitar and who is searching for his stolen left eye, taken from him in infancy by his grandfather, the supernatural Moon King (Ralph Fiennes); the child's mother and father, whose atypicality is rendered literally through their identities as a talking monkey and a giant beetle; and the subtle references to Ray Harryhausen (an animated skeleton) and even Luis Buñuel and Salvador Dalí's classic avant-garde short, *An Andalusian Dog* (1929), in the initial scene's shot of a full moon being partially obscured by shards of cloud and ocean waves. Despite its many oddities, the child protagonist is similar to those of Laika's other films in that his physical and psychological differences ultimately prove to be strengths rather than weaknesses. Rather more abstract than the traditional wrongdoers of children's fiction, the Moon King, the film's villain, is nonetheless typical of Laika's overarching worldview. Described as 'cold and hard and perfect', he is a representation of brutal, unthinking conformity. It is Kubo's father's qualities of love and compassion that transform his mother from the ruthless, unemotional realm governed by his grandfather, and which define Kubo, who vows, 'I'll never be like him – never,' and defeats the Moon King by drawing strength from the realisation that 'For every wretched thing down here, there is something far more beautiful. My mother saw it. So did my father. I see it. Even with just one eye.'

Like *9*, *Kubo and the Two Strings* is perhaps most radical in the context of mainstream Hollywood cinema in its partial disavowal of the happy ending. The theft of Kubo's left eye in the opening scene establishes the film's central thematic, that of the child's/human's need to come to terms with loss. The nature of the film's quest narrative might create an anticipation in audiences that he will eventually recover his stolen eye, thereby healing himself and making himself 'whole' in some kind of idyllic fulfilment of the children's literary trope of narrative closure. However, Kubo does not regain his eye, and in the distinctly bittersweet final scenes, he must learn to cope with the death of both of his mother and father. Although this is an unspeakably tragic loss for a child, the emotional impact on Kubo – and on the audience – is nonetheless carefully mediated. The fantasy setting avails the possibility of ambiguity; in the final scene Kubo is able somehow to summon the ghostly images of his mother and father as they sit, facing the camera, as the credits roll (Figure 5.4). Family, in some form, therefore survives, even if this scene can also be read metaphorically as part of Kubo's conception of keeping the dead alive through memory. The story is explicitly allegorical, and the film's preferred reading seems to be that the virtues embodied by the parents – love, hope, tolerance and humanity – have been inherited by Kubo.

Just as contemporary fairy tale films such as *Shrek* (Andrew Adamson and Vicky Jenson, 2001) and *Frozen* (Chris Buck and Jennifer Lee, 2013) lampoon or rewrite structural conventions that no longer appear sustainable, so *Kubo and the Two Strings* is one of the few Hollywood animated features that deliberately problematises the fabled 'happy ending'. Yet while those fairy tale films self-consciously reinterpret the *political* conventions of the genre, *Kubo* is attempting something more complex in rewriting part of the fundamental syntax of the family film and its emotive resonances – the near inevitability

Figure 5.4   Kubo's plangent reunion with the apparitions of his dead parents (*Kubo and the Two Strings*, Laika, 2016). Frame grab.

that such a film will end happily for its characters (and, thereby, for audiences). Tellingly, perhaps, the final scenes exhibit a large degree of self-consciousness, with Kubo's address to his absent parents also addressing viewers: 'This was a happy story. But it could still be a whole lot happier . . . I still need you. So I can say this has been a happy story, or I could feel it – we could all feel it. Then we could end this story together.' The final image, of Kubo and his deceased parents sitting together in silence, both reaffirms the film's humanistic view of immortality through collective memory and signals a degree of ambivalence towards the ending. What audiences are left with, perhaps, is closer to pensiveness than indulgent sentimentality.

Conclusion

Several features link the films discussed in this chapter. Firstly, and most obviously, they cater to demographic sections that Disney, Pixar, DreamWorks, and other producers of 'mainstream' computer-generation Hollywood animation do not. Their storylines, and their major characters, are deliberately offbeat, and this is part of an industrial strategy of product differentiation. A historical parallel is that of the Warner Bros. shorts of the 1930s and 1940s, where the films' strategies of comic anarchism and narrative circularity asserted important points of difference from the overt sentimentalism and moralism of Disney's shorts of the period. Secondly, the films evidence increasing generic hybridisation, with multiple textual and iconographic references to recognised conventions of other (primarily adult-oriented) cinematic forms, such as horror, westerns, and post-1990s indie films. Admittedly, some of these intertextual borrowings are parodic, while some others can be attributed to the familiar strategy in contemporary Hollywood animation of programmed allusiveness in a bid to extend the films' popular appeal. However, the considerable narrative continuities between the live-action and animated films of directors such as Tim Burton and Wes Anderson point to the dubious distinctions between what continue to be termed – increasingly anachronistically – 'live-action' and 'animation'. Thirdly, there is an ongoing process of internationalisation in contemporary Hollywood animation. To some degree, this is an organic process; in an age of global transmedia exchange, filmmakers in North America are exposed to a wider range of animation than in previous generations. However, there is considerable evidence to suggest that US animators deliberately incorporate stylistic practices from other international traditions, not simply for artistic reasons but also to boost their films' commercial prospects in the international market.[53] Finally, as we have seen, despite their aesthetic innovations, the films under discussion here are largely conventional in narrative and ideological terms.

The placement of these films within the industrial and creative contexts of contemporary Hollywood cinema is not straightforward. Hollywood has always absorbed the production practices (as well as creative personnel) of rival cinemas, from the German Expressionist influence on 1940s *film noir* to the French New Wave influence on the 1960s 'Hollywood Renaissance' and beyond. What is not entirely clear is whether the children's horror and 'indiewood' films are an inevitable part of this ongoing process, or isolated, abortive forays into less commercial territory. While most of the films discussed in this chapter were highly successful in critical terms, none of them have broken $250 million at the global box office; indeed, *Fantastic Mr. Fox*, *Frankenweenie*, *Kubo and the Two Strings* and *Isle of Dogs* all grossed substantially less than $100 million worldwide. (The most profitable of the indiewood films, *Rango*, received a substantial commercial boost when it won the Academy Award for Best Animated Feature.) It may be useful to view the children's horror cycle as a relatively coherent body of films with its own recognisable syntax, and indiewood animation as a much broader category that encompasses *any* commercial film predicated on formal, thematic or ideological differentiation from the Disney/Pixar centre ground. It may be that the children's horror cycle has temporarily run its course (at least as a sub-genre within contemporary Hollywood animated family films), but the wider category of indiewood animation remains open-ended, subject to new aesthetic and thematic innovations.

The box office underperformance of most of these films relates to a broader point concerning the commercial viability of experimentalism in US animation, even in the relatively mild forms seen here. The North American commercial market is notoriously parochial, with very few international animated features receiving wide distribution. Furthermore, although a handful of non-Hollywood films tend to be nominated for the Best Animated Film

Oscar each year, including more complex and experimental productions such as *The Red Turtle* (Michaël Dudok de Wit, 2016) and *Loving Vincent* (Dorota Kobiela and Hugh Welchman, 2017), only one such film – *Spirited Away* (Hayao Miyazaki, 2001) – has ever won the award, and it did so only after a high-profile release by Disney and an English-language dub featuring several big stars. It may be, then, that the inherent parochialism of North American audiences and the deep-set conservatism of the major Hollywood studios are mutually supporting.

CONCLUSION

The aim of this book has been to provide a comprehensive overview of post-1990s Hollywood animation, taking in major changes and continuities in style and aesthetics, narrative and story structure, and industry contexts, while considering how the films operate in relation to broader currents in US culture and society. It is not the first word on the subject, and it will not be the last: film and animation studies have, in recent years, shown a deep interest in mainstream Hollywood animation. The resulting scholarship has gone a long way to overturning the traditional antipathy which 'serious' critics have often expressed towards it. On the opening page of this book, I made the observation that animation is at the heart not only of the Hollywood machine, but of contemporary popular culture more broadly. This point has, I hope, been proven beyond reasonable doubt, and not just on account of the critical success that continues to meet Hollywood animation or its lofty position in international box office tables. Its importance can also be gauged by the ways it instantiates current and foundational mythologies of the nation while ascribing to broader mythological structures and resonating with worldwide audiences from all kinds of backgrounds. However, as I have argued throughout, this cultural centrality has important implications for how the form has developed since the 1990s, with the emergence of new narrative and stylistic strategies that update many of the principles of classical-era Hollywood animation.

Firstly, we must acknowledge the extent to which the narrative style of mainstream Hollywood animation is a product of the commercial ambitions of the major studios. These films are produced for the consumption of a diverse global market. This has led to the cultivation of a 'transparent' narrative style that offers familiar pleasures, not just in the aesthetic sense, but also in the recurrence of specific thematic and ideological patterns. Almost all mainstream Hollywood animated features are made for all-inclusive 'family audiences', a fact that some scholars have tended to elide with claims that animation possesses an inherent, unique ability to liberate artists from technological constraints and physical laws, and thus represents a 'high' art far removed from its popular associations with children's culture.

This argument possesses obvious attractions to those who work in and study the discipline. But while it is true in the abstract sense, all but the most avant-garde animators in the United States operate in the business of commercial narrative cinema; consequently, they remain bound by conventions of form, structure, ideology, and even the potentialities and the constraints of technology and human imagination. These limitations need not be viewed as compromising the essential 'purity' of the medium. As Andrew Darley argues, technical and stylistic constraints (many of which are self-imposed) are necessary in any artistic form.[1] However, I suspect that scholarly prejudice towards children's culture has played a large part in some of the more extravagant claims to the artistic superiority of animation. Early film scholarship was similarly preoccupied with asserting the formal uniqueness and the artistic potentiality of the medium as a means of challenging claims to its 'lowness' and vulgarity.

The explicit claim that children's film is an arena that animation has 'transcended' is unfortunate.[2] It appears to rest on two presumptions: that animation is inherently radical and creative, and that films for children are simplistic, inherently conservative, and necessarily devoid of artistic worth. This is plainly a false opposition. A substantial body of recent scholarship has shown how children's film has the capacity for stylistic and ideological innovation; equally, of course, animation (for children and for adults) can be blandly formulaic.[3] Even if it were true that child-oriented cinema is intrinsically conservative (and I have tried to argue otherwise), it would still remain worthy of study, not simply in terms of how it negotiates and transcends its apparent formal constraints, but also how its conventions speak to the collective desires, fantasies and anxieties of the society that produces it and which it serves.

In this book I have argued in favour of a different approach. The fact that almost all Hollywood animated features are produced for mixed audiences of children and adults ('family films') is neither an inconvenient truth nor a minor detail. In fact, it is absolutely central to understanding the form. It means that films must respond, at a fundamental level, to socio-cultural constructions of childhood; as we saw in the opening chapter, the need for films to remain 'suitable' and 'appealing' for children has led to the cultivation of specific formal and ideological conventions, such as the tendency towards coming-of-age narratives, the need to avoid prolonged depictions of traumatic realities, and, broadly speaking, upbeat and unambiguous endings. Sometimes, of course, this results in conservative productions that justify popular prejudices against child-oriented cinema as a medium for artistry. Just as often, though, films succeed in engaging creatively with the inherited conventions of the genre in ways that emphasise its plurality rather than its homogeneity (the same is true of musicals, westerns, and most other genres with well-established, recognisable tropes). And indeed, as we have seen, some films renegotiate or rewrite apparently fundamental elements of the narrative syntax of family-oriented animation. *Shrek* (Andrew Adamson and Vicky Jenson, 2001), for instance, deconstructs the classical-era Disney fairy tale, just as *Frozen* (Chris Buck and Jennifer Lee, 2013) revises the classical-era convention for heterosexual romantic union and *Kubo and the Two Strings* (Travis Knight, 2016) resists the unambiguous 'happy ending'.

To what degree, then, is post-1990s Hollywood animation recognisably distinct from its classical precursors? To answer this question, it is useful to return to the various threads considered in Chapter 1, particularly industry, style and narrative. In industrial terms, Hollywood animation continues to address a broad, cross-demographic audience in much the same way as the films of Walt Disney's era did. However, films now reside within much larger, multimedia (and sometimes transmedia) family entertainment franchises built around instantly recognisable brand properties. At their core, brands such as Universal's Minions continue to embody the utopian inflections of classical Hollywood animation: family, friendship, community, fun, play, consensus, and so on. However, the stakes are now much higher. In many ways, this is a logical commercial development that responds to ongoing processes of industrial conglomeration and horizontal integration, as well as recent tendencies towards multimedia convergence. Films are no longer self-contained entities (in truth, Disney's features never were), but rather components within larger fictional 'universes' that also encompass TV shows, games, theme-park rides, toys, books, comics, clothes, food, and any number of licensable properties. In turn, this has implications for film form, with an increasing trend towards serialisation, where individual films become, in essence, 'chapters' within larger, multimedia narratives.

In stylistic terms, of course, the major change since the 1990s is that computer animation has become the dominant medium, replacing the traditional pre-eminence of cel animation. To some degree, this has led to greater standardisation in the visual aesthetic of Hollywood animation, since most studios use similar principles and technologies to animate their films. However, as scholars such as Christopher Holliday argue, computer animation is a relatively new art form with its own unique idiom, and it is still in the process of being written. Already, computer animation has begun to diverge radically from the inherited style of live-action film, particularly in terms of cinematography (e.g. the increasing proliferation of fluidic camera moves unconstrained by physical laws). However, as we saw in the first chapter, computer animation continues to draw on recognisable continuity editing conventions of the kind used both in live-action cinema and in classical-era Hollywood animation. Indeed, some directors prefer to foreground these conventions, mindful of the need to retain strategies of familiarisation in a medium that might otherwise lean too heavily towards abstraction. Again, there is a balancing act between the need to innovate, dazzling audiences with aesthetic attractions that they are unable to access elsewhere, and the parallel need to retain the engagement of a pluralistic, multi-demographic global audience. That is to say, post-1990s computer animation remains a hybrid style comprising elements of traditional animation, live-action cinema, and its own evolving formal characteristics.

The narrative aesthetic of post-1990s Hollywood is more ambivalently situated in relation to classical traditions. On the one hand, like the early Disney films, most releases are recognisable as coming-of-age quest narratives that reaffirm traditional values of family, community and consensus, address mass audiences through the provision of familiar attractions (song, spectacle, comedy) and serve an important ritualistic function of bringing people – particularly family and friends – together through a shared viewing experience. On the other hand, there have been some important semantic changes in the narrative ideology of Hollywood animation since the 1990s. Representations of family, everyday life and modernity have been brought to the forefront, partially superseding the fantastical or fairy tale worlds of most classical Disney animated films. Equally, many of the dominant values of contemporary US society have been emphasised: the weighing of family responsibilities with individualist desires; the importance of upholding individual uniqueness, group identities, sexual equality and multiculturalism; and allusions to social issues, ranging from expensive chain coffee to climate change and the possibility of human extinction. All of these form part of a broader embedding of contemporary culture, driven by the perceived need to make Hollywood animation 'real' and 'relatable' to mass audiences, particularly the tweens, teenagers and young adults that drive box office trends and consumer spending.

As with the films produced during Walt Disney's lifetime, the dominant characteristic of post-1990s Hollywood animation is utopianism. Political values may vary from film to film and generation to generation, but the format remains closely aligned with the perceived interests, beliefs and aesthetic requirements of the majority. Innovative and significant films continue to be made; sustaining critical as well as popular interest is part of the art of producing mainstream Hollywood animation. Yet the goal is always the same: mobilising mass audiences through the recapitulation of universalistic (or almost universalistic) patterns of fantasy, usually as part of a wider attempt to feed a franchise machine predicated upon the exploitation of widely accessible, family-oriented brand properties.

Substantive deviations from this aesthetic are rarely successful (at least not on a comparable level), partly because the major Hollywood studios are wholly committed to producing films in the hyper-realist, family-oriented mode of computer animation. Certainly, the comparatively limited horizons of Hollywood family entertainment are evident in the fact that a highly acclaimed production such as *My Life as a Courgette* (Claude Barras, 2016), a French–Swiss stop-motion feature widely seen as a children's film on continental Europe, was almost universally received as an 'adult animation' in the United States.[4] Consequently, the commercial prospects of films of this kind, and even those produced by US studios such as Laika, are limited. In this way, the North American system of production, distribution, marketing and reception continues, systematically, to ghettoise animated films that do not conform to the dominant narrative ideology of mainstream Hollywood animation. This ideology is flexible enough to promote and sustain change from within (and, occasionally, to absorb elements from other traditions), but it has proven stubbornly resistant to films that threaten to violate the fundamentals of Hollywood family-oriented cinema.

At this point, I would like to suggest some possible avenues for future research in the field of contemporary Hollywood animation. It seems to me that the current trajectory of scholarship leans heavily towards form and aesthetics – naturally enough, given that computer animation is still an emergent medium. However, there are two areas of substantial interest that, thus far, have been relatively unexplored and would benefit from further enquiry. The first is the placement of contemporary animation within paratextual industry structures, such as theme parks, licensing and other outlets for the brands at the heart of theatrically released films. The second is children's engagement with the form, both individually and within family and kinship structures (here I am repeating a call I have made on a number of occasions).[5] Although there has been a great deal of valuable research on children's engagement with other media,[6] almost all the relevant audience studies on Hollywood animation to date have surveyed adults. There are good reasons for this: animation, as we have seen, does appeal enormously to grown-up sensibilities, and adults are also a good deal more accessible to researchers (who have to contend with various practical and ethical issues when studying children as audiences). However, if we are to get fully to grips with the child–adult 'doubleness' that underpins Hollywood animation, then we need to understand how children relate to it a good deal better than we currently do.

Nevertheless, in taking a larger view on contemporary Hollywood animation, we might recall G. K. Chesterton's famous observation that 'in everything that matters, the inside is much larger than the outside'.[7] As in many texts putatively intended for children, close scrutiny of the form reveals complexities and ambiguities lying beneath more conventional surface pleasures. This is not to decry the value of entertainment for entertainment's sake, nor to question the ability of such films to forge deep emotional and intellectual connections with mass audiences. Hollywood animation is a democratic art that represents one of the purest distillations of US society as it imagines itself, how it wishes it were, and (occasionally) what it fears it may be: a nation that is highly individualistic, but pre-eminently concerned with upholding family and kinship structures; that is industrious, progressive and forward-thinking yet still beset by old prejudices; that is diverse and multicultural, but committed to traditional value structures; that is meritocratic, but resolutely hierarchical and unequal; that is patriotic and optimistic, but sometimes fractious, divided, opportunistic and self-absorbed; and that is ever-changing, but recognisably still the country of Washington, Jefferson and Lincoln.

NOTES

1. Paul Wells, *Animation and America* (Edinburgh: Edinburgh University Press, 2002), pp. 16–17.
2. Paul Wells, *Understanding Animation* (London and New York: Routledge, 1998), pp. 7–8.
3. In adopting such (loaded) terms as 'classical' and 'post-classical' to describe these production eras, I do not suggest that the 'classical' era of production is marked by aesthetic and ideological uniformity, nor do I deny that the post-1990s 'post-classical' era exhibits many profound continuities from earlier traditions of Hollywood animation.
4. Statistics in this chapter are drawn from several sources, primarily IMDb (details of film production companies) and film statistics website The Numbers (box office statistics). I have included only narrative feature films that received a wide theatrical release, thereby excluding shorts, documentaries and films that are either non-commercial or which received only very limited theatrical distribution.
5. Christopher Holliday, *The Computer-Animated Film: Industry, Style and Genre* (Edinburgh: Edinburgh University Press, 2018), pp. 10–11.
6. Richard Neupert, *John Lasseter* (Urbana: University of Illinois Press, 2016), pp. 170–1.
7. Peter Krämer, '"The Best Disney Film Disney Never Made": Children's Films and The Family Audience in American Cinema since the 1960s' in Steve Neale (ed.), *Genre And Contemporary Hollywood* (London: British Film Institute, 2002), pp. 185–200 (p. 188).
8. Janet Wasko, *Understanding Disney: The Manufacture of Fantasy* (Cambridge: Polity Press, 2001), p. 4.

9. 'Walt Disney Grows Up', *The Economist*, 23 July 1983, pp. 86–7.
10. Peter Krämer, *The New Hollywood: From Bonnie and Clyde to Star Wars* (London and New York: Wallflower, 2005), p. 102.
11. James B. Stewart, *DisneyWar: The Battle for the Magic Kingdom* (London and New York: Simon & Schuster, 2005), p. 44.
12. Peter Biskind, *Easy Riders, Raging Bulls: How the Sex-Drugs-and-Rock Roll Generation Saved Hollywood* (New York: Simon & Schuster, 1998), p. 328.
13. Ibid., p. 334.
14. Marcus Hearn, *The Cinema of George Lucas* (New York: Harry N. Abrams, Inc., 2005), p. 107.
15. 'Star Wars: The Year's Best Movie', *Time*, 30 May 1977.
16. David A. Cook, *Lost Illusions: American Cinema in the Shadow of Watergate and Vietnam, 1970–1979* (Berkeley, Los Angeles and London: University of California Press, 2000), p. 51.
17. Peter Krämer, 'Disney, George Lucas und Pixar: Animation und die US-amerikanische Filmindustrie seit den 1970er Jahren', *Film-Konzepte*, no. 33 (February 2014), pp. 6–21.
18. Peter Krämer, 'Would You Take Your Child to See This Film?: The Cultural and Social Work of the Family Adventure Movie' in Steve Neale and Murray Smith (eds), *Contemporary Hollywood Cinema* (London: Routledge, 1998), pp. 294–311.
19. Peter Krämer, '"It's Aimed at Kids – The Kid in Everybody": George Lucas, *Star Wars* and Children's Entertainment' in Yvonne Tasker (ed.), *Action and Adventure Cinema* (London and New York: Routledge, 2004), pp. 358–70 (pp. 366–7).
20. Noel Brown, *The Hollywood Family Film: A History, from Shirley Temple to Harry Potter* (London and New York: I. B. Tauris, 2012); Noel Brown, 'Hollywood, Children's Cinema and the Family Audience', Ch. 2 in *The Children's Film: Genre, Nation and Narrative* (New York: Columbia University Press, 2017), pp. 35–60.
21. Robert C. Allen, 'Home Alone Together: Hollywood and the "Family" Film' in Melvyn Stokes and Richard Maltby (eds), *Identifying Hollywood's Audiences: Cultural Identity and the Movies* (London: BFI Publishing, 1999), pp. 109–34 (p. 127).
22. Quoted in Krämer, '"The Best Disney Film Disney Never Made"', p. 192.
23. Christopher Finch, *The Art of Walt Disney* (New York: Harry N. Abrams, Inc., 1995), p. 372.
24. Stewart, *DisneyWar*, p. 45.
25. Ibid., p. 44.
26. Ibid., pp. 72–3.
27. Ibid., pp. 68–9.
28. Ibid., p. 96.
29. Tino Balio, *Hollywood in the Age of Television* (Boston: Unwin Hyman, 1990), p. 268.
30. Stewart, *DisneyWar*, pp. 92–3.
31. Cook, *Lost Illusions*, p. 65.
32. Kristin Thompson, *The Frodo Franchise: The Lord of the Rings and Modern Hollywood* (Berkeley and London: University of California Press, 2007), p. 219.

33. Frederick Wasser, *Veni, Vidi, Video: The Hollywood Empire and the VCR* (Austin: University of Texas Press, 2001), p. 165.
34. Stewart, *DisneyWar*, p. 86.
35. Ibid., p. 88.
36. Ibid.
37. Ibid., pp. 104–5.
38. 'New Plan to Put Warners in Family Way', *Variety*, 9 December 1991, pp. 1, 3.
39. Ryan Murphy, 'The Kids Are All Right', *Entertainment Weekly*, 16 April 1993, unpaginated.
40. Kenneth M. Chanko, 'Who Says a Movie Sequel Can't Be Made for Home Video?', *The New York Times*, 19 June 1994.
41. Scott Hettrick, 'Video Bows Mint Coin: Pic Franchises Mine Straight-to-Video Gold', *Variety*, 23 June 2000.
42. Marc Graser, 'H'Wood's Direct Hits: DVD Preems Boffo, But Biz Frets over Sequel-Mania', *Variety*, 13 September 2004, p. 1.
43. John Brodie and Jay Greene, 'Dwarfs Tell Disney: Draw! – Rival Studios Get Serious about Animation', *Variety*, 11 July 1994, p. 1.
44. John Brodie, 'Disney Wannabes Play Copycat-and-Mouse', *Variety*, 2 January 1995, p. 3.
45. Ibid.
46. Ben Fritz and Pamela McClintock, 'Animation World Gets Competitive: Studios Challenging Pixar for Toon Throne', *Variety*, 21 March 2008.
47. David A. Price, *The Pixar Touch: The Making of a Company* (New York: Vintage Books, 2009), p. 5.
48. Noel Brown, '"Family" Entertainment and Contemporary Hollywood Cinema', *Scope: An Online Journal of Film and Television Studies*, no. 25 (2013), pp. 1–22, <https://www.nottingham.ac.uk/scope/documents/2013/february-2013/brown.pdf> (accessed 8 June 2020)
49. Jonathan Knee, Bruce A. Greenwald and Ava Seave, *The Curse of the Mogul: What's Wrong with the World's Leading Media Companies* (New York: Portfolio, 2009), pp. 236–7.
50. Allen, 'Home Alone Together: Hollywood and the "Family" Film', p. 121.
51. Ben Fritz, 'Disney Animation Gets Pixar-ization: Catmull Thinks a Radical Shift is Needed', *Variety*, 24 February 2007.
52. Marc Graser, 'Disney Buys Lucasfilm, New "Star Wars" Planned', *Variety*, 30 October 2012.
53. Price, *The Pixar Touch*, pp. 259–60.
54. Nigel M. Smith, 'Universal's Marketing Campaign Has Minions Taking Over the World', *The Guardian*, 8 July 2015.
55. Marc Graser, 'Partners Serve up Stack of Toon Tie-Ins', *Variety*, 1 June 2010, p. 1.
56. Smith, 'Universal's Marketing Campaign Has Minions Taking Over the World'.
57. Ben Fritz, 'Hollywood Sees Star Qualities in Classic Games and Toys', *Los Angeles Times*, 28 September 2009.
58. Meredith Hamilton, '"Minions" Takes in $115.2 Million. What's Driving the Appeal?', *The Christian Science Monitor*, 12 July 2015.

59. Dann Gire, 'Looney Cartoony', *The Chicago Daily Herald*, 10 July 2015, p. 39; Brian Truitt, 'Manic "Minions" Manages Just Enough Charm', *USA Today*, 10 July 2015, p. 4D; Kyle Smith, 'Dumb-minion!', *The New York Post*, 9 July 2015, p. 35.

60. Siobhan O'Flynn, 'Data Science, Disney, and the Future of Children's Entertainment' in Casie Hermansson and Janet Zepernick (eds), *The Palgrave Handbook of Children's Film and Television* (Cham: Palgrave Macmillan, 2019), pp. 507–31 (p. 521).

61. Brian Lowry, '"Cars" Spins its Wheels', *Variety*, 12 June 2006, p. 27.

62. Ben Fritz, *The Big Picture: The Fight for the Future of Movies* (New York: Houghton Mifflin Harcourt, 2018), p. xxv.

63. Dave McNary, 'Fantasy Movies a Hit Overseas: "Compass" is Latest Family-Friendly Pic to Thrive', *Variety*, 3 March 2008.

64. Fritz, *The Big Picture*, p. 204.

65. Chris Pallant, *Demystifying Disney: A History of Disney Feature Animation* (London: Continuum, 2011), pp. 94–5.

66. Fritz, *The Big Picture*, pp. 161–2.

67. Bettina Kümmerling-Meibauer, 'Never-Ending Sequels? Seriality in Children's Films' in Casie Hermansson and Janet Zepernick (eds), *The Palgrave Handbook of Children's Film and Television* (Cham: Palgrave Macmillan, 2019), pp. 533–47 (p. 541).

68. Henry Jenkins, 'The Aesthetics of Transmedia: In Response to David Bordwell (Part Two)', *Confessions of an Aca-Fan: The Official Weblog of Henry Jenkins*, 13 September 2009, <http://henryjenkins.org/2009/09/the_aesthetics_of_transmedia_i_1.html> (accessed 28 December 2019).

69. Price, *The Pixar Touch*, p. 213.

70. Wells, *Animation and America*, p. 46.

71. Pallant, *Demystifying Disney*, p. 35.

72. See particularly Wells, *Animation and America*, and Pallant, *Demystifying Disney*.

73. Quoted in Pallant, *Demystifying Disney*, pp. 96–7.

74. Ibid., pp. 98–101.

75. J. P. Telotte, *The Mouse Machine: Disney and Technology* (Urbana and Chicago: University of Illinois Press, 2010), p. 162.

76. Ibid., p. 207; Price, *The Pixar Touch*, p. 41.

77. Andrew Darley, *Visual Digital Culture: Surface Play and Spectacle in New Media Genres* (New York: Routledge, 2000), pp. 84–5.

78. Ibid., p. 83.

79. Maureen Furniss, *Art in Motion: Animation Aesthetics* (New Barnet: John Libbey, 1998), pp. 5–6.

80. Holliday, *The Computer-Animated Film*, p. 15.

81. Aside from the photorealistic CGI used in nominally live-action films, an obvious (but so far isolated) counter-example is Disney's near-photorealistic computer-animated remake of *The Lion King* (2019), which *has* often been mistaken for live-action. At the time of writing, it is too early to judge whether this is part of a wider trend towards mimetic animation in Hollywood.

82. Ibid., p. 16.

83. Darley, *Visual Digital Culture*, p. 85.
84. Price, *The Pixar Touch*, p. 134.
85. Holliday, *The Computer-Animated Film*, p. 177.
86. Ian Failes, 'Brick by Brick: How Animal Logic Crafted *The LEGO Movie*', *FX Guide*, 7 February 2014, <https://www.fxguide.com/featured/brick-by-brick-how-animal-logic-crafted-the-lego-movie/> (accessed 12 July 2017).
87. David Bordwell, *The Way Hollywood Tells It: Story and Style in Modern Movies* (Berkeley, Los Angeles and London: University of California Press, 2006), pp. 121–3.
88. Ibid., p. 123.
89. Holliday, *The Computer-Animated Film*, p. 32.
90. Ibid., pp. 35–6.
91. Ibid., pp. 102–3.
92. Ibid., p. 32.
93. David Bordwell, *Narration in the Fiction Film* (Madison: University of Wisconsin Press, 1985), p. 157.
94. Ibid., p. 157.
95. Jack Zipes, *The Enchanted Screen: The Unknown History of Fairy-Tale Films* (New York: Routledge, 2011), pp. 20–1.
96. Christopher Vogler, *The Writer's Journey: Mythic Structure for Storytellers and Screenwriters*, 2nd edn (London: Pan Books, 1999), p. 11.
97. Ibid., p. 296; Susan Mackey-Kallis, *The Hero and the Perennial Journey Home in American Film* (Philadelphia: University of Pennsylvania Press, 2001), pp. 6, 202.
98. Brown, *The Children's Film*, pp. 13–15.
99. Wasko, *Understanding Disney*, pp. 111, 190.
100. Nicholas Sammond, *Babes in Tomorrowland: Walt Disney and the Making of the American Child 1930–1960* (Durham: Duke University Press, 2005), p. 13.
101. Wasko, *Understanding Disney*, p. 190.
102. Janet Wasko and Eileen R. Meehan, 'Dazzled by Disney? Ambiguity in Ubiquity' in Janet Wasko, Mark Phillips and Eileen R. Meehan (eds), *Dazzled by Disney? The Global Disney Audiences Project* (London: Leicester University Press, 2001), pp. 329–43 (p. 334).
103. Steven Watts, *The Magic Kingdom: Walt Disney and the American Way of Life* (Boston and New York: Houghton Mifflin Company, 1997), pp. 448–9.
104. Jack Zipes, 'Once Upon a Time Beyond Disney: Contemporary Fairy-Tale Films for Children' in Cary Bazalgette and David Buckingham (eds), *In Front of the Children: Screen Entertainment and Young Audiences* (London: British Film Institute, 1995), pp. 109–26 (pp. 110–12).
105. Watts, *The Magic Kingdom*, p. 451.
106. Stewart, *DisneyWar*, pp. 101–2.
107. Wells, *Animation and America*, pp. 104–6.
108. Ibid.
109. Judith Halberstam, 'Animating Revolt and Revolting Animation', Ch. 1 in *The Queer Art of Failure* (Durham: Duke University Press, 2011), pp. 27, 29.
110. Ibid., pp. 43–4.

111. Ibid.
112. Ibid., p. 43.
113. Ibid., pp. 46–7.
114. Ellen Scott, 'Pixar, Deniability, and the Adult Spectator', *The Journal of Popular Film and Television*, vol. 42, no. 3 (2014), pp. 150–62; Katrina Onstad, 'Pixar Gambles on a Robot in Love', *The New York Times*, 22 June 2008, p. A13. Stephen Prince has made a similar argument of Reagan-era cinema in *Visions of Empire: Political Imagery in Contemporary Hollywood Film* (New York: Praeger, 1992).
115. It is worth noting that 'relatability' is a vulgarisation of the literary studies concept of 'identification', which itself has been criticised for its vagueness as an all-encompassing theory of spectatorial engagement by scholars such as Noël Carroll, Murray Smith and others. See particularly Carroll, *The Philosophy of Horror* (New York: Routledge, 1990) and Smith, *Engaging Characters* (Oxford: Oxford University Press, 1995).
116. 'The Most Relatable Disney Character Moment', Huffington Post, 12 September 2013, <https://www.huffingtonpost.co.uk/2013/09/12/the-most-relatable-disney_n_3916449.html> (accessed 19 April 2019); Sam Stryker, 'Here's Why the Villains are Actually the Relatable Heroes of Disney Movies', BuzzFeed, 29 July 2018, <https://www.buzzfeed.com/samstryker/relatable-disney-villains> (accessed 19 April 2019).
117. Mark Harrison, 'Chris Buck and Jennifer Lee Interview: On Making Frozen', Den of Geek, 6 December 2013, <https://www.denofgeek.com/movies/frozen/28495/chris-buck-and-jennifer-lee-interview-on-making-frozen> (accessed 25 April 2019). See also Katie Baillie, 'Disney Producer Reveals How Frozen Could Have Ended VERY Differently', *Metro*, 30 March 2017, <https://metro.co.uk/2017/03/30/disney-producer-reveals-how-frozen-could-have-ended-very-differently-6542449/> (accessed 19 April 2019).
118. Rebecca Mead, 'The Scourge of "Relatability"', *The New Yorker*, 1 August 2014, <https://www.newyorker.com/culture/cultural-comment/scourge-relatability> (accessed 19 April 2019).
119. Pallant, *Demystifying Disney*, p. 123.
120. Sergei Eisenstein, *Eisenstein on Disney* (London: Methuen, 1988), p. 42.
121. Ibid., pp. 41, 2, 46.
122. Oliver Lindman, 'From Operatic Uniformity to Upbeat Eclecticism: The Musical Evolution of the Princess in Disney's Animated Features' in Amy M. Davis (ed.), *Discussing Disney* (New Barnet: John Libbey, 2019), pp. 151–72.
123. These include Celine Dion and Peabo Bryson's 'Beauty and the Beast' (#9, 1991), Peabo Bryson and Regina Belle's 'A Whole New World' from *Aladdin* (#1, 1992), Elton John's 'Can You Feel the Love Tonight' from *The Lion King* (#4, 1994), Vanessa Williams's 'Colors of the Wind' from *Pocahontas* (#4, 1995) and Idina Menzel's 'Let it Go' from *Frozen* (#5, 2013).
124. Price, *The Pixar Touch*, p. 128.
125. Finch, *The Art of Walt Disney*, p. 287.
126. Ibid., pp. 312, 319.
127. See particularly Pallant, *Demystifying Disney*; J. P. Telotte, *Animating Space: From Mickey to Wall-E* (Lexington: University Press of Kentucky, 2010).

128. See, for instance, Wells, *Understanding Animation*; Holliday, *The Computer-Animated Film*; Eric Herhuth, *Pixar and the Aesthetic Animation: Animation, Storytelling, and Digital Culture* (Oakland: University of California Press, 2017).

129. M. Keith Booker, *Disney, Pixar and the Hidden Messages of Children's Films* (California: Praeger, 2010).

130. Brown, *The Hollywood Family Film*.

131. Deitmar Meinel, *Pixar's America: The Re-Animation of American Myths and Symbols* (New York: Palgrave Macmillan, 2016); Lilian Munk Rösing, *Pixar with Lacan: The Hysteric's Guide to Animation* (London and New York: Bloomsbury, 2016).

132. Sam Summers, 'Intertextuality and the Break from Realism in DreamWorks Animation' (PhD thesis submitted to the University of Sunderland, April 2018).

133. See particularly Johnson Cheu (ed.), *Diversity in Disney Films: Critical Essays on Race, Ethnicity, Gender, Sexuality and Disability* (Jefferson: McFarland, 2012).

134. Neupert, *John Lasseter*.

135. See, for instance, Susan Smith, Noel Brown and Sam Summers (eds), *Toy Story: How Pixar Reinvented the Animated Feature* (New York: Bloomsbury, 2018).

CHAPTER 2

1. Peter Krämer, '"The Best Disney Film Disney Never Made": Children's Films and The Family Audience in American Cinema since the 1960s' in Steve Neale (ed.), *Genre And Contemporary Hollywood* (London: British Film Institute, 2002), pp. 185–200 (p. 193).

2. Tino Balio, 'Hollywood Production Trends in the Era of Globalisation, 1990–1999' in Steve Neale and Murray Smith (eds), *Genre and Contemporary Hollywood* (London: Routledge, 1998), pp. 165–84.

3. James B. Stewart, *DisneyWar: The Battle for the Magic Kingdom* (London and New York: Simon & Schuster, 2005), p. 104.

4. I am excluding heterosexual romance, which may be seen as 'pre-familial' in its promise of marriage and children, from this equation.

5. Jessica D. Zurcher, Sarah M. Webb and Tom Robinson, 'The Portrayal of Families Across Generations in Disney Animated Films', *Social Sciences*, vol. 7, no. 3 (2018).

6. *Meet Me in St. Louis* press book (BFI).

7. Carl DiOrio and Frank Segers, '"Up" Cleared for Big Overseas Landing', *The Hollywood Reporter*, 24 August 2009, p. 1.

8. See Noel Brown, *British Children's Cinema: From The Thief of Bagdad to Wallace and Gromit* (London: I. B. Tauris, 2016), pp. 264–5.

9. For more on the historical relationship between Hollywood and the so-called 'family audience', see Noel Brown, '"A New Movie-Going Public": 1930s Hollywood and the Emergence of the "Family" Film', *The Historical Journal of Film, Radio and Television*, vol. 33 (1), 2013, pp. 1–23.

10. '2017 THEME Report' (New York: Motion Picture Association of America, 2018), p. 19.

11. Karl Marx, *A Contribution to the Critique of Political Economy*, trans. S. W. Ryazanskaya (London: Lawrence & Wishart, 1971).

12. 'Interview of Walt Disney by Cecil B. DeMille' in Kathy Merlock Jackson (ed.), *Walt Disney: Conversations* (Jackson: University Press of Mississippi, 2006), pp. 13–14.
13. Talcott Parsons, 'The American Family: Its Relations to Personality and the Social Structure' [1954] in Michael Anderson (ed.), *Sociology of the Family* (Middlesex: Penguin, 1971), pp. 43–62 (p. 61).
14. Sigmund Freud, 'Delusions and Dreams in Jenson's *Gradiva*' in *Psychological Writings and Letters* (London: Continuum, 1995), p. 29.
15. For greater elaboration on different modes of audience address in children's films and family films, see Noel Brown and Bruce Babington, 'Introduction: Children's Films and Family Films' in Noel Brown and Bruce Babington (eds), *Family Films in Global Cinema: The World Beyond Disney* (London and New York: I. B. Tauris, 2015), pp. 1–15; Noel Brown, *The Children's Film: Genre, Nation and Narrative* (New York: Columbia University Press, 2017), Ch. 1.
16. Peter Krämer, '"It's Aimed at Kids – The Kid in Everybody': George Lucas, *Star Wars* and Children's Entertainment' in Yvonne Tasker (ed.), *Action and Adventure Cinema* (London and New York: Routledge, 2004), pp. 358–70 (pp. 366–7).
17. Ellen Scott, 'Pixar, Deniability, and the Adult Spectator', *The Journal of Popular Film and Television*, vol. 42, no. 3 (2014), pp. 150–62. Whilst I find much to admire in Scott's article, I take issue with her claim (on p. 161) that the uplifting endings of films such as *WALL-E* do little 'to reassure the viewers or to repair the damage done by the darkness, edginess, or social disturbance announced by the earlier image'. Such a reading is not only against the grain, but highly subjective: a professional film critic is likely to infer more problematic subtextual elements than the average movie-goer; this is especially true of young viewers who may be less able or less inclined to engage in 'deep' readings of family films. The evidence gathered by audience research into Disney films has tended to register not only a widespread perception that such films are both happy and ideologically straightforward, but also a deep-seated resistance to analysing them in detail, so Scott's interpretation of the endings of Pixar films would not appear to be widely shared.
18. Lewis Beale, 'At Long Last, Disney is Shooting for the Hip', *New York Daily News*, 20 November 1995, p. 36.
19. 'Interview of Walt Disney by Cecil B. DeMille'.
20. '2017 THEME Report', p. 19; '2018 THEME Report' (New York: Motion Picture Association of America, 2019), p. 26.
21. Carl DiOrio, '"Up" Rises above Boxoffice Competition', *The Hollywood Reporter*, 31 May 2009; Rebecca Rubin, 'How "Incredibles" Became Animation's Hottest Franchise', *Variety*, 18 June 2018.
22. Brian Fuson, '"Cars" Smokes Competition', *Variety*, 12 June 2006.
23. Jeremy Fuster, 'The Pixar Generation Just Helped "Incredibles 2" Make Box Office History', The Wrap, 19 June 2018, <https://www.thewrap.com/pixar-generation-incredibles-2-millennials/> (accessed 2 March 2019).
24. Gregg Kilday, '"Dragon" Makes Weekend Debut at No. 1', *The Hollywood Reporter*, 28 March 2010.
25. Paul Wells, *Understanding Animation* (London and New York: Routledge, 1998), p. 239; Mark Phillips, 'The Global Disney Audiences Project: Disney

Across Cultures' in Janet Wasko, Mark Phillips and Eileen R. Meehan (eds), *Dazzled by Disney? The Global Disney Audiences Project* (London: Leicester University Press, 2001), pp. 31–61 (pp. 42, 46); Janet Wasko and Eileen R. Meehan, 'Dazzled by Disney? Ambiguity in Ubiquity' in Wasko, Phillips and Meehan (eds), *Dazzled by Disney?*, pp. 329–43 (p. 334).

26. Stewart, *DisneyWar*, p. 108.

27. Christopher Vogler, *The Writer's Journey: Mythic Structure for Storytellers and Screenwriters*, 2nd edn (London: Pan Books, 1999), pp. 271–2.

28. Martin Barker, *From Antz to Titanic: Reinventing Film Analysis* (London: Pluto Press, 2000), p. 110.

29. Ibid., p. 117.

30. Robin Wood, *Hollywood from Vietnam to Reagan* (New York: Columbia University Press, 1986), p. 172.

31. Ibid.

32. J. Hoberman, 'The Mouse Roars', *Village Voice*, 21 June 1994, p. 45.

33. Jamie Portman, 'Toy Story is Success Story for Disney', *The Gazette*, 21 December 1995, p. D5.

34. Beale, 'At Long Last, Disney is Shooting for the Hip'.

35. Brown and Babington, 'Introduction: Children's Films and Family Films', p. 9.

36. Jack Zipes, 'Once Upon a Time Beyond Disney: Contemporary Fairy-Tale Films for Children' in Cary Bazalgette and David Buckingham (eds), *In Front of the Children: Screen Entertainment and Young Audiences* (London: British Film Institute, 1995), pp. 109–26 (pp. 110–12).

37. Chelsie Lynn Akers, 'The Rise of Humour: Hollywood Increases Adult Centred Humour in Animated Children's Films' (unpublished Master's thesis submitted to Brigham Young University, July 2013), pp. 3–4.

38. Benjamin Barber, *Consumed: How Markets Corrupt Children, Infantilise Adults and Swallow Citizens Whole* (London and New York: W. W. Norton & Company, 2007).

39. Janet Maslin, 'There's A New Toy in the House. Uh Oh', *The New York Times*, 22 November 1995, p. C9; David Ansen, 'Disney's Digital Delight', *Newsweek*, 27 November 1995, p. 89; Leonard Klady, 'Toy Story', *Variety*, 20 November 1995, p. 2.

40. See 'Top Rated Movies', IMDb, <http://www.imdb.com/search/title?groups=top_250&sort=user_rating&start=1> (accessed 5 January 2020); the critics' list of top hundred films on Metacritic includes *Ratatouille* (#38), *Beauty and the Beast* (#48), *Toy Story* (#50), *WALL-E* (#61), and *Inside Out* (#75). See 'Movie Releases by Score', Metacritic, <https://www.metacritic.com/browse/movies/score/metascore/all/filtered> (accessed 5 January 2020).

41. Eli Zaretsky, *Capitalism, the Family and Personal Life* (New York: Harper & Row, 1976), p. 51.

42. Jay D. Teachman, Lucky M. Tedrow, and Kyle D. Crowder, 'The Changing Demography of America's Families', *Journal of Marriage and Family*, vol. 62, no. 4 (2000), pp. 1234–46 (pp. 1240–1).

43. Ibid., p. 1239.

44. Shawn Haley, 'The Future of the Family in North America', *Futures*, no. 32 (2000), pp. 777–82 (p. 781).

45. Ibid., pp. 779–80.
46. This reading accords with Martin Barker's proposition that post-1990s Hollywood animation offers up 'a new kind of star relationship in which the star becomes a *contracted semiotician*, i.e. a star in effect sub-contracts his/her accumulated star presence to a film'. See Martin Barker, 'Introduction' in Thomas Austin and Martin Barker (eds), *Contemporary Hollywood Stardom* (London: Arnold, 2003), pp. 1–24 (p. 21).
47. Roger Ebert, 'Finding Nemo', Roger Ebert.com, 30 May 2003, <https://www.rogerebert.com/reviews/finding-nemo-2003> (accessed 26 February 2019).
48. See, for instance, Lincoln Geraghty's essay 'Mischief and Mayhem: A Cultural History of the Relationship Between Children and Old People in the Contemporary Family Film' in Vanessa Joosen (ed.), *Connecting Childhood and Old Age in Popular Media* (Jackson: University Press of Mississippi, 2018), pp. 146–67.
49. *As You Like It*, Act II, Scene VII. It is worth adding that Shakespeare views this 'second childishness' as perverse, so clearly there has been a major shift in attitudes towards childish grown-ups in the intervening time.
50. Haley, 'The Future of the Family in North America', pp. 778–9, 779–80.
51. Landon Y. Jones, *Great Expectations: America and the Baby Boom Generation* (New York: Coward, McCann & Geoghegan, 1980), p. 212.
52. Ibid., p. 207.
53. It may be significant, in this regard, that Brad Bird claims to have devised the basic story for *The Incredibles* in the early 1990s, the period at which fantasies of masculine dysfunction were almost inescapable.
54. Frank F. Furstenberg, 'Good Dads – Bad Dads: Two Faces of Fatherhood' in Andrew J. Cherlin (ed.), *The Changing American Family and Public Policy* (Washington: The Urban Institute Press, 1988), pp. 193–218.
55. Andrew J. Cherlin, 'The Changing American Family and Public Policy' in Andrew J. Cherlin (ed.), *The Changing American Family and Public Policy* (Washington: The Urban Institute Press, 1988), pp. 1–29; Russell Duncan and Joseph Godard, *Contemporary America*, 2nd edn (New York: Palgrave Macmillan, 2005), p. 137.
56. Tom Wolfe, 'The "Me" Decade and the Third Great Awakening', *New York*, 23 August 1976.
57. Lisa Damour, 'Inside Out: Pixar's Convincing Argument Against Childhood Happiness', *The New York Times*, 19 June 2005.
58. Jacqueline Rose, *The Case of Peter Pan, or The Impossibility of Children's Fiction* (Basingstoke: Macmillan, 1984).
59. To some degree, these films respond to widespread popular familiarity with Freudian psychoanalysis, which posits that personality formation occurs mainly during the formative periods of childhood development.

Chapter 3

1. To this extent, both forms can be related to the textual strategies discussed in Chapter 2 aimed to maximise the potential audience base for these films.
2. Geoff King, *Film Comedy* (London: Wallflower, 2002), p. 22.

3. Raymond Durgnat, *The Crazy Mirror: Hollywood Comedy and the American Image* (New York: Horizon Press, 1970), p. 102; Paul Wells, *Understanding Animation* (London and New York: Routledge, 1998), p. 185.

4. Paul Wells, *Understanding Animation* (London and New York: Routledge, 1998), p. 140.

5. David Bordwell, *The Way Hollywood Tells It: Story and Style in Modern Movies* (Berkeley, Los Angeles and London: University of California Press, 2006), pp. 8, 10.

6. Sam Summers, 'Intertextuality and the Break from Realism in DreamWorks Animation' (PhD thesis submitted to the University of Sunderland, April 2018). Summers outlines four categories of authorial intertextuality: extra-diegetic intertexts, diegetic intertexts, contra-diegetic intertexts, and tele-diegetic intertexts (pp. 40–2).

7. Ibid., p. 35.

8. Ibid.

9. Pierre Bourdieu, *Distinction: A Social Critique of the Judgement of Taste* (New York and London: Routledge, [1979] 2009), pp. 270, 281–2.

10. Noël Carroll, 'The Future of Allusion: Hollywood in the Seventies (and Beyond), *October*, vol. 20 (Spring 1982), pp. 51–81 (p. 54).

11. Ibid., p. 52.

12. Gary R. Edgerton, *American Film Exhibition and an Analysis of the Motion Picture Industry's Market Structure 1963–1980* (New York and London: Garland Publishing, Inc., 1983), p. 175.

13. See Noel Brown, *The Hollywood Family Film: A History, from Shirley Temple to Harry Potter* (London and New York: I. B. Tauris, 2012), Ch. 6.

14. David Buckingham, *After the Death of Childhood: Growing Up in the Age of Electronic Media* (Cambridge: Polity, 2000), p. 88.

15. Timothy Shary, 'Reification and Loss in Postmodern Puberty: The Cultural Logic of Fredric Jameson and American Youth Movies' in Cristina Degli-Esposti (ed.), *Postmodernism in the Cinema* (New York and Oxford: Berghahn, 1998), pp. 73–89 (pp. 73–4).

16. Bordwell, *The Way Hollywood Tells It*, pp. 184, 24–5.

17. Ibid., p. 184.

18. David Weinstein, 'Of Mice and Bart: *The Simpsons* and the Postmodern' in Cristina Degli-Esposti (ed.), *Postmodernism in the Cinema* (New York and Oxford: Berghahn, 1998), pp. 61–72.

19. Andrew Britton, 'Blissing Out: The Politics of Reaganite Entertainment' in Barry Keith Grant (ed.), *Britton on Film* (Detroit: Wayne State University Press, 2009), pp. 97–154 (p. 100).

20. Summers, 'Intertextuality and the Break from Realism in DreamWorks Animation', p. 77.

21. Wells, *Understanding Animation*, pp. 185–6.

22. Marwan M. Kraidy, 'Intertextual Manoeuvres Around the Subaltern: *Aladdin* as a Postmodern Text' in Cristina Degli-Esposti (ed.), *Postmodernism in the Cinema* (New York and Oxford: Berghahn, 1998), pp. 45–59 (p. 58).

23. Summers, 'Intertextuality and the Break from Realism in DreamWorks Animation', p. 81; Wells, *Understanding Animation*, pp. 185–6.

24. Lewis Beale, 'At Long Last, Disney Is Shooting for the Hip', *New York Daily News*, 20 November 1995, p. 36.
25. Ibid.
26. David Denby, 'This Toy's Life', *New York*, November 1995, pp. 126–9.
27. Mike Featherstone, *Consumer Culture and Postmodernism* (London: Sage, 1991), pp. 7–8.
28. Fredric Jameson, 'Postmodernism and Consumer Society' in Hal Foster (ed.), *The Anti-Aesthetic: Essays on Postmodern Culture* (Port Townsend: Bay Press, 1983), pp. 111–25.
29. On the pleasures of cognitive play for film audiences, see Carl Plantinga, *Moving Viewers: American Film and the Spectator's Experience* (Berkeley: University of California Press, 2009), pp. 21–5.
30. Chelsie Lynn Akers, 'The Rise of Humour: Hollywood Increases Adult Centred Humour in Animated Children's Films' (unpublished Master's thesis submitted to Brigham Young University, July 2013.
31. Christine Wilkie-Stibbs, 'Intertextuality and the Child Reader' in Peter Hunt (ed.), *Understanding Children's Literature* (London: Routledge, 2005), pp. 168–79 (pp. 169–70).
32. Sue Chambers, Nicki Karet and Neil Samson, 'Cartoon Crazy?: Children's Perception of "Action" Cartoons', Independent Television Commission (March 1998); Jennifer Cunningham, 'Children's Humour' in W. George Scarlett et al. (eds), *Children's Play* (London and New Delhi: Sage, 2005), pp. 93–109 (pp. 106–8).
33. Ibid.
34. Chris Woodyard, 'DreamWorks Puts "Prince" to Test', *USA Today*, 25 November 1998, p. 1B.
35. Summers, 'Intertextuality and the Break from Realism in DreamWorks Animation', pp. 78–9, 86.
36. Josh Young, 'Jeffrey's Wild Kingdom', *Variety*, 16 May 2005, p. 60.
37. Michael Mallory, 'When Big Toons Attack', *Variety*, 10 November 1998, p. A1.
38. Susan Wloszczyna, '"Antz" Joins the Picnic', *USA Today*, 2 October 1998, p. 1E.
39. Martin Barker, *From Antz to Titanic: Reinventing Film Analysis* (London: Pluto Press, 2000), p. 78.
40. Andy Seiler, '"Shrek" Treks Through Fairyland', *USA Today*, 15 May 2001, p. 1D.
41. Ibid.
42. Todd McCarthy, '"Shrek Will Charm Kids, Adults on Road to Cannes', *Variety*, 7 May 2001, p. 49.
43. Both films will be discussed in greater depth in Chapter 5.
44. Stan Beeler, 'Songs for the Older Set: Music and Multiple Demographics in *Shrek*, *Madagascar* and *Happy Feet*' in Karin Beeler and Stan Beeler (eds), *Children's Film in the Digital Age: Essays on Audience, Adaptation and Consumer Culture* (Jefferson: McFarland, 2015), pp. 28–36 (p. 30).
45. Ibid., p. 35.
46. Summers, 'Intertextuality and the Break from Realism in DreamWorks Animation', p. 134.

47. Todd McCarthy, '"Shrek Will Charm Kids, Adults on Road to Cannes', p. 49.
48. Elvis Mitchell, 'So Happily Ever After, Beauty and the Beasts', *The New York Times*, 16 May 2001, p. E1.
49. Summers, 'Intertextuality and the Break from Realism in DreamWorks Animation', pp. 8–9.
50. Ibid., pp. 255–6.
51. Ibid., p. 222.
52. Richard McCulloch, 'Towards Infinity and Beyond: Branding, Reputation, and the Critical Reception of Pixar Animated Studios' (PhD thesis submitted to University of East Anglia, 2013), pp. 128–9.
53. Matthew Beloni and Noela Hueso, 'THRs Animation Roundtable', *The Hollywood Reporter*, 22 December 2011, unpaginated.
54. Summers, 'Intertextuality and the Break from Realism in DreamWorks Animation', p. 261.
55. Heather Havrilesky, 'All Hail Lord Business', *The New York Times*, 2 March 2014, p. 46.
56. Kevin McCoy, 'Everything's Awesome: Lego Claims No. 1 Spot', *USA Today*, 5 September 2014, p. 3B.
57. Steven Zeitchik, '"The Lego Movie": Six Lessons from its Box Office Success', *Los Angeles Times*, 10 February 2014, unpaginated.
58. Havrilesky, 'All Hail Lord Business'.
59. Christopher Stern, 'WB Asks for "Giant" Favor', *Variety*, 4 November 1999, p. 5.
60. '"The Iron Giant" Lands on Capitol Hill', *Business Wire*, 4 November 1999, unpaginated.
61. Stern, 'WB Asks for "Giant" Favor'; '"The Iron Giant" Lands on Capitol Hill'.
62. Claudia Puig, 'Family-Friendly Concept Crashes as "Giant" Falls to Earth', *USA Today*, 30 August 1999, p. 4D.
63. Ibid.
64. Lawrence Van Gelder, 'The Attack of the Human Paranoids', *The New York Times*, 4 August 1999, p. E11; Steve Persall, '"Iron Giant" May Spark a Few Recoils', *St. Petersburg Times*, 6 August 1999, p. 11.
65. Stephen Hunter, '"Iron Giant": A Little Rusty', *The Washington Post*, 6 August 1999, p. C1.
66. Ellen Scott, 'Pixar, Deniability, and the Adult Spectator', *The Journal of Popular Film and Television*, vol. 42, no. 3 (2014), pp. 150–62 (pp. 151, 152).
67. Herbert Marcuse, *One-Dimensional Man: Studies in the Ideology of Advanced Industrial Society* (London and New York: Routledge, [1964] 2002), p. 59.
68. Daniel Bell, *The Cultural Contradictions of Capitalism* (London: Heinemann, 1976), p. 21.
69. Lou Lumenick, 'Bot Stuff!', *The New York Post*, 26 June 2008, p. 59.
70. Katrina Onstad, 'Pixar Gambles on a Robot in Love', *The New York Times*, 22 June 2008, p. A13.
71. Todd McCarthy, 'Pixar Aces Space', *Variety*, 30 June 2008, p. 40.
72. Van Gelder, 'The Attack of the Human Paranoids'.

CHAPTER 4

1. Jack Zipes, *The Enchanted Screen: The Unknown History of Fairy-Tale Films* (New York: Routledge, 2011), p. 24.
2. Ibid.
3. Janet Wasko and Eileen R. Meehan, 'Dazzled by Disney? Ambiguity in Ubiquity' in Janet Wasko, Mark Phillips and Eileen R. Meehan (eds), *Dazzled by Disney? The Global Disney Audiences Project* (London: Leicester University Press, 2001), pp. 329–43 (pp. 334–5).
4. Amy M. Davis, *Handsome Heroes and Vile Villains: Men in Disney's Feature Animation* (New Barnet: John Libbey, 2013), p. 7.
5. James R. Mason, 'Disney's Adult Audiences' in Noel Brown (ed.), *The Oxford Handbook of Children's Film* (Oxford and New York: Oxford University Press, 2021).
6. It should be noted, at this point, that Amy M. Davis's study of the role of women in Disney feature animation perceives greater ambiguity in the sexual politics of these films than is widely acknowledged, while Rebecca-Anne C. Do Rozario, more optimistically, reads pre-1990s Disney princesses as central characters in whom narrative authority is generally invested, with the greatest dramatic tension between virtuous and villainous women rather than between the sexes. See Amy M. Davis, *Good Girls and Wicked Witches: Women in Disney's Feature Animation* (New Barnet: John Libbey, 2007); Rebecca-Anne C. Do Rozario, 'The Princess and the Magic Kingdom: Beyond Nostalgia, the Function of the Disney Princess', *Women's Studies in Communication*, vol. 27, no. 1 (2004), pp. 34–59.
7. Davis, *Good Girls and Wicked Witches*, p. 172.
8. Ibid., p. 170.
9. Do Rozario, 'The Princess and the Magic Kingdom', p. 57.
10. Susan Wloszczyna, 'Muscle Behind "Hercules": Disney Duo Musker, Clements do it Again', *USA Today*, 13 June 1997, p. 1D.
11. Roberta Trites, 'Disney's Sub/Version of Andersen's *The Little Mermaid*', *Journal of Popular Film and Television*, vol. 18, no. 4 (1991), pp. 145–52 (p. 145).
12. Ibid., p. 146.
13. Davis, *Good Girls and Wicked Witches*, pp. 219, 171.
14. Ibid., pp. 178, 181.
15. Ibid., p. 182.
16. Ibid., p. 194.
17. Linda Haugsted, 'Disney Puts Diversity on Display', *Multichannel News*, 21 July 2008, p. 15.
18. 'The Walt Disney Company Recognized for Diversity Leadership', The Walt Disney Company, 16 December 2014, <https://www.thewaltdisneycompany.com/the-walt-disney-company-recognized-for-diversity-leadership/> (accessed 7 May 2019).
19. Yohana Desta, 'The Year Disney Started to Take Diversity Seriously', *Vanity Fair*, 23 November 2016, <https://www.vanityfair.com/hollywood/2016/11/disney-films-inclusive> (accessed 7 May 2019); Rebecca Ford, 'Disney Doubles Down on Diversity', *The Hollywood Reporter*, 11 November 2016, p. 20.

20. 'Our Diversity & Inclusion Journey', The Walt Disney Company, September 2019, <https://www.thewaltdisneycompany.com/app/uploads/2019/09/DiversityAndInclusionCommitment.pdf> (accessed 29 May 2019).
21. Janet Wasko, *Understanding Disney: The Manufacture of Fantasy* (Cambridge: Polity Press, 2001), pp. 63, 99–101.
22. Don Groves, 'Disney Goes Ape on Tarzan Dubs', *Variety*, 14 June 1999, p. 12.
23. Mark Phillips, 'The Global Disney Audiences Project: Disney Across Cultures' in Janet Wasko, Mark Phillips and Eileen R. Meehan (eds), *Dazzled by Disney? The Global Disney Audiences Project* (London: Leicester University Press, 2001), pp. 31–61 (p. 50).
24. Mason, 'Disney's Adult Audiences'.
25. Ibid.
26. On this point, it is notable that a single line of dialogue in Pixar's *Onward* (Dan Scanlon, 2020) alluding to a lesbian relationship resulted in the film being banned or censored in numerous countries, even as it was mostly lauded for its 'progressive' acceptance of queer families in Western discourses. See Andreas Wiseman, 'Disney/Pixar's "Onward" Banned in Multiple Middle Eastern Countries Due to Lesbian Reference', Deadline, 6 March 2020, <https://deadline.com/2020/03/disney-onward-banned-multiple-middle-east-markets-lesbian-lgbt-reference-1202876168/> (accessed 11 March 2020).
27. Marie Moran, 'Identity and Identity Politics: A Cultural Materialist History', *Historical Materialism*, vol. 26, no. 2 (2018), <http://www.historicalmaterialism.org/articles/identity-and-identity-politics> (accessed 21 March 2020).
28. Ronald Inglehart and Wayne E. Baker, 'Modernisation, Cultural Change, and the Persistence of Traditional Values', *American Sociological Review*, vol. 65, no. 1 (Feb 2000), pp. 19–51 (pp. 25–6, 28).
29. Ibid., pp. 25–6.
30. Wayne E. Baker, *America's Crisis of Values: Reality and Perception* (Princeton and Oxford: Princeton University Press, 2005), p. 35; Moran, 'Identity and Identity Politics'.
31. Baker, *America's Crisis of Values*, p. 60.
32. Moran, 'Identity and Identity Politics'.
33. Ibid.
34. Ibid.
35. Ibid.
36. Ibid.
37. Benjamin R. Barber, *Consumed: How Markets Corrupt Children, Infantilize Adults, and Swallow Citizens Whole* (New York and London: W. W. Norton & Company, 2007), p. 117.
38. Desta, 'The Year Disney Started to Take Diversity Seriously'; Keka Araujo, 'Disney Signed Contract to Respectfully Portray Indigenous People for Hit Movie "Frozen 2"', Diversity Inc, 2 December 2019, <https://www.diversityinc.com/disney-signed-contract-to-respectfully-portray-indigenous-people-for-hit-movie-frozen-2/> (accessed 5 January 2020).
39. Sabrina Santoro, 'Bringing the Land of the Dead to Life: "Coco" Director Talks Filmmaking Process', *The Panther: Chapman University*, 3 November, 2017, p. 1.

40. A. O. Scott, 'Death the Pixar Way', *The New York Times*, 22 November 2017, p. C1.
41. Tara O'Leary, 'Disney's Diversity Deficiency', *University Wire*, 5 October 2018, p. 1.
42. Stacy L. Smith, Marc Choueiti and Katherine Pieper, 'Inclusion or Invisibility?: Comprehensive Annenberg Report on Diversity in Entertainment', USC Annenberg, February 2016.
43. Ibid., p. 14.
44. Ibid., p. 16.
45. I am excluding *Aladdin*, in which Princess Jasmine plays second fiddle to the title character.
46. Janet P. Palmer, 'Animating Cultural Politics: Disney, Race, and Social Movement in the 1990s', unpublished dissertation submitted to the University of Michigan, 2000, p. 187. Janet Maslin, writing in the *New York Times*, detailed some of the film's most egregious deviations from established history: 'Pocahontas later married a different Englishman and was christened Rebecca. John Smith was punished for insubordination en route from England to Virginia. Pocahontas's saving his life may have been more politic than the melodramatic gesture Captain Smith later made famous'; Janet Maslin, '"Pocahontas", Romantic and Revisionist', *The New York Times*, 23 June 1995, p. C6.
47. Maslin, '"Pocahontas", Romantic and Revisionist'.
48. Sarah Vradenburg, 'Disney Should Stick to Fairy Tales', *The San Jose Mercury News*, 6 July 1995, p. 7B.
49. See Michelle Anya Anjirbag, 'Mulan and Moana: Embedded Coloniality and the Search for Authenticity in Disney Animated Film', *Social Sciences*, vol. 7, no. 11 (2018), pp. 1–15.
50. Georg Szalai, 'Disney Exec Discusses "Princess" Toy Line', *The Hollywood Reporter*, 17 February 2009.
51. Brooks Barnes, 'Her Prince Has Come. Critics Too', *The New York Times*, 31 May 2009, p. ST1. Criticisms of the film's politics have not been restricted to race; the figure of the gap-toothed, idiot savant firefly, Ray (Jim Cummings), has been interpreted as a crude stereotype of a working-class Southern hick.
52. See Joel Best and Kathleen S. Lowney, 'The Disadvantage of a Good Reputation: Disney as a Target for Social Problems Claims', *The Sociological Quarterly*, no. 50 (2009), pp. 431–49.
53. Caitlin Moore, 'Despite Familiar Formula, Disney's "Moana" is a Breath of Fresh Air', *The Washington Post*, 23 November 2016, p. C3.
54. Bryan Alexander, 'Let's Talk About That Surprising "Moana" Ending', *USA Today*, 29 November 2016, p. 3D.
55. Indeed, it might be argued that *Moana* more closely maps on to the so-called 'heroine's journey', a female-centred iteration of Joseph Campbell's 'hero's journey', as delineated by Maureen Murdock in *The Heroine's Journey: Woman's Quest for Wholeness* (Boston: Shambhala Publications, Inc., 1990). Amy M. Davis argues in favour of the presence of the 'heroine's journey' across both films in the *Frozen* franchise; see 'On "Love Experts", Evil Princes, Gullible Princesses, and *Frozen*'

in Noel Brown (ed.), *The Oxford Handbook of Children's Film* (Oxford and New York: Oxford University Press, 2021).

56. Robert Ito, 'How (And Why) Maui Got so Big in "Moana"', *The New York Times*, 15 November 2016.
57. Anjirbag, 'Mulan and Moana', p. 3.
58. Ibid.
59. Ibid., p. 6.
60. Ibid., p. 4.
61. Ibid.
62. Ed Catmull, *Creativity, Inc: Overcoming the Unseen Forces That Stand in the Way of True Inspiration* (London: Transworld Publishers, 2009), p. 269.
63. Mekado Murphy, 'Evolution of a Feisty Pixar Princess', *The New York Times*, 17 June 2012, p. 14.
64. Claudia Puig, '"Brave" Embraces Girl Power Boldly', *USA Today*, 22 June 2012, p. 2D. It should be noted that Chapman considered that the original design of the Merida doll in the 'Disney Princess' merchandising line – in which she appears slimmer, leggier and with straightened hair – was 'atrocious': 'Merida was created to break that mould – to give young girls a better, stronger role model, a more attainable role model, something of substance, not just a pretty face that waits around for romance'; in response to these criticisms, Disney redesigned the doll; see Ben Child, 'Brave Director Criticises Disney's "Sexualised" Princess Merida Redesign', *The Guardian*, 13 May 2013.
65. Pamela McClintock, '"Brave" Hits Bullseye with $66.7 mil', *The Hollywood Reporter*, 24 June 2012.
66. Ibid.; Brooks Barnes, 'Boys Don't Run Away From These Princesses', *The New York Times*, 2 December 2013, p. C1.
67. Murphy, 'Evolution of a Feisty Pixar Princess'.
68. Dan Harries, 'Film Parody and the Resuscitation of Genre' in Steve Neale (ed.), *Genre and Contemporary Hollywood* (London: BFI, 2002), pp. 281–93.
69. Dan Harries, *Film Parody* (London: BFI, 2000), p. 122.
70. Thomas Schatz, *Hollywood Genres: Formulas, Filmmaking, and the Studio System* (New York: Random House, 1981).
71. Harries, 'Film Parody and the Resuscitation of Genre', p. 286.
72. Rick Altman, 'A Semantic/Syntactic Approach to Film Genre' in Barry Keith Grant (ed.), *Film Genre Reader III* (Austin: University of Texas Press, 2003), pp. 27–41.
73. Indeed, in early 2018, when asked to comment on the rumour that Elsa will have a girlfriend in the then-forthcoming *Frozen II* (Chris Buck and Jennifer Lee, 2019), co-director Lee was defiantly non-committal, merely responding that: 'For me [. . .] Elsa's every day telling me where she needs to go, and she'll continue to tell us. I always write from character-out, and where Elsa is and what Elsa's doing in her life, she's telling me every day. We'll see where we go'; see Dory Jackson, 'Will Elsa Have a Girlfriend in "Frozen 2"? Director Responds to Gay Rumours', *Newsweek*, 28 February 2018, <https://www.newsweek.com/disneys-froze-elsa-girlfriend-frozen-2-frozen-directors-elsa-lesbian-824055> (accessed 4 July 2019). Then, in late 2019, Lee defended the decision not to disambiguate

Elsa's sexuality, claiming that the character was subjected to the Myers–Briggs personality test, which revealed that she is 'not ready for a relationship'; see Maureen Dowd, 'Jennifer Lee, Queen of the "Frozen" Franchise', *The New York Times*, 7 November 2019, <https://www.nytimes.com/2019/11/07/style/jennifer-lee-frozen.html> (accessed 1 January 2020).

74. John G. Cawelti, *Adventure, Mystery and Romance: Formula Stories as Art and Popular Culture* (Chicago: Chicago University Press, 1976), pp. 11–12.

75. Ken Gillam and Shannon R. Wooden, 'Post-Princess Models of Gender: The New Man in Disney/Pixar', *The Journal of Popular Film and Television*, vol. 36, no. 1 (2008), pp. 2–8.

76. Ibid., p. 3.

77. Ibid., p. 4.

78. Indeed, contemporary media discourses positioned the film as a watermark in the history of Disney animation, with the more team-oriented 'brain-trust' dynamic of Pixar supplanting Disney's traditionally executive-driven approach.

79. Zipes, *The Enchanted Screen*, p. 23.

80. Richard Dyer, 'Entertainment and Utopia', Ch. 5 in *Only Entertainment* (New York: Routledge, 1992), pp. 19–35 (p. 20).

81. Baker, *America's Crisis of Values*, pp. 34–5.

CHAPTER 5

1. I should point out that some animated features continue to be made in the United States that can, legitimately, be called independent, not just on narrative and aesthetic levels but in their separateness from the industrial sphere of the major Hollywood studios. These include the primarily adult-oriented productions *My Dog Tulip* (Paul Fierlinger, 2009), *It's Such a Beautiful Day* (Don Hertzfeldt, 2012), *An Oversimplification of Her Beauty* (Terence Nance, 2012), *Cheatin'* (Bill Plympton, 2013), and *Anomalisa* (Charlie Kaufman, 2015).

2. Sarah J. Smith, *Children, Cinema and Censorship: From Dracula to the Dead End Kids* (London and New York: I. B. Tauris, 2005).

3. Catherine Lester, 'The Children's Horror Film: Characterizing an "Impossible" Subgenre', *The Velvet Light Trap*, no. 78 (2016), pp. 22–37 (p. 24).

4. Ibid.

5. Filipa Antunes, 'Rethinking PG-13: Ratings and the Boundaries of Childhood and Horror', *Journal of Film and Video*, vol. 69, no. 1 (2017), pp. 27–43.

6. Ibid.

7. James M. Curtis, '"This is Halloween": The History, Significance and Cultural Impact of Tim Burton's The Nightmare Before Christmas' in Noel Brown and Bruce Babington (eds), *Family Films in Global Cinema: The World Beyond Disney* (London and New York: I. B. Tauris, 2015), pp. 69–84 (p. 70).

8. Judith Halberstam, 'Animating Revolt and Revolting Animation', Ch. 1 in *The Queer Art of Failure* (Durham: Duke University Press, 2011), p. 27.

9. Maureen Furniss, *Art in Motion: Animation Aesthetics* (New Barnet: John Libbey, 1998).

10. Sam Summers, 'Intertextuality and the Break from Realism in DreamWorks Animation' (PhD thesis submitted to the University of Sunderland, April 2018).
11. Steven Rea, 'On Movies: "Coraline" Animator Started with the Story', *The Philadelphia Inquirer*, 1 February 2009, p. H2.
12. Paul Wells, *Understanding Animation* (London: Routledge, 1998), p. 6.
13. A. O. Scott, 'Cornered in a Parallel World', *The New York Times*, 6 February 2009, p. C1.
14. Maria Nikolajeva, 'Children's Literature as a Cultural Code: A Semiotic Approach to History' in Maria Nikolajeva (ed.), *Aspects and Issues in the History of Children's Literature* (Westport: Greenwood Press, 1995), pp. 39–48 (p. 46).
15. As noted in Chapter 1, this story pattern closely conforms to what mythologist Joseph Campbell called the 'hero's journey', a three-part structure composed of 'separation', 'initiation' and 'return'; see *The Hero with a Thousand Faces* (Princeton: Princeton University Press, [1949] 2004).
16. Bruno Bettelheim, *The Uses of Enchantment: The Meaning and Importance of Fairy Tales* (New York: Vintage Books, 1976), p. 7.
17. Chris Hewitt, 'The directors of the stop-action "ParaNorman" call it "John-Carpenter-meets-John-Hughes"', *St. Paul Pioneer Press*, 15 August 2012.
18. Manohla Dargis, 'Seeing Ghosts Wherever He Looks', *The New York Times*, 17 August 2012, p. C4.
19. Lester, 'The Children's Horror Film', pp. 28–9.
20. Kyle Smith, 'Animated Film "The Boxtrolls" Has a Twee Victorian Vibe', *The New York Post*, 24 September 2014.
21. Xan Brooks, quoted in Jim Hillier, 'American Independent Cinema Since the 1980s' in Linda Ruth Williams and Michael Hammond (eds), *Contemporary American Cinema* (Maidenhead: McGraw-Hill, 2006), pp. 247–64 (p. 255).
22. Geoff King, *Indiewood USA: Where Hollywood Meets Independent Cinema* (London: I. B. Tauris, 2009), p. 2.
23. Yannis Tzioumakis, *Hollywood's Indies: Classics Divisions, Speciality Labels and the American Film Market* (Edinburgh: Edinburgh University Press, 2012), p. 8.
24. James MacDowell, 'Quirky: Buzzword or Sensibility' in Geoff King, Claire Molloy and Yannis Tzioumakis (eds), *American Independent Cinema: Indie, Indiewood and Beyond* (London and New York: Routledge, 2013), pp. 53–64.
25. Michael Z. Newman, 'Movies for Hipsters' in Geoff King, Claire Molloy and Yannis Tzioumakis (eds), *American Independent Cinema: Indie, Indiewood and Beyond* (London and New York: Routledge, 2013), pp. 71–82.
26. MacDowell, 'Quirky: Buzzword or Sensibility', p. 54.
27. Ibid., p. 51.
28. Newman, 'Movies for Hipsters', p. 75.
29. Newman, 'Movies for Hipsters'; Benjamin Barber, *Consumed: How Markets Corrupt Children, Infantilize Adults, and Swallow Citizens Whole* (New York and London: W. W. Norton & Company, 2007); Noel Brown, 'Spielberg and the Kidult' in Adrian Schober and Debbie Olson (eds), *The Child in the Films of Steven Spielberg* (New York: Lexington Books, 2016), pp. 19–44.
30. Newman, 'Movies for Hipsters', p. 71.

31. Peter C. Kunze, 'From the Mixed-Up Films of Mr. Wesley W. Anderson: Children's Literature as Intertexts' in Peter C. Kunze (ed.), *The Films of Wes Anderson: Critical Essays on an Indiewood Icon* (New York: Palgrave Macmillan, 2014), pp. 91–107.

32. Newman, 'Movies for Hipsters', p. 76.

33. Barber, *Consumed*, pp. 3–4.

34. Ibid., pp. 7–8.

35. Newman, 'Movies for Hipsters', p. 77.

36. Pierre Bourdieu, *Distinction: A Social Critique of the Judgement of Taste* (New York and London: Routledge, [1979] 2009), pp. 270, 281–2.

37. Todd McCarthy, 'Fantastic Mr. Fox', *Variety*, 15 October 2009, p. 4.

38. Ibid.

39. A. O. Scott, 'Don't Count Your Chickens', *The New York Times*, 13 November 2009, p. C1.

40. McCarthy, 'Fantastic Mr. Fox'; Lou Lumenick, '"Fox" is Worthy', *The New York Post*, 13 November 2009, p. 44.

41. Scott, 'Don't Count Your Chickens'; McCarthy, 'Fantastic Mr. Fox'.

42. Ann Oakley, 'Conventional Families' in Robert N. Rapoport et al. (eds), *Families in Britain* (London: Routledge and Kegan Paul, 1982), pp. 123–37.

43. Pamela McClintock, '"Rango" Tops Weekend with $38 Million', *The Hollywood Reporter*, 6 March 2011.

44. A. O. Scott, 'There's a New Sheriff in Town, and He's a Rootin' Tootin' Reptile', *The New York Times*, 4 March 2011, p. C8.

45. Michael Cavna, 'In a Land of Allusion, Here's Why "Rango" Impresses us with Double Barrels', *The Washington Post*, 10 March 2011, p. C10.

46. Peter Debruge, '*Rango*: The Lizard of Awes', *Variety*, 7 March 2011, p. 15.

47. Claudia Puig, '*Rango*: The Colours Can't Fool Us', *USA Today*, 4 March 2011, p. 3D.

48. McClintock, '"Rango" Tops Weekend with $38 Million'.

49. MacDowell, 'Quirky: Buzzword or Sensibility', p. 55.

50. Ellen Scott, 'Pixar, Deniability, and the Adult Spectator', *The Journal of Popular Film and Television*, vol. 42, no. 3 (2014), pp. 150–62.

51. Todd McCarthy, '9', *Variety*, 18 August 2009, p. 2.

52. A. O. Scott, 'In a Grim, Mysterious World, a Burlap Hero With a Heart of Golden Fuzz', *The New York Times*, 9 September 2009, p. C9.

53. Ben Fritz, *The Big Picture: The Fight for the Future of Movies* (New York: Houghton Mifflin Harcourt, 2018), Ch. 13.

CONCLUSION

1. Andrew Darley, 'Bones of Contention: Thoughts on the Study of Animation', *Animation: An Interdisciplinary Journal*, vol. 2, no. 1 (2007), pp. 63–76 (p. 69).

2. This kind of language is visible in a number of studies. For instance, Paul Wells has claimed that Disney's popularity 'consigns' animation to 'its traditional child audience', as if its popularity with children is automatically a bad thing for the credibility

of the medium. Equally, Christopher Holliday has noted that recent studies of Hollywood animation have allowed scholarship to 'move beyond' the children's film and family film labels. See Paul Wells, *Understanding Animation* (London: Routledge, 1998), p. 6; Christopher Holliday, *The Computer-Animated Film: Industry, Style and Genre* (Edinburgh: Edinburgh University Press, 2018), p. 20.

3. See, for instance, Noel Brown, *The Children's Film: Genre, Nation and Narrative* (New York: Columbia University Press, 2017); Casie Hermansson and Janet Zepernick (eds), *The Palgrave Handbook of Children's Film and Television* (Cham: Palgrave Macmillan, 2019); Filipa Antunes, *Children Beware! Childhood, Horror and the PG-13 Rating* (Jefferson: McFarland, 2020); Noel Brown (ed.), *The Oxford Handbook of Children's Film* (Oxford and New York: Oxford University Press, 2021).

4. Noel Brown, 'Change and Continuity in Contemporary Children's Film' in Casie Hermansson and Janet Zepernick (eds), *The Palgrave Handbook of Children's Film and Television* (Cham: Palgrave Macmillan, 2019), pp. 225–44.

5. Noel Brown, *The Hollywood Family Film: A History, from Shirley Temple to Harry Potter* (London and New York: I. B. Tauris, 2012); Noel Brown, *British Children's Cinema: From The Thief of Bagdad to Wallace and Gromit* (London and New York: I. B. Tauris, 2016).

6. Exemplary studies in this regard include David Buckingham's various investigations into the child television audience, especially *Children Talking Television: The Making of Television Literacy* (London and Washington: The Falmer Press, 1993), as well as Maya Gotz et al., *Media and the Make-Believe World of Children: When Harry Potter Meets Pokémon in Disneyland* (New York: Routledge, 2005) and Becky Parry, *Children, Film and Literacy* (Basingstoke: Palgrave Macmillan, 2013).

7. G. K. Chesterton, *Autobiography* (San Francisco: Ignatius Press, 1988), p. 47.

SELECT FILMOGRAPHY

Adventures of Tintin, The. Dir. Steven Spielberg. Paramount, 2011.
Aladdin. Dirs Ron Clements and John Musker. Disney, 1992.
An American Tale. Dir. Don Bluth. Universal, 1986.
Bambi. Dirs David Hand et al. Disney, 1942.
Antz. Dirs Eric Darnell and Tim Johnson. DreamWorks, 1998.
Back to the Future. Dir. Robert Zemeckis. Universal, 1985.
Beauty and the Beast. Dirs Gary Trousdale and Kirk Wise. Disney, 1991.
Big Hero 6. Dirs Don Hall and Chris Williams. Disney, 2014.
Black Cauldron, The. Dirs Ted Berman and Richard Rich. Disney, 1985.
Boxtrolls, The. Dirs Graham Annable and Anthony Stacchi. Laika, 2014.
Brave. Dirs Mark Andrews and Brenda Chapman. Pixar, 2012.
Bug's Life, A. Dirs John Lasseter and Andrew Stanton. Pixar, 1998.
Cars. Dir. John Lasseter. Pixar, 2006.
Chicken Little. Dir. Mark Dindal. Disney, 2005.
Cinderella. Dir. Clyde Geronimi et al. Disney, 1950.
Close Encounters of the Third Kind. Dir. Steven Spielberg. Columbia, 1977.
Cloudy with a Chance of Meatballs. Dirs Phil Lord and Christopher Miller. Sony, 2009.
Coco. Dir. Lee Unkrich. Pixar, 2017.
Coraline. Dir. Henry Selick. Laika, 2009.
Corpse Bride. Dir. Tim Burton. Warner Bros., 2005.
Croods, The. Dirs Kirk DeMicco and Chris Sanders. Blue Sky, 2013.
Despicable Me. Dirs Pierre Coffin and Chris Renaud. Illumination, 2010.
Despicable Me 2. Dirs Pierre Coffin and Chris Renaud. Illumination, 2013.
Dumbo. Dirs Ben Sharpsteen et al. Disney, 1941.
E.T. The Extra-Terrestrial. Dir. Steven Spielberg. Universal, 1982.
Fantasia. Dirs Ben Sharpsteen et al. Disney, 1940.

Fantastic Mr. Fox. Dir. Wes Anderson. Fox, 2009.
Finding Nemo. Dirs Andrew Stanton and Graham Walters. Pixar, 2003.
Finding Dory. Dir. Andrew Stanton. Pixar, 2016.
Frankenweenie. Dir. Tim Burton. Disney, 2012.
Fritz the Cat. Dir. Ralph Bakshi. Cinemation, 1972.
Frozen. Dirs Chris Buck and Jennifer Lee. Disney, 2013.
Frozen II. Dirs Chris Buck and Jennifer Lee. Disney, 2019.
Happy Feet. Dir. George Miller. Warner Bros., 2006.
Hook. Dir. Steven Spielberg. Sony, 1991.
Hotel Transylvania. Dir. Genndy Tartakovsky. Sony, 2012.
How to Train Your Dragon. Dirs Chris Sanders and Dean DeBlois. DreamWorks, 2010.
Ice Age. Dir. Chris Wedge. Blue Sky, 2002.
Ice Age: Continental Drift. Dirs Steve Martino and Michael Thurmeier. Blue Sky, 2012.
Ice Age: Dawn of the Dinosaurs. Dir. Carlos Saldanha. Blue Sky, 2009.
Ice Age: The Meltdown. Dir. Carlos Saldanha. Blue Sky, 2006.
Incredibles, The. Dir. Brad Bird. Pixar, 2004.
Incredibles 2. Dir. Brad Bird. Pixar, 2018.
Inside Out. Dir. Pete Docter. Pixar, 2015.
Iron Giant, The. Dir. Brad Bird. Warner Bros., 1999.
Isle of Dogs. Dir. Wes Anderson. Fox, 2018.
Kubo and the Two Strings. Dir. Travis Knight. Laika, 2016.
Kung Fu Panda. Dirs John Stevenson and Mark Osborne. DreamWorks, 2008.
Lego Movie, The. Dirs Phil Lord and Christopher Miller. Warner Bros., 2014.
Lego Movie 2, The: The Second Part. Dir. Mike Mitchell. Warner Bros., 2019.
Lion King, The. Dirs Roger Allers and Rob Minkoff. Disney, 1994.
Lion King, The. Dir. Jon Favreau. Disney, 2019.
Little Mermaid, The. Dirs Ron Clements and John Musker. Disney, 1989.
Madagascar. Dirs Eric Darnell and Tom McGrath. DreamWorks, 2005.
Maleficent. Dir. Robert Stromberg. Disney, 2014.
Mars Needs Moms. Dir. Simon Wells. Disney, 2011.
Meet Me in St. Louis. Dir. Vincente Minnelli. MGM, 1944.
Minions. Dirs Pierre Coffin and Kyle Balda. Illumination, 2015.
Moana. Dirs Ron Clements and John Musker. Disney, 2016.
Monsters, Inc. Dir. Pete Docter. Pixar, 2001.
Monsters University. Dir. Dan Scanlon. Pixar, 2013.
Mrs Doubtfire. Dir. Chris Columbus. Fox, 1993.
Mulan. Dirs Barry Cook and Tony Bancroft. Disney, 1998.
Nightmare Before Christmas, The. Dir. Henry Selick. Disney, 1993.
9. Dir. Shane Acker. Focus Features, 2009.
Oliver & Company. Dir. George Scribner. Disney, 1988.
ParaNorman. Dirs Sam Fell and Chris Butler. Laika, 2012.
Pocahontas. Dirs Mike Gabriel and Eric Goldberg. Disney, 1995.
Polar Express, The. Dir. Robert Zemeckis. Warner Bros., 2004.
Princess and the Frog, The. Dirs Ron Clements and John Musker. Disney, 2009.
Ralph Breaks the Internet. Dirs Rich Moore and Phil Johnston. Disney, 2018.

Rango. Dir. Gore Verbinski. Paramount, 2011.

Ratatouille. Dir. Brad Bird. Pixar, 2007.

Rescuers Down Under, The. Dirs Hendel Butoy and Mike Gabriel. Disney, 1990.

Rio. Dir. Carlos Saldanha. Blue Sky, 2011.

Robots. Dir. Chris Wedge. Blue Sky, 2005.

Secret of NIMH, The. Dir. Don Bluth. MGM/UA, 1982.

Shrek. Dirs Andrew Adamson and Vicky Jenson. DreamWorks, 2001.

Shrek 2. Dirs Andrew Adamson, Kelly Asbury and Conrad Vernon. DreamWorks, 2004.

Shrek the Third. Dirs Chris Miller and Raman Hui. DreamWorks, 2007.

Shrek Forever After. Dir. Mike Mitchell. DreamWorks, 2010.

Simpsons Movie, The. Dir. David Silverman. Fox, 2007.

Sleeping Beauty. Dir. Clyde Geronimi et al. Disney, 1959.

Snow White and the Seven Dwarfs. Dirs David Hand et al. Disney, 1937.

Spider-Man: Into the Spider-Verse. Dirs Bob Persichetti et al. Sony, 2018.

SpongeBob SquarePants Movie, The. Dir. Stephen Hillenberg. Paramount, 2004.

Star Wars. Dir. George Lucas: Fox, 1977.

Tangled. Dirs Nathan Greno and Byron Howard. Disney, 2010.

Tarzan. Dirs Kevin Lima and Chris Buck. Disney, 1999.

Toy Story. Dir. John Lasseter. Pixar, 1995.

Toy Story 2. Dir. John Lasseter. Pixar, 1999.

Toy Story 3. Dir. Lee Unkrich. Pixar, 2010.

Toy Story 4. Dir. Josh Cooley. Pixar, 2019.

Tron. Dir. Steven Lisberger. Disney, 1982.

Up. Dir. Pete Docter. Disney, 2009.

Wallace and Gromit: The Curse of the Were-Rabbit. Dirs Nick Park and Steve Box. Aardman, 2005.

WALL-E. Dir. Andrew Stanton. Pixar, 2008.

Who Framed Roger Rabbit. Dir. Robert Zemeckis. Touchstone, 1988.

Wizard of Oz, The. Dir. Victor Fleming. MGM, 1939.

Wreck-It Ralph. Dir. Rich Moore. Disney, 2012.

Zootopia. Dirs Byron Howard and Rich Moore. Disney, 2016.

SELECT BIBLIOGRAPHY

Allen, Robert C., 'Home Alone Together: Hollywood and the "Family Film"' in Melvyn Stokes and Richard Maltby (eds), *Identifying Hollywood's Audiences: Cultural Identity and the Movies* (London: BFI Publishing, 1999), pp. 109–34.

Antunes, Filipa, 'Rethinking PG-13: Ratings and the Boundaries of Childhood and Horror', *Journal of Film and Video*, vol. 69, no. 1 (2017), pp. 27–43.

Barber, Benjamin R., *Consumed: How Markets Corrupt Children, Infantilize Adults, and Swallow Citizens Whole* (New York and London: W. W. Norton & Company, 2007).

Barker, Martin, *From Antz to Titanic: Reinventing Film Analysis* (London: Pluto Press, 2000).

Barrier, Michael, *Hollywood Cartoons: American Animation in its Golden Age* (Oxford: Oxford University Press, 1999).

Barrier, Michael, *The Animated Man: A Life of Walt Disney* (Berkeley: University of California Press, 2008).

Batkin, Jane, *Identity in Animation: A Journey into Self, Difference, Culture and the Body* (New York: Routledge, 2017).

Beck, Jerry, *Animation Art: From Pencil to Pixel, the History of Cartoon, Anime, and CGI* (London: Flame Tree, 2004).

Bell, Elizabeth, Lynda Haas and Laura Sells (eds), *From Mouse to Mermaid: The Politics of Film, Gender, and Culture* (Bloomington: Indiana University Press, 1995).

Beeler, Karin and Stan Beeler (eds), *Children's Film in the Digital Age: Essays on Audience, Adaptation and Consumer Culture* (Jefferson: McFarland, 2015).

Booker, M. Keith, *Disney, Pixar and the Hidden Messages of Children's Films* (California: Praeger, 2010).

Bordwell, David, *The Way Hollywood Tells It: Story and Style in Modern Movies* (Berkeley, Los Angeles and London: University of California Press, 2006).

Brown, Noel, *The Hollywood Family Film: A History, from Shirley Temple to Harry Potter* (London and New York: I. B. Tauris, 2012).

Brown, Noel, '"Family" Entertainment and Contemporary Hollywood Cinema', *Scope: An Online Journal of Film and Television Studies*, no. 25 (February 2013).

Brown, Noel, '"A New Movie-Going Public": 1930s Hollywood and the Emergence of the "Family" Film', *The Historical Journal of Film, Radio and Television*, vol. 33 (1), 2013, pp. 1–23.

Brown, Noel, *British Children's Cinema: From The Thief of Bagdad to Wallace and Gromit* (London and New York: I. B. Tauris, 2016).

Brown, Noel, *The Children's Film: Genre, Nation and Narrative* (New York: Columbia University Press, 2017).

Brown, Noel (ed.), *The Oxford Handbook of Children's Film* (Oxford and New York: Oxford University Press, 2021).

Brown, Noel and Bruce Babington (eds), *Family Films in Global Cinema: The World Beyond Disney* (London and New York: I. B. Tauris, 2015).

Byrne, Eleanor and Martin McQuilan, *Deconstructing Disney* (London: Pluto Press, 1999).

Campbell, Joseph, *The Hero with a Thousand Faces* (Princeton: Princeton University Press, [1949] 2004).

Catmull, Ed, *Creativity, Inc: Overcoming the Unseen Forces That Stand in the Way of True Inspiration* (London: Transworld Publishers, 2009).

Cheu, Johnson (ed.), *Diversity in Disney Films: Critical Essays on Race, Ethnicity, Gender, Sexuality and Disability* (Jefferson: McFarland, 2012).

Crafton, Donald, *Before Mickey: The Animated Film, 1898–1928* (Chicago: University of Chicago Press, 1993).

Darley, Andrew, *Visual Digital Culture: Surface Play and Spectacle in New Media Genres* (New York: Routledge, 2000).

Davis, Amy M., *Good Girls and Wicked Witches: Women in Disney's Feature Animation* (New Barnet: John Libbey, 2006).

Davis, Amy M., *Handsome Heroes and Vile Villains: Men in Disney's Feature Animation* (New Barnet: John Libbey, 2013).

Davis, Amy M., *Discussing Disney* (New Barnet: John Libbey, 2019).

Featherstone, Mike, *Consumer Culture and Postmodernism*, 2nd edn (London: Sage, 2007).

Finch, Christopher, *The Art of Walt Disney* (New York: Harry N. Abrams, Inc., 1995).

Fritz, Ben, *The Big Picture: The Fight for the Future of Movies* (New York: Houghton Mifflin Harcourt, 2018).

Furniss, Maureen, *Art in Motion: Animation Aesthetics* (New Barnet: John Libbey, 1998).

Giroux, Henry A. and Grace Pollock, *The Mouse That Roared: Disney and the End of Innocence* (Plymouth: Rowman and Littlefield Publishers, Inc., 2010).

Halberstam, Judith, *The Queer Art of Failure* (Durham: Duke University Press, 2011).

Herhuth, Eric, *Pixar and the Aesthetic Animation: Animation, Storytelling, and Digital Culture* (Oakland: University of California Press, 2017).

Hermansson, Casie and Janet Zepernick (eds), *The Palgrave Handbook of Children's Film and Television* (Basingstoke: Palgrave Macmillan, 2019).

Holliday, Christopher, *The Computer-Animated Film: Industry, Style and Genre* (Edinburgh: Edinburgh University Press, 2018).

Jackson, Kathy Merlock (ed.), *Walt Disney: Conversations* (Jackson: University Press of Mississippi, 2006).

Krämer, Peter, 'Would You Take Your Child to See This Film?: The Cultural and Social Work of the Family Adventure Movie' in Steve Neale and Murray Smith (eds), *Contemporary Hollywood Cinema* (London: Routledge, 1998), pp. 294–311.

Krämer, Peter, '"The Best Disney Film Disney Never Made": Children's Films and The Family Audience in American Cinema since the 1960s' in Steve Neale (ed.), *Genre and Contemporary Hollywood* (London: British Film Institute, 2002), pp. 185–200.

Krämer, Peter, '"It's Aimed at Kids – The Kid in Everybody": George Lucas, *Star Wars* and Children's Entertainment' in Yvonne Tasker (ed.), *Action and Adventure Cinema* (London and New York: Routledge, 2004), pp. 358–70.

Krämer, Peter, 'Disney, George Lucas und Pixar: Animation und die US-amerikanische Filmindustrie seit den 1970er Jahren', *Film-Konzepte*, no. 33 (February 2014), pp. 6–21.

Lester, Catherine, 'The Children's Horror Film: Characterizing an "Impossible" Subgenre'. *The Velvet Light Trap*, no. 78 (2016), pp. 22–37.

Maltin, Leonard, *Of Mice and Magic: A History of American Animated Cartoons* (New York: Plume, 1987).

McCulloch, Richard, *Towards Infinity and Beyond: Branding, Reputation, and the Critical Reception of Pixar Animated Studios* (PhD thesis submitted to the University of East Anglia, 2013).

McGowan, David, *Animated Personalities: Cartoon Characters and Stardom in American Theatrical Shorts* (Austin: University of Texas Press, 2019).

Meinel, Deitmar, *Pixar's America: The Re-Animation of American Myths and Symbols* (New York: Palgrave Macmillan, 2016).

Pallant, Chris, *Demystifying Disney: A History of Disney Feature Animation* (London: Continuum, 2011).

Pallant, Chris and Steven Price, *Storyboarding: A Critical History* (Basingstoke: Palgrave Macmillan, 2015).

Pilling, Jayne (ed.), *A Reader in Animation Studies* (New Barnet: John Libbey, 1999).

Price, David A., *The Pixar Touch: The Making of a Company* (New York: Vintage Books, 2009).

Rösing, Lilian Munk, *Pixar with Lacan: The Hysteric's Guide to Animation* (London and New York: Bloomsbury, 2016).

Sammond, Nicholas, *Babes in Tomorrowland: Walt Disney and the Making of the American Child, 1930–1960* (Durham: Duke University Press, 2005).

Schickel, Richard, *The Disney Version: The Life, Times, Art and Commerce of Walt Disney* (Chicago: Elephant Paperbacks, 1997).

Scott, Ellen, 'Pixar, Deniability, and the Adult Spectator', *The Journal of Popular Film and Television*, vol. 42, no. 3 (2014), pp. 150–62.

Smoodin, Eric, *Animating Culture: Hollywood Cartoons from the Sound Era* (Oxford: Roundhouse Publishing, 1993).

Smith, Susan, Noel Brown and Sam Summers (eds), *Toy Story: How Pixar Reinvented the Animated Feature* (New York: Bloomsbury, 2018).

Sperb, Jason, *Disney's Most Notorious Film: Race, Convergence, and the Hidden Histories of Song of the South* (Austin: University of Texas Press, 2012).

Stewart, James B., *DisneyWar: The Battle for the Magic Kingdom* (London and New York: Simon & Schuster, 2005).

Summers, Sam, 'Intertextuality and the Break from Realism in DreamWorks Animation' (PhD thesis submitted to the University of Sunderland, April 2018).

Telotte, J. P., *Animating Space: From Mickey to Wall-E* (Lexington: University Press of Kentucky, 2010).

Vogler, Christopher, *The Writer's Journey: Mythic Structure for Storytellers and Screenwriters*, 2nd edn (London: Pan Books, 1999).

Ward, Annalee R., *Mouse Morality: The Rhetoric of Disney Animated Film* (Austin: University of Texas Press, 2002).

Wasko, Janet, *Understanding Disney: The Manufacture of Fantasy* (Cambridge: Polity, 2001).

Wasko, Janet, Mark Phillips and Eileen R. Meehan (eds), *Dazzled by Disney? The Global Disney Audiences Project* (London: Leicester University Press, 2001).

Watts, Steven, *The Magic Kingdom: Walt Disney and the American Way of Life* (Boston and New York: Houghton Mifflin Company, 1997).

Wells, Paul, *Understanding Animation* (London and New York: Routledge, 1998).

Wells, Paul, *Animation and America* (Edinburgh: Edinburgh University Press, 2002).

Wells, Paul, *Animation: Genre and Authorship* (London: Wallflower Press, 2002).

Wood, Robin, *Hollywood from Vietnam to Reagan* (New York: Columbia University Press, 1986).

Zipes, Jack, 'Once Upon a Time Beyond Disney: Contemporary Fairy-Tale Films for Children' in Cary Bazalgette and David Buckingham (eds), *In Front of the Children: Screen Entertainment and Young Audiences* (London: British Film Institute, 1995), pp. 109–26.

Zipes, Jack, *The Enchanted Screen: The Unknown History of Fairy-Tale Films* (New York: Routledge, 2011).

INDEX

Printed and bound by CPI Group (UK) Ltd, Croydon, CR0 4YY

28/01/2025

01827061-0006